THE SCIENCE OF CLIMBING TRAINING

AN EVIDENCE-BASED GUIDE TO IMPROVING YOUR CLIMBING PERFORMANCE

THE SCIENCE OF CLIMBING TRAINING

AN EVIDENCE-BASED GUIDE TO IMPROVING
YOUR CLIMBING PERFORMANCE

SERGIO CONSUEGRA
TRANSLATED BY ROSIE STAINTHORPE

Vertebrate Publishing, Sheffield
www.adventurebooks.com

The Science of Climbing Training
Sergio Consuegra
Translated by Rosie Stainthorpe

First published in English in 2023 by Vertebrate Publishing. Originally published in Spanish in 2020 by Ediciones Desnivel as *Entrenamiento de Escalada basado en la Evidencia Científica*.

 Vertebrate Publishing
Omega Court, 352 Cemetery Road, Sheffield S11 8FT, United Kingdom.
www.adventurebooks.com

Copyright © 2023 Sergio Consuegra Gómez.

Front cover: Svana Bjarnason during golden hour on *Homage a Catalunya*, a F7b+ slab in Abella de la Conca, Spain. Photo: Lena Drapella.

Photography by Rubén Crespo unless otherwise credited.

Graphics by Javier Fernández de Cara, unless otherwise credited.

Original design by Lluís Palomares.

Sergio Consuegra Gómez has asserted his rights under the Copyright, Designs and Patents Act 1988 to be identified as author of this work.

A CIP catalogue record for this book is available from the British Library.

ISBN 978-1-83981-182-1 (Paperback)
ISBN 978-1-83981-183-8 (Ebook)

10 9 8 7 6 5 4 3 2 1

All rights reserved. No part of this work covered by the copyright herein may be reproduced or used in any form or by any means – graphic, electronic, or mechanised, including photocopying, recording, taping or information storage and retrieval systems – without the written permission of the publisher.

Every effort has been made to obtain the necessary permissions with reference to copyright material, both illustrative and quoted. We apologise for any omissions in this respect and will be pleased to make the appropriate acknowledgements in any future edition.

Vertebrate Publishing is committed to printing on paper from sustainable sources.

Printed and bound in Europe by Latitude Press.

Every effort has been made to achieve accuracy of the information in this guidebook. The author, translator, publisher and copyright owners can take no responsibility for: loss or injury (including fatal) to persons; loss or damage to property or equipment; trespass, irresponsible behaviour or any other mishap that may be suffered as a result of following the advice offered in this guidebook.

Climbing is an activity that carries a risk of personal injury or death. Participants must be aware of and accept that these risks are present and they should be responsible for their own actions and involvement. Nobody involved in the writing and production of this guidebook accepts any responsibility for any errors that it may contain, nor are they liable for any injuries or damage that may arise from its use. All climbing is inherently dangerous and the fact that individual descriptions in this volume do not point out such dangers does not mean that they do not exist.
Take care.

CONTENTS

Introduction IX

PART I: UNDERSTANDING TRAINING

1 THE PROCESS OF TRAINING 1
  Definition 1
  Intensity and thresholds 2
  Homeostasis, GAS and supercompensation 4
  The principles of training 5
  What to train 6

2 UNDERSTANDING THE IMPORTANCE OF STRENGTH 9
  What is strength? 9
  Types of muscle contraction 11
  Types of muscle fibre and recruitment 11
  Causes of fatigue 12
  Muscle failure: is it really necessary? 13
  Ways to develop strength: hypertrophy and neural 14
  Strength training for injury prevention 16

3 UNDERSTANDING AND OPTIMISING MOBILITY 19
  What is mobility? Flexibility, elasticity and stiffness 19
  Active vs passive flexibility and mobility reserve 20
  Myotatic reflex and autogenic inhibition/inverse myotatic reflex 21
  Threat perception as a limiting factor of ROM 22
  Brain maps, SIMs and DIMs 22
  Options for optimising mobility 24

4 BRIEF NOTES ON ANATOMY 33
Upper body: pulling muscles 34
Core: the connecting chain 39
Lower body: pushing muscles 43
Connective tissue: tendons and ligaments 46

5 FASCIA, MUSCLE CHAINS AND BIOTENSEGRITY 47
Fascial anatomy: superficial fascia and deep fascia 47
Main muscle chains 49
The body as a biotensegrity structure 50

6 BIOENERGETICS AND METABOLISM 51
Focus: energy production 51
The ATP–PCr system 52
Anaerobic glycolysis 52
Aerobic glycolysis 53
Fat oxidation or lipolysis 53
The energy continuum 55

7 ANALYSIS OF THE MAIN PHYSIOLOGICAL FACTORS IN CLIMBING PERFORMANCE 57
The old paradigm of performance: intensity and energy systems according to number of moves 58
New findings about limiting factors in climbing performance: routes and bouldering 59

PART II: OPTIMISATION OF TRAINING

8 WHAT CAN I OPTIMISE IN MY TRAINING SESSIONS? 69
Definition of training goals 69
General warm-up. Joint mobilisation. Coordination-based cardio. Increasing ROM. Muscle activation 72
Core activation 75
Specific wall-based exercises 76
    Traversing. Introducing the session's target technique 76
    Wall-based core work. Resistance band exercises and body tension 77

Enhancing performance: post-activation potentiation 81
Climbing-specific training needs 82
   Maximum strength training 83
Maximum grip strength. Deadhangs. Evidence and protocols.
Adaptation for different levels of training 84
Maximum pulling strength. Pull-ups. Velocity-based strength training.
Maximum intensity methods and calculating your RM 89
Maximum isometric strength. Lock-offs 94
Recovery time during and between sessions 95
   Power and RFD training 96
Campus board training 97
Recovery time during and between sessions 105
   Integrated strength, power and RFD training: bouldering 105
   Endurance training 107
Physiological effects of different intensities 108
Increasing forearm blood flow. Continuous, long interval and
intermittent methods. Blood flow restriction training (BFR) 110
Improving recovery. High-intensity interval methods.
Active wall-based recovery. Intermittent deadhangs 114
   Physical conditioning for climbing 119
      Strength training to maximise performance.
      Methods and techniques for upper body, core and lower body exercises 119
      Strength training for injury prevention 148
      Cardiovascular endurance training for climbing.
      Base endurance, HIIT, body composition and SIT 153
      Mobility training for climbing 155

PART III: PLANNING YOUR TRAINING

9 TRAINING SESSION DESIGN **161**
   Single-focus sessions. Example session 161
   Criteria for planning a multi-focus session.
   Transfer and interference 164

10 PERIODISATION MODELS: IN SEARCH OF OPTIMAL PEAK FORM ... **167**

Basic concepts: macrocycle, mesocycle and microcycle ... 168
Linear periodisation: traditional and reverse. General and specific preparation period. Competition and tapering period. Advantages and disadvantages. Example periodisation ... 169
ATR periodisation. Accumulation, transmutation and realisation mesocycles. Types and order of microcycles. Advantages and disadvantages. Example periodisation ... 177

11 DETRAINING ... **183**

Bibliography ... 187
Acknowledgements ... 203

INTRODUCTION

There is an overwhelming amount of information available to us about training for climbing. The rapid growth of sports culture, bigger and better climbing walls, easy access to climbing-related content, the internet ... All have played a huge part in advancing the incredible sport of climbing. However, due to the sheer quantity of information, it's not always easy to sift through and select the most accurate sources. Most people – and not only in the world of climbing – base their training on word of mouth, what friends or influencers are doing, the 'no pain, no gain' mantra, what they've always done, or so-called 'bro science'.

The aim of this book is to provide quality information for a broad range of readers: from climbers taking the next step in their training (whether they're climbing F6a or F8a) to coaches looking to optimise their athletes' training.

It boasts no revolutionary or magic training methods (although you might be shocked by the science behind some popular methods). Instead, it analyses the sporting needs of climbers from the perspective of exercise and sports science to provide an evidence-based approach to climbing training.

The first part explains what training is and how different training methods are governed by the physiological and biomechanical processes that occur in the body.

The second part looks at how to improve specific needs (such as finger strength and forearm muscle endurance) and general needs (basic physical conditioning, pulling strength, pushing strength, strength training for injury prevention, and so on) for the different demands and types of climbing.

The third and final part, after gathering together all the pieces of the puzzle, suggests the best ways in which you can fit them together. It looks at adjusting training volume and intensity and tapering to encourage supercompensation, all to achieve improved performance, a higher grade, ticking your long-standing project or climbing your dream route.

To sum up the contents of this book in just a few words, I'd go with my personal training philosophy: 'don't train more: train better'. And I'd like to think this book will, in the words of Alvin Toffler, help you to 'learn, unlearn and relearn'.

PART I

UNDERSTANDING TRAINING

THE PROCESS OF TRAINING

DEFINITION

To begin, it's important to set a common understanding of what 'training' is. According to Bernal Ruiz (2006), training is a voluntary process that entails a transformation of physical and psychological functional systems. It occurs through the application of external stresses and in reaction to specific internal conditions in the body, and it's designed to improve performance in a particular situation.

Let's break this down into several key points.

The first thing to note is that training is a *process*; it is not a one-off session at the wall or the gym. It's also *voluntary*, meaning it's not going to happen while you're sitting on the sofa, scrolling through social media or talking about climbing at the pub. You have to get out there and train.

Then we get to the *transformation* of both *physical* and, especially in climbing, *psychological* systems. There's a clear and proven link between these two factors. Without sufficient physical training, no athlete will ever perform at their best. However, all the physical training in the world means nothing without the motivation, focus or resolution to win, take that next step, stick to the training or give that final push at the end of a race. And vice versa, regardless of how well prepared we are on a psychological level, without physical training, we'll never reach our full potential. What's more, with poor physical form, we start to doubt whether we can keep going or make that next move ... a vicious cycle that we'd do well to avoid.

The *external stresses* and *internal conditions* are two of the most important factors, and so we'll look at these in greater depth later on in the book. Basically, training must require genuine effort and the difficulty (technical, physical, psychological, and so on) of training exercises needs to vary according to the climber's level of training. For example, doing 10 pull-ups is not as hard for a F8a climber as it would be for a complete beginner whose previous hobbies amount to lying on the sofa and eating junk food.

The final thing to note is that our training should lead to a *higher level of performance*. If it doesn't, then something's gone wrong and we'll have wasted precious time and energy.

So, to get better at climbing, we just need to climb more and try harder routes? Unfortunately, it doesn't quite work like that, and it's the same for any sport: unless we're just starting out and don't climb very often, doing more won't make us any better and we won't climb any harder, no matter how hard we try.

Repeatedly doing any sport with no variation or evolution and, above all, no additional physical conditioning, leads to two possible scenarios: plateauing as we fail to master new techniques, or injury. If we never leave our comfort zone, where we climb and train comfortably, enjoy ourselves, feel proficient and capable, never try too hard or ever get frustrated, we'll never see any evolution or improvement because we're always doing the same thing. It would be like trying to train by brushing our teeth or drinking a glass of water. It's outside of this comfort zone where the magic happens: things evolve, changes occur ... However, without the necessary physical conditioning for the demands of our sport, we'll overload the most commonly used muscles, tendons, and so on. This can lead to excessive wear, agonist/antagonist imbalance and, most probably, to an injury that could stop us from climbing at all.

So, to climb better we need to train for climbing: we should dedicate our midweek sessions to training at the wall or the gym, and save climbing outdoors for the weekends (unlike many climbers who just tend to climb outdoors).

INTENSITY AND THRESHOLDS

How hard should I train? To answer this question, we must first understand the term 'threshold'. According to the *Oxford English Dictionary*, it is: 'a level, rate or amount at which something comes into effect'. Remember that functional adaptations are achieved by exposure to successively greater training stimuli. This is based on the Arndt–Schulz law,

which basically states: 'stimuli that fall short of the threshold have no [training] effect'.
This can be seen in the following graph:

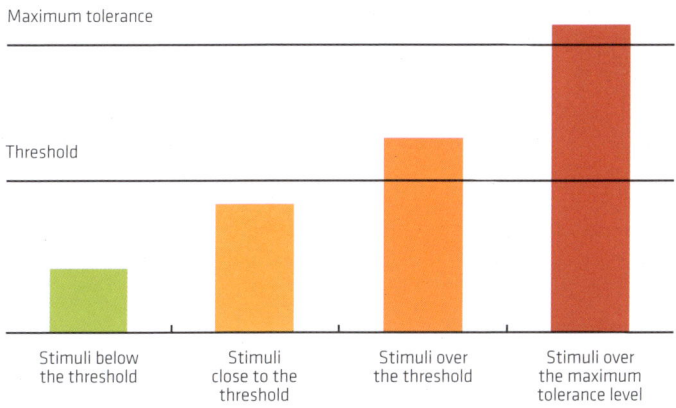

This graph demonstrates four possible scenarios:
- Stimuli below the threshold: no training effect. If our training doesn't require much effort, if it feels easy, then we're wasting our time.
- Stimuli close to the threshold: training effect if repeated, although some authors believe this only has a maintenance effect.
- Stimuli over the threshold: TRAINING EFFECT. These are the stimuli that we want. They take us out of our comfort zone and require just the right amount of effort. They make us dig deep and give that little bit extra.
- Stimuli over the maximum tolerance level: risk of overtraining syndrome and injury. If we need a few days to recover from a training session, we're probably over this level.

This should explain how hard to train: just hard enough, neither too little nor too much. As I said in the introduction: 'don't train more: train better'. Now let's look at how our bodies respond to stimuli that exceed the threshold to just the right degree, which is precisely what it means to 'train'.

4 | THE SCIENCE OF CLIMBING TRAINING

HOMEOSTASIS, GAS AND SUPERCOMPENSATION

Homeostasis is when the body is in a state of equilibrium. In other words, when synthesis and degeneration are in balance (remember the body is in a constant state of regeneration: from our skin to the cells in our bones). If something, in this case training, disrupts homeostasis, the body will establish a new state of balance through regenerative or anabolic processes. This is known as general adaptation syndrome (GAS), a theory developed by Hans Selye.

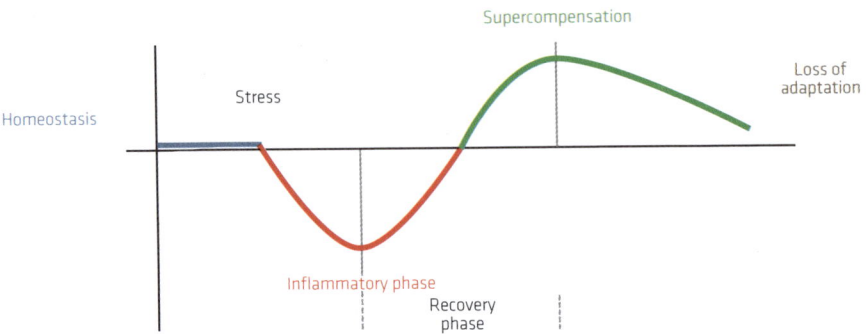

As seen in this graph, external stress disrupts the level of homeostasis in the body, leading to the inflammatory phase. During this phase, our body releases stress hormones such as adrenaline and steroid hormones such as corticosteroid (of which cortisol is the most well known). These hormones trigger physiological processes that allow us to withstand the *external stress* – the training – at the expense of 'damaging' our body, by creating what's known as *internal stress*.

When the external stress stops, the body tries to recover as quickly as possible. In other words, you're already recovering in the changing room after your session. To better withstand any similar external stress in the future, the body supercompensates to a heightened level of homeostasis, making you stronger than you were before the training session.

The bad news is that you'll lose the resulting adaptations if more stress isn't applied soon after the supercompensation phase. This is because the body adapts to the actual demands of our everyday lives. Logically, if something isn't needed and takes energy to maintain, the body will simply get rid of it to best adapt to our day-to-day needs. In even more bad news, the more extreme the adaptations (the harder you train), the faster they are lost because they're of least use. For example, the external stress that a sprinter would need to shave an extra hundredth of a second off a 100-metre sprint isn't really that useful for their body on a day-to-day basis. Training is like building a house: it can take years to build, but can be demolished in a matter of minutes.

That said, we have to be very careful about when we apply subsequent stress. If the body is still in the inflammatory phase, we risk entering a process called catabolism (degradation). If we don't realise this is happening, we could end up with overtraining syndrome and risk spending far more time at the doctor's than out at the crag, which is exactly what we don't what to happen. Luckily, it's difficult to fall into this trap unless you're training far too much and far too often.

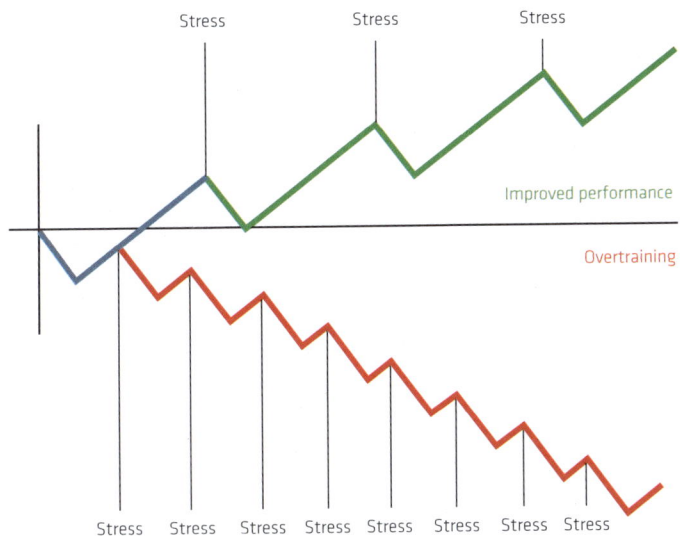

THE PRINCIPLES OF TRAINING

The principles of training are a set of rules that help us to develop and manage our training. For me, the most important of these are:
- *The principle of active and mindful participation:* perhaps the very reason behind this book. Understanding why we do things a certain way when training.
- *The principle of individualisation:* one that is often ignored. It means that any training should be adapted to the trainee's morpho-functional characteristics and level of ability. In other words, doing something just because it works for a friend is a big mistake.

- *The principle of specificity:* one of the most disheartening. It means that the gains from a certain exercise are not transferable to other situations. For example, training on a bike to improve aerobic capacity won't dramatically improve your aerobic capacity for long mountain walks. Similarly, the strength gained from doing pull-ups on a bar is only transferable to pulling down vertically on a bar-type hold.
- *The principle of continuity:* as the name suggests, only going to the gym once a month is simply a waste of membership fees.
- *The principle of variety:* training the same things in the same way is not going to work. You can't just repeat the same exercises for an entire season as the body will adapt and you'll see no improvement in performance. In the words of Albert Einstein: 'If you want different results [in our case, improved performance], do not do the same things.'

WHAT TO TRAIN

Now we know what training is, the logical thing to ask is: 'What should I train?'

In climbing, as in all sports, there are two types of training: visible training (physical factors) and invisible training (rest, nutrition, psychology, and so on). They are very closely linked and completely interdependent. Let's look that the specific factors that affect climbing performance:
- The technical factor (technique)
- The psychological factor (motivation, activation or arousal, fear, and so on)
- The physical factor (the physical condition of the climber)

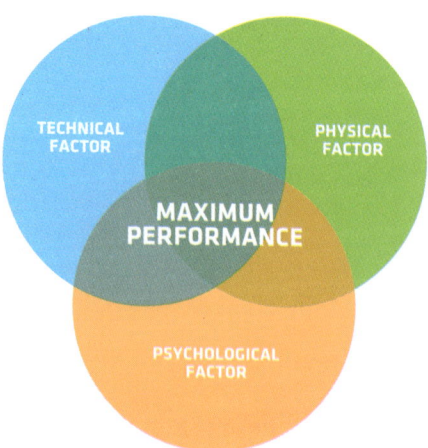

The ability to maximise and synchronise each of these factors is key to achieving the best possible performance.

This book deals exclusively with the physical factor of climbing. If you want to explore the other two factors, there's lots of information out there about mental training and technique, although it's always best to seek advice from a qualified professional.

In the simple yet meaningful words of renowned American football coach Vince Lombardi: 'Fatigue makes cowards of us all.' We could say that in climbing, a sport where these factors are so deeply connected, you need good physical form not only for individual moves but to respond to the wider challenges of any given climb. For example, imagine you're totally spent on the ninth pitch of a route, graded say F7a, and there are still five pitches to go: one F7b+ and four at F6b or above. It's going to be a real fight to finish the climb. Imagine you're also in a pretty committed situation, where you can't just abandon the route … things are really not looking good. This will of course affect your mental game. So, in this simple example, we've already touched on two of the three factors.

This book will analyse what to train to avoid these situations (at a higher or lower grade, on single or multi-pitch routes, alpine routes, boulder problems, and so on). Simply put, the physical factor is shaped by the following physical qualities: strength, endurance (cardiovascular), speed and flexibility. As you'll see throughout this book, strength and flexibility are the most important in climbing. Speed, in this context, is determined by strength and technique. Endurance, except when the approach to the crag is so strenuous that poor cardiopulmonary capacity will in fact affect climbing performance, is not a limiting factor *per se*. In any case, this will all be explored in greater depth.

UNDERSTANDING THE IMPORTANCE OF STRENGTH

WHAT IS STRENGTH?

Strength is the 'ability to overcome or counteract external resistance by muscular effort' (Zatsiorsky, 1995). And in the words of Tony Yaniro (the first person to climb F8a): 'If you can't do the moves, then there's nothing to endure.'

Strength manifests in countless (and at times incomprehensible and unrealistic) ways, and it can be hard to tell what type of strength is involved in any given action. In truth, it all comes down to a single type of strength: maximum strength.

According to the *Oxford English Dictionary*, 'maximum' is defined as: 'the greatest amount, extent or intensity possible, permitted or recorded'. Maximum strength sports are usually thought of as powerlifting and weightlifting, which have nothing to do with climbing. But this doesn't mean that max strength isn't used in other sports. According to Balsalobre-Fernández and Jiménez-Reyes (2014), in reality, anyone in any sport will try to use as much strength as possible, as often as possible and as fast as possible. To understand this, González-Badillo (2002) gives two examples. Firstly, a marathon isn't won by the runner with the best endurance but by the fastest runner, as they can move their body more quickly, exert greater force with each step and therefore produce more speed. Secondly, a 100-metre sprint is won by the runner who has spent the least amount of time exerting force, the least amount of time in contact with the ground and who has needed the least amount of time to propel themselves towards the finish line. This would suggest that any given movement in sport is not just about (maximum) strength, but the crucial link between max strength and speed.

Based on this, we could say any one person has as many different measures of max strength as there are movements or actions in their sport. Maximum strength can therefore be defined as the maximum amount of strength that can be applied by an individual in response to a specific stress or load within a specific movement in sport (Balsalobre-Fernández and Jiménez-Reyes, 2014).

However, maximum strength isn't only connected to speed, it's also closely connected to endurance. This is based on the idea that increasing our maximum strength also increases our submaximal strength. For example, imagine someone who can squat a maximum of 100 kilograms in a single rep (known as 1RM or one-repetition maximum). If they then squat 80 kilograms, they'll be using 80 per cent of their max strength. If they subsequently increase their 1RM to 160 kilograms, squatting 80 kilograms becomes 50 per cent of their max strength instead of 80 per cent. In other words, it's the same workload but less effort, meaning they can do more reps at this weight.

Let's apply this to climbing. If a climber struggles to do one pull-up, each time they need to pull when climbing they'll use a very high percentage of their strength, or even their max strength, and they'll fatigue quickly. If this climber could do a pull-up with say 50 kilograms of added weight, then a pull-up with no added weight wouldn't be much effort at all and they'd be able to do lots of them. As a result, pulling when climbing wouldn't be nearly so tiring.

This clearly shows that greater max strength equals greater endurance – and why strength is the mother of all physical qualities!

Endurance could also be defined as the ability to keep producing the necessary force to move mass through space over a set period of time. In other words, the ability to produce enough force to move your body at 13 miles per hour if you want to run a two-hour marathon, or to climb a 40-metre overhang without resting on the rope.

TYPES OF MUSCLE CONTRACTION

How do muscles contract to generate force? There are three different types of muscle contraction:
- *Isometric:* the muscle comes under tension but remains the same length. This happens when we push against an unmovable object (like a wall) or when we hold a certain body position (like a lock-off). In climbing, it's the main type of forearm muscle contraction: when we grip a hold, our forearm flexor muscles contract but remain the same length as we move the rest of our body.
- *Isotonic:* the muscle comes under tension and the length of the muscle changes. Concentric isotonic contractions are when the points of origin and insertion move closer together and enough force is generated to move an object (for example, the upward phase of a pull-up). Eccentric isotonic contractions are when the points of origin and insertion move further apart as sufficient force cannot be maintained or we want to return to the initial position (the downward phase of a pull-up).
- *Auxotonic:* this is a mixture of all the above, which is what happens in reality in all sports. With auxotonic contractions, a muscle could start off under isometric tension, instantly switch to concentric and then back to isometric or to eccentric, depending on how the action or movement evolves. Muscle contractions like to mix things up a little!

TYPES OF MUSCLE FIBRE AND RECRUITMENT

Sticking with types ... Each muscle contains different types of fibres. The body decides which fibres to contract or recruit depending on the action that we want to perform.
- *Type I fibres:* also known as slow-twitch, aerobic or red fibres. These muscle fibres are used for actions like walking or jogging that don't require a sudden burst of energy. They mainly use the aerobic energy system, and they are red because they contain red blood cells. As such, they're highly vascularised with a large number of capillaries for the supply of blood and nutrients, and they are highly resistant to fatigue.
- *Type II fibres:* also known as fast-twitch, anaerobic or white fibres. These include the subtypes IIa, IIb and IIx. Basically, IIb fibres have a higher recruitment threshold than IIa fibres, meaning they're only activated in more intense muscle contractions, and IIx fibres are indeterminate (they're transformed into IIa or IIb fibres as needed).

Type II fibres mainly use the anaerobic energy system and are white because they don't need the oxygen that is carried in red blood cells to produce energy. Although they can produce lots of energy, they fatigue much more quickly than type I fibres.

The percentage of type II fibres in our muscles is determined by our genetics. Through training, we can change type II muscle fibres into type I, but there's no scientific evidence that we can change type I into type II. This can be problematic in sports that require both strength and endurance, such as mountaineering. A mountaineer needs lots of type I fibres to get them through gruelling approaches, long routes and descents, but they also need type II fibres to do technical and difficult moves while carrying all their gear.

To adjust the percentage of each type of muscle fibre to best suit our needs, we need to follow an effective and well-designed training plan. We'll look at this in more depth after piecing together the other parts of the puzzle.

CAUSES OF FATIGUE

Why do we run out of steam? Why does our strength fail us? Why can't we maintain our energy levels? What turns off the supply? Firstly, it's important to distinguish between the type of fatigue caused by an 800-metre route, after a four-hour approach with 1,500 metres of elevation, and the type of fatigue caused by a six-move boulder problem. Secondly, it's important to distinguish between general or central fatigue and peripheral or local fatigue. Even then, it's not that simple, and in reality there are many factors that can contribute to fatigue (Cairns, 2013):

- *Build-up of lactate:* although in the past lactate has been blamed for causing fatigue, recent studies suggest that neither intracellular nor extracellular lactate reduces performance.
- *Metabolic acidosis:* at body temperature, acidosis reduces the ability to generate force, it significantly reduces the speed of muscle contractions and it causes a slight loss of calcium sensitivity on a cellular level.
- *Muscle hypoxia:* high-intensity muscle contractions need a good supply of oxygen to be sustained over time. Hypoxia refers to a lack of oxygen, where the muscle runs out of oxygen and can't draw any energy from its fuel supply. The muscle then competes with the brain for oxygen, lowering the brain's oxygen supply and leading to central fatigue.

- *Phosphates:* high-intensity exercise depletes adenosine triphosphate (ATP) and creatine phosphate (PCr) energy reserves, increasing the presence of inorganic phosphates. This affects the function of contractile proteins, inhibiting the production of force and speed.
- *Carbohydrate availability:* the availability of muscle and liver glycogen stores is a key factor in central fatigue but has little effect on local fatigue.
- *Build-up of hydrogen ions (H^+):* there's strong scientific evidence that the acidosis caused by a build-up of hydrogen ions significantly inhibits force, power and shortening velocity in muscle cells.
- *Build-up of ammonium:* the production of ammonium has also been linked to fatigue. Ammonium is produced when concentrations of ATP/PCr fall below critical levels and branched-chain amino acids are catabolised. This occurs in high-intensity training (for example, strength training, sprints, powerful boulder problems). In these cases, ammonium build-up is partly responsible for and an indicator of local muscle fatigue, and it can also contribute to central fatigue (Balsalobre-Fernández and Jiménez-Reyes, 2014).

However, between a movement command leaving the cerebral cortex, travelling through the motor neurons in the spinal cord, entering the muscle cell and arriving at the actin and myosin muscle fibres, there are many different places where fatigue could appear. As such, in reality we should be thinking about neuromuscular fatigue.

MUSCLE FAILURE: IS IT REALLY NECESSARY?

The 'no pain, no gain' mantra, training until you can't do another rep or move ... Is training to failure really necessary? Before we decide, let's look at some scientific evidence:
- Training to failure causes excessive fatigue, the stimulus creates muscle fibre transformation (IIx to IIa) and lowers the rate of force development (RFD) (Andersen and Aagaard, 2010; Marshall *et al.*, 2011; Schuenke *et al.*, 2012; Pareja-Blanco *et al.*, 2017).
- Training at half the possible number of reps leads to greater intra-set speed, lower performance loss and better neuromuscular recovery post-training. It results in less hormonal stress (cortisol, prolactin, GH, IGF-1), less muscle damage (creatine kinase (CK)) and a lower reduction in heart rate variability and complexity (HRV/HRC) post-training (González-Badillo *et al.*, 2016).

- Pareja-Blanco *et al.* (2017) compared the strength gains in two groups tasked with training squats: one group trained at half the possible number of reps, at 20 per cent velocity loss (VL20), while the other group trained at 40 per cent velocity loss (VL40), almost to muscle failure. Both groups made the same strength gains, but VL20 showed greater improvement in the countermovement jump test and VL40 showed greater hypertrophy with more type IIx to IIa muscle-fibre transformation.

So, what do we think? To build strength, it seems obvious that we should steer well clear of muscle failure, high levels of fatigue and the 'no pain, no gain' approach. (Don't worry if you don't know what velocity loss or RFD is, as we'll look at these later on in chapter 7.)

Training for any sport (with the exception of bodybuilding and very few others) should focus on the maximum performance of each rep, set and exercise. If we train to failure or exhaustion, fatigue will significantly limit the intensity at which we're able to perform these actions: we won't be able to perform at maximum intensity because we're tired. This doesn't just apply to intra-session fatigue: intra-microcycle fatigue, day-to-day fatigue and inter-session fatigue also have a significant effect. We should train in a way that creates the least possible fatigue so that we can come back and give it our all in our next session. As Yoda says: 'Do ... or do not. There is no try.' It's all or nothing: maximum intensity or it's not worth it. And you can't do this when you're tired.

WAYS TO DEVELOP STRENGTH: HYPERTROPHY AND NEURAL

We can all agree that Adam Ondra and Arnold Schwarzenegger are both really strong, but they couldn't look any less alike. This is because they use different training methods.

One of the aims of this book is to debunk the idea that you should only train strength if you want to look like Arnie. Traditionally, we've viewed bodybuilding practices as the only type of strength training and physical conditioning, leading to unwanted weight gain and perpetuating the myth that weight training makes you slow and heavy. Fortunately, this is gradually starting to change.

There are a few different options for making our muscles stronger:
- *Hypertrophy (sarcoplasmic/aesthetic or myofibrillar/functional):* enhancing contractile capacity by increasing the size of muscle fibres and contractile proteins (actin and myosin). Larger muscles ... just like Arnie.

- *Hyperplasia:* increasing the number of muscle fibres instead of the size. However, there's no evidence that it's possible to increase the number of muscle fibres in human beings, so this isn't an option.
- *Neural hypertrophy:* the best option for climbers. The following analogy can explain this type of training. A Ferrari won't use its full horsepower to drive around a city; it'll save maximum power for overtaking or racing. Our muscles are similar: they have a set number of muscle fibres (horsepower) and will use more or less of them as needed. The difference, and the problem, is that when some of these fibres aren't fired up or recruited, they're still there but we can't use them. This is where neural hypertrophy comes into play. It increases the *pool* (quantity) of fibres that are activated or innervated by a single motor neuron, aiming to maximise the innervation ratio and make use of every last gram of muscle. Greater fibrillar recruitment requires a more intense signal to be transmitted from motor neurons to muscle fibres. This electrical impulse is known as the action potential. We can't make our nervous system transmit a stronger action potential to the muscle fibres, but we can make it send more action potentials per unit of time. This is how we can recruit new fibres and get stronger without getting heavier.

The following table shows the key variables of strength training (adapted from Benito, 2008):

Rate of protein degradation (INTENSITY)	Mechanical workload (REPETITIONS)	Total amount of degraded proteins (HYPERTROPHY)
Low (<60% 1RM)	High (15+)	Low
Moderate (60–85% 1RM)	Moderate (6–12)	High
High (85–100% 1RM)	Low (1–4)	Low

As the table shows, both a high number of reps with lighter weights and a low number of reps with heavier weights will achieve a low degree of hypertrophy. And since the aim of strength training for climbing should be to improve our strength-to-weight ratio, we should be training as per the last row of the table: heavy weight and low reps.

STRENGTH TRAINING FOR INJURY PREVENTION

Is strength training also useful for injury prevention? Absolutely. Let's use another car analogy. Imagine driving a 70-horsepower car over a mountain pass. You'll be in a very low gear, going very slowly, burning a load of fuel and pushing the revs into the red. If you do this often or you want to go faster than the car can handle, you'll risk blowing the engine. Then think back to our Ferrari: with 500 horsepower, it will cruise over the pass at 60 miles per hour and at barely 2,000 revs per minute. Basically, a lot faster and with a lot less effort: it's unlikely you'll blow the engine. The same applies with the human body and the idea behind maximum strength training: the stronger you are, the less relative effort will be required for the same workload. Imagine a weaker and a stronger climber trying a hard move: the weaker climber is less likely to do the move, they'll fatigue faster and to a higher degree, will inflict greater damage on their muscles and tendons, and will be more likely to injure themselves.

Let's take a look at some scientific research:
- A study performed by Lauersen *et al.* (2014) analysed 26,610 subjects and a total of 3,464 injuries. It concluded that an appropriate strength programme was the most effective way to reduce injury, leading to a 30 per cent reduction in the number of injuries and a 50 per cent reduction in injuries related to overloading. Multicomponent and proprioception training programmes had a moderate effect but were significantly less effective than strength training. In turn, stretching proved to have no effect whatsoever on reducing injury.
- A study performed by Malone *et al.* (2019) explored the link between training load, physical condition and injury in amateur team sports (two to three training sessions a week). Participants who were relatively stronger (strength-to-weight ratio), faster over 5-metre, 10-metre and 20-metre sprints, and able to do more sprints in a short period of time showed greater tolerance of higher training loads and were less likely to injure themselves than participants with less well-developed physical qualities.

These findings suggest a new paradigm that many people are still unaware of: strength training is a more effective means of injury prevention than stretching. If this is news to you, steady yourself for the findings of Jenkins *et al.* (2016). They concluded that higher training loads (80 per cent 1RM) lead to greater strength gains as they produce greater neural adaptation than lower training loads (30 per cent 1RM). So, training heavy is even more effective than training light and much more effective than stretching for injury prevention.

In short, it is our focus on strength training that will help minimise the risk of injury. We can do this in two ways:
- *Training to maximise climbing performance:* if a climber can hang an 8-millimetre edge, using a 22-millimetre edge will cause minimal stress on their muscles and tendons. However, for novices or climbers at lower grades, using a 22-millimetre edge could be a huge challenge (even with feet on) for both the climber and their tendons. So, by training to maximise performance, we'll be less likely to injure ourselves.
- *Training to prevent/correct strength imbalance:* like any other sport, climbing involves the repetition of a specific set of movements or actions (for example, gripping holds, pulling up, pulling over). This means that the muscles used to perform these movements (agonists) become stronger. As these muscles increase in strength, they exert an increasingly strong pull on the corresponding joint. If the muscles that stabilise these joints (antagonists) can't respond with sufficient opposing force, this imbalance will result in joint instability. In turn, this can lead to poor posture, contracture or spasm in the antagonist muscles as they attempt to stabilise the joint by resisting the pull of the agonist muscles, and a significantly higher risk of injury.

UNDERSTANDING AND OPTIMISING MOBILITY

WHAT IS MOBILITY? FLEXIBILITY, ELASTICITY AND STIFFNESS

Mobility is a broader and more useful concept than others which we tend to use in the world of sport, such as flexibility or elasticity. Although mobility is affected to a certain degree by flexibility and elasticity, it cannot be defined solely by these terms. Mobility or range of motion (ROM) is, in fact, 'the amount of movement that exists in a joint and that is determined by the design of the joint' (Leal, Martínez and Sieso, 2012; Tortora and Derrickson, 2011; within Peláez Maza, 2015a).

There are several factors that affect the amount of movement in our joints:
- *The design of the joint itself:* this is determined by evolution and genetics so it's not something we can change. For example, the shape of our femoral neck bone will determine whether it's possible for us to do the splits.
- *Elasticity:* this is the ability of something (in this case, soft tissue) to return to its original state without deforming or breaking. Therefore, we can't be more elastic or less elastic: we either are or we aren't. There's no in between.

- *Muscle stiffness, tightness or tension:* this occurs when our muscles try to resist any form of deformation (or stretching). It is determined by the number of collagen fibres in our bodies (which is also genetic and so something else we can't change) and by our nervous system. There are numerous receptors in our muscles and tendons (we'll explore this later on in the book) that continually send sensory signals to the brain, providing information about how our muscles should move. If these mechanoreceptors detect that a joint may be unstable, they'll send a danger signal to the brain, and the brain will send a stop signal to the relevant muscles to stop this joint from moving. This prevents the joint from entering a potentially dangerous range of motion, protecting it from harm. Thus, some authors believe that stiffness (as a mechanical factor) is not a limiting factor of ROM and that mobility is instead limited by the nervous system (Piepoli, 2019).
- *Flexibility:* this is the ability of a material to bend without breaking (Nacleiro, 2011, within Peláez Maza, 2015a). By definition, improving flexibility is not the same as improving mobility, which in reality is what any athlete wants to do (although good mobility does require muscular flexibility to prevent injury).

So, do we really get 'tight' muscles? If tightness is a defence mechanism (against injury) and (static/passive) stretching attempts to turn off this mechanism, does it make any sense to stretch when that might increase our risk of injury? And will this help improve our ROM?

ACTIVE VS PASSIVE FLEXIBILITY AND MOBILITY RESERVE

The brain is like an overprotective parent who's obsessed with keeping us safe, but sometimes this excessive protection can have the opposite effect.

Luckily, the brain is constantly being fed information about the body (such as body position, tension, muscle length) and using this information to instruct us to move or not move, or perform a certain action or not. For example, if you sprain your ankle, the brain will not only issue pain signals to stop you from fully weighting your foot but will also orchestrate a new pattern of movement (limping) so you can still walk. All this information comes from numerous sensory receptors (proprioceptors) that are located around the body (in muscles, tendons, ligaments, joint capsules, and so on) and which are directly connected to the nervous system. To keep things simple, we'll just mention three different types:

- *Muscle spindles:* receptors which measure and report on variations in muscle length and the speed at which these variations occur.
- *Golgi tendon organs:* receptors found in tendons, next to the bone–tendon junction, which report on variations in muscle contractions.
- *Joint receptors:* receptors that are embedded in joint capsules, ligaments, and so on, which report on the position of the joint.

Using the information sent by these receptors, the brain controls the mobility of each and every joint in the human body. In practice, this range of motion is divided into:

- *Active flexibility:* the ROM we can achieve voluntarily. How far apart we can spread our legs or if we can bend over and touch our knees, our toes or get our hands flat on the floor. As muscle tension is determined by the brain based on the information received from mechanoreceptors, active ROM will vary depending on what action is being performed and when it is being performed (Latash and Zatsiorsky, 1993).
- *Passive flexibility:* the ROM we can achieve with the assistance of an external force that moves the joint into a certain position, such as a band, or our hands. However, there's a difference between the limit of our active ROM and the point at which the joint is at immediate risk of injury. This difference exists so when any sort of external force is applied (for example, a fall or a collision), the joint has a small margin of extra mobility before reaching breaking point.

The difference in mobility between active and passive ROM is referred to by some authors as our mobility reserve. It is the range of motion that we can't access voluntarily but which we could tap into with training.

MYOTATIC REFLEX AND AUTOGENIC INHIBITION/INVERSE MYOTATIC REFLEX

The body uses two basic reflexes, among other things, to control muscle tone:
- *Myotatic reflex:* this measures and controls muscle length. In response to stretching, this reflex causes the muscle to contract in order to resist the stretch.
- *Autogenic inhibition or inverse myotatic reflex:* this measures and controls muscle tension. In response to intense and prolonged tension (as created by passive stretching), the proprioceptors send signals to the brain to relax the muscle in order to prevent any damage. By relaxing the muscle, the brain inhibits its ability

to produce force. As such, it doesn't seem that sensible to activate this reflex in climbing or in any other sport. In fact, inhibiting muscle response to improve joint mobility, precisely when we want the best possible response from our muscles (during sport or training), doesn't make any sense at all. This is why we should avoid passive or static stretching of agonist muscles before or during training as it would send contradictory signals to the brain (contract, relax, contract, relax, and so on), which can easily lead to injury.

THREAT PERCEPTION AS A LIMITING FACTOR OF ROM

Why would the brain limit a joint's range of motion? The brain is an expert at making predictions. It anticipates all possible outcomes and will attempt to give the best possible response based on past experience. For example, if you're about to jump from a certain height, your brain will assess this height and produce what it thinks is the right amount of force to break your fall. This calculation is based on past experiences of you jumping from the same or similar heights. In response to stretching, mobilisation or the need to move, the brain considers all possible factors (such as how comfortable you are, if you're in a safe environment, the necessity of the action, good or bad past experiences) and forms a response. If, for whatever reason, it decides that moving a joint into a certain position means it will lose control of the joint, and if this lack of control could lead to injury, it will react in two ways: inhibiting the muscles responsible for moving the joint, and creating tension and pain in another place in order to bypass the 'zona incerta' in the brain, which it is proposed plays a role in gating sensory input and controlling pain.

BRAIN MAPS, SIMS AND DIMS

The brain is home to millions of interconnected neurons. It is the control centre for the whole body and decides how and when we move. To do this, it contains a representation of every muscle in the human body. When a group of neurons – a neural circuit – is activated, it controls a certain muscle. To perform a specific movement, several of these circuits are activated at the same time (to use a crimp above your head, you need to raise your arm, turn your hand, move your fingers, and so on). To perform a movement that you've done before, the brain uses a 'map' of these circuits to produce this movement.

3 UNDERSTANDING AND OPTIMISING MOBILITY | 23

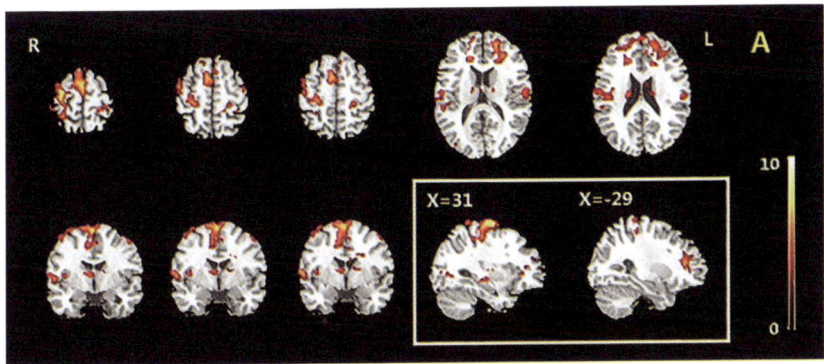

ACTIVATION IN DIFFERENT AREAS OF THE BRAIN FOR FINGER FLEXION (LI *ET AL.*, 2015)

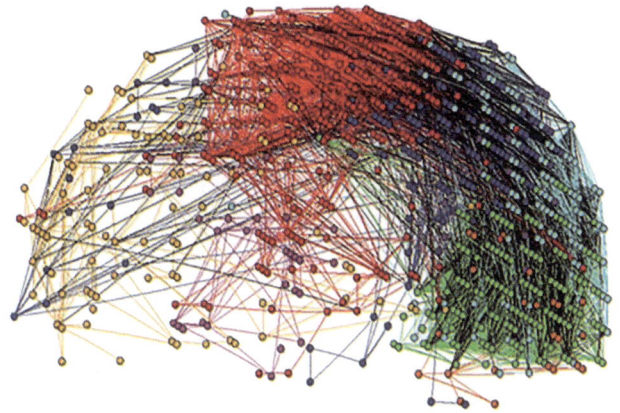

REPRESENTATION OF BRAIN CONNECTIVITY (MEUNIER *ET AL.*, 2010)

These maps are closely linked to the brain's powers of prediction as they are continually updated with new experiences. For example, when you throw for a hold on a new route, your brain activates its map for holding an edge. However, since you've never held this specific hold before, it doesn't know if this is the right map. Using the information it receives about visual perception, body position, and so on, it decides on what it thinks will be the best map for the job. When you make contact with the hold, your brain will readjust its map or create a new one, depending on the information received about the size, depth, texture and other characteristics of the hold.

But what's this got to do with mobility? It's simple: the brain will perceive a potential threat if it has to rely on a damaged or corrupted map of the movement that we want to perform (if an injury, awkward body movement or bad experience has damaged the map). A damaged map could be missing key information about the joint, in which case the brain will restrict its movement in order to prevent injury. Likewise, if there's no map for the movement we want to perform, this will also be seen as a potential threat and we'll need to inform the brain that the movement is safe.

This is where things get interesting, with the appearance of SIMs and DIMs (Moseley and Butler, 2015). SIMs (Safety In Me) are things that make us feel strong, happy, more secure, and suchlike. DIMs (Danger In Me) are things that we feel might endanger our body, life, happiness, and so on. They function as positive or negative neurotags that are attached to actions or feelings and which activate different sets of brain maps. As such, they affect how the brain responds to different situations. As this is quite a complicated topic, let's use an example based on climbing. Helen was training at the climbing wall a few days ago. She did a drop-knee on a boulder problem, slipped and hurt her knee. She had some physiotherapy for the pain in her knee and she's now made a full recovery. She goes back to the wall and is about to try the same problem again. Her brain starts predicting what might happen: it knows that she hurt herself on this move before and, what's more, the brain map for this move is now damaged. This is when a DIM will appear, signalling danger: be on alert, watch out. She tenses up, her muscles become stiff and she can't move fluidly. She pulls on the problem and can't even get to the move to try the drop-knee. She needs to retrain her brain and create a SIM so that she isn't afraid of drop-knees and can move fluidly and confidently through them.

OPTIONS FOR OPTIMISING MOBILITY

After all this, what can we do to improve mobility? There are a number of options, and each works in a different way and is more or less useful depending on the person:
- *Breathing and relaxation techniques:* although it seems like the simplest thing in the world, breathing and relaxation can help improve joint mobility. Feeling stressed puts the sympathetic nervous system in a state of high alert, anticipating danger. As we saw earlier, if the brain senses danger, it won't let us do anything that it doesn't think is safe. What's more, on a cellular level, the shape and density of the fibroblasts in our fascia are affected by incoming electrical impulses (a phenomenon known as piezoelectricity), meaning they're affected by emotions and, of course, anxiety is a powerful emotion.

- *Techniques to reduce descending inhibition:* many physiotherapy techniques and paraphernalia such as foam rollers, massage sticks and different size/texture balls are based on the age-old principle of massage. This helps increase blood flow in the massaged area and therefore boosts oxygen supply (improving the predisposition of this area to exercise). It also stimulates the proprioceptors, creating a signal to activate the mechanisms of descending pain inhibition (meaning less pain information reaches the brain). In turn, this can improve stretch tolerance and therefore ROM (Støve *et al.*, 2019).

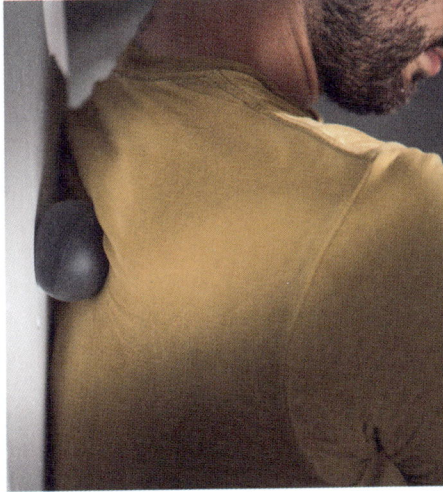

- *Flossing:* this technique involves wrapping a stretchy band around a joint and moving the joint as much as possible for a set period of time (usually no more than two minutes). There are numerous benefits to this type of compression. It holds the joint firmly in place, so the brain knows that the joint is secure and under control. It also holds the superficial fascia in place and pulls on it when the joint moves. This causes the fascia to glide over the muscle, reducing adhesions and therefore improving both the transmission of force through the superficial and deep fascia system and the sliding of muscle fibres. Finally, flossing affects the blood supply to the targeted area. By moving the joint, we're increasing blood supply to the area, but by compressing it at the same time, we're stopping the blood from entering the area. (Warning: this is an effective technique but it can be highly uncomfortable, especially if the joint is injured in any way.) When the compression stops, this build-up

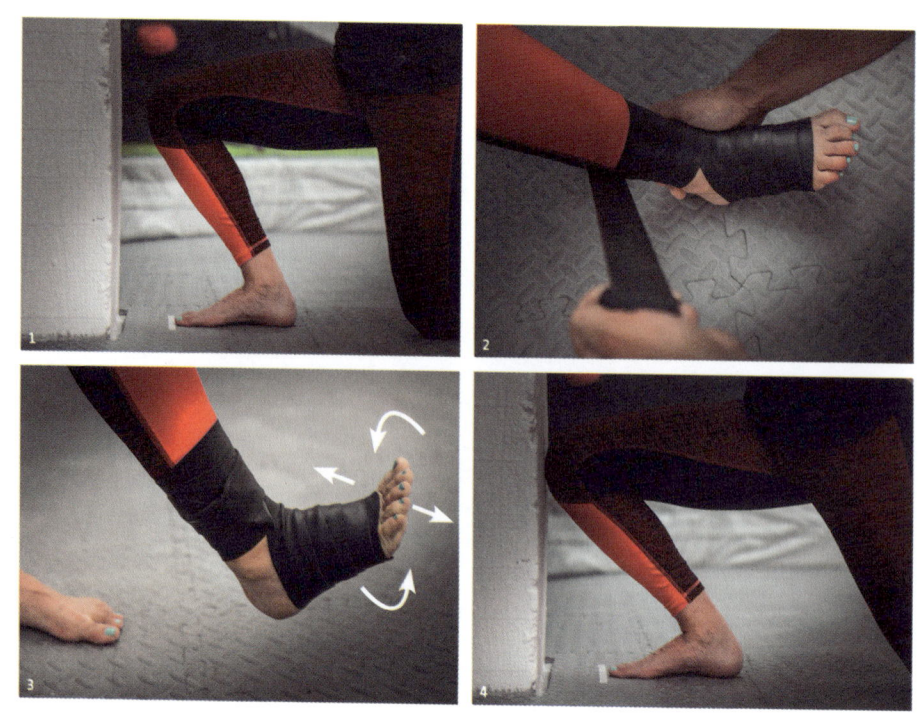

1. ASSESSING ANKLE MOBILITY (DORSIFLEXION). 2. WRAPPING THE JOINT FOR FLOSSING. 3. MOVING THE JOINT TO END RANGE OF MOTION IN ALL POSSIBLE DIRECTIONS. 4. MEASURING THE INCREASE IN ANKLE MOBILITY AFTER FLOSSING.

of blood rushes through the area, carrying away metabolic waste and inflammatory substances, which also significantly reduces pain. This technique is also highly effective for recovering from injuries (Clements, 2015).
- *Improving end-range strength:* another example of the importance of strength. High-intensity isometric exercises (70 per cent of 1RM) have been proven to reduce intracortical inhibition in the contracted muscle, to reduce pain for up to 45 minutes after training and to increase corticospinal excitability, improving maximum voluntary contraction (Rio *et al.*, 2015, within Peláez Maza, 2016). In other words, these exercises give the brain control over the muscle, reducing the perception of threat. There is also strong evidence that submaximal eccentric exercises are highly effective for increasing muscle strength at a low risk of injury as they allow for greater motor control. (In fact, these types of exercises have been used for years

in physiotherapy treatments.) As such, doing a few sets of submaximal eccentric contractions at the end range of movement will increase muscle strength and give the brain confidence and control in this range, therefore improving joint mobility. What is intracortical inhibition? As we already know, the brain can detect when a joint is in a potentially dangerous position and will send a pain signal and a signal that inhibits muscular force. The brain 'puts the brakes on' to stop the joint from moving towards the threat. To do this, it sends inhibition signals from the cerebral cortex. Through strength training, proprioception training and local vibration therapy, we can send a message to the brain to 'ease off the brake' and to 'give it some gas' instead, resulting in intracortical facilitation. This makes the area more sensitive, enhancing proprioceptive control, motor control and therefore strength, by reducing the effects of threat perception in the brain.

- *Local vibration:* most coaches won't have heard of this technique as it's more common in rehabilitation than in sports performance. There's an increasing amount of research into the benefits of this technique, although the exact details of how it works remain unclear. A study performed by Souron *et al.* (2017) found that after eight weeks of local vibration therapy at 100Hz, on three non-consecutive days of the week, maximum strength increased in both the vibrated muscle and in the opposing muscle (vibration not applied). To explain these findings, it was suggested that the increase in signals sent by the proprioceptors to the brain led to greater activation of the corticospinal pathways. That is, it improved the interconnecting 'highway' between the brain and the muscles, allowing for more information to be sent and received, therefore improving motor control.

28 | THE SCIENCE OF CLIMBING TRAINING

INITIAL ROM IN HIP ABDUCTION

LOCAL VIBRATION + ISOMETRIC CONTRACTIONS IN ABDUCTOR MUSCLES

ROM IN HIP ABDUCTION POST INTERVENTION

- *Motor imagery:* recent studies have shown that in addition to mechanical factors, the nervous system and especially the brain also have a significant impact on ROM. Motor imagery (visualisation, imagery training, mental imagery, and suchlike) is defined as a cognitive task based on the internal reproduction, in this case mental, of a specific movement with no other type of motor stimulation (Cicinelli *et al.*, 2006, within Peláez Maza, 2015b). Athletes have been using these techniques for years to improve the quality of an action or movement and consolidate new techniques. In elite sport, visualisation is considered a fundamental part of training. But what's visualisation got to do with mobility? Although it might seem unlikely that you could improve your range of motion by simply imagining it, mental imagery does have an impact on brain maps. As such, it could be really useful in repairing damaged maps and in increasing cerebral control over our muscles.

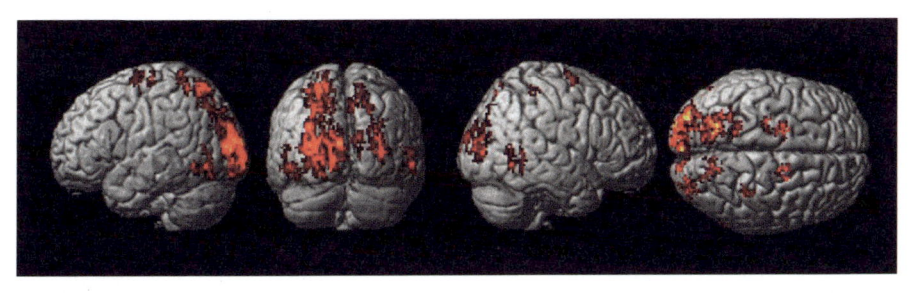

CEREBRAL ACTIVATION OF HAND MOTOR MAPS DURING MOTOR IMAGERY EXERCISES (PILGRAMM *ET AL.*, 2016).

So where does this leave stretching? It's important to distinguish between the two main types of stretching: active stretching (resulting from our own actions – we stretch) and passive stretching (resulting from the application of external force – we get stretched).

The aim of passive stretching is to increase the length of the muscle by reducing muscular tension. But what really happens? In response to external force, the myotatic reflex shortens the muscle to protect it and stop it from tearing. And here's our first contradiction: you try to lengthen a muscle but end up shortening it. So how does this type of stretching work? It inhibits the muscle spindle, inhibits the myotatic reflex and activates the autogenic inhibition reflex. This means that the muscle can't respond, contract or produce any force. Although this can be useful in some situations, it definitely does more harm than good if you're about to do any type of sport.

As for active stretching, let's clear up a common misconception about the mechanics of stretching. The brain doesn't send a signal to stretch the targeted muscle, it sends a signal to shorten the opposing muscle. For example, if you sit on the floor with your legs straight and try to touch your toes, your brain won't send a signal to stretch your back and your hamstrings, but instead to contract the hip flexors. Therefore, the stretching of one muscle is an indirect consequence of the shortening of another.

Now let's distinguish between static stretching, and dynamic or ballistic stretching. Static stretching involves the isometric contraction of the opposing group of muscles to those which we want to stretch. There's different advice on how long to hold these stretches, but a standard duration would be around 30 seconds. This is enough time to inhibit the myotatic reflex in the targeted muscle. However, as we've already seen, this isn't recommended if you're about to do any form of sport, except in very specific cases, and especially not for agonist muscles. The following studies show the effects of static stretching prior to physical exercise:

- Baxter *et al.* (2017) studied the effects of static stretching before running. The results showed that it decreased musculotendinous stiffness and elastic potential energy, reducing running economy and performance for up to an hour after stretching. It didn't reduce the duration or intensity of muscle stiffness or the prevalence of running-related injuries.
- Jelmini *et al.* (2018) performed a maximum strength test on the flexor muscles in both hands using a hand-held dynamometer. They then stretched the dominant hand only and repeated the test. The stretched hand lost 17.3 per cent of its strength. The non-stretched hand lost 10.8 per cent of its strength. This loss of strength continued for up to 15 minutes after stretching.
- Reduced performance after stretching has also been observed in other studies (Lauersen *et al.*, 2014; Kay and Blazevich, 2012; Thacker *et al.*, 2004). These studies found that stretching not only failed to reduce the risk of injury but could trigger an inflammatory response, which would damage soft tissue and therefore increase the risk of injury.

To conclude, static or passive stretching is simply not a good idea (either before or during training). Stretches that are held beyond the myotatic reflex (for longer than eight seconds) reduce the muscle's contractile capacity. They slow down the generation and transmission of electrical impulses. This can cause up to a 30 per cent loss in performance, which can continue for up to an hour after stretching and result in an increased risk of injury. So be very careful with this type of stretching.

Active stretches are repeated concentric contractions of the opposing muscles to those which we want to stretch. Instead of inhibiting the muscle spindle, these stretches activate the antagonist muscles. This generates intracortical facilitation, reduces inhibition and strengthens the muscles, while the brain feels safe and in control and therefore increases the range of motion: a much better scenario for performing at our best! Now we've covered mobility, let's turn our attention to how we can use movement to maximise the efficiency of our training.

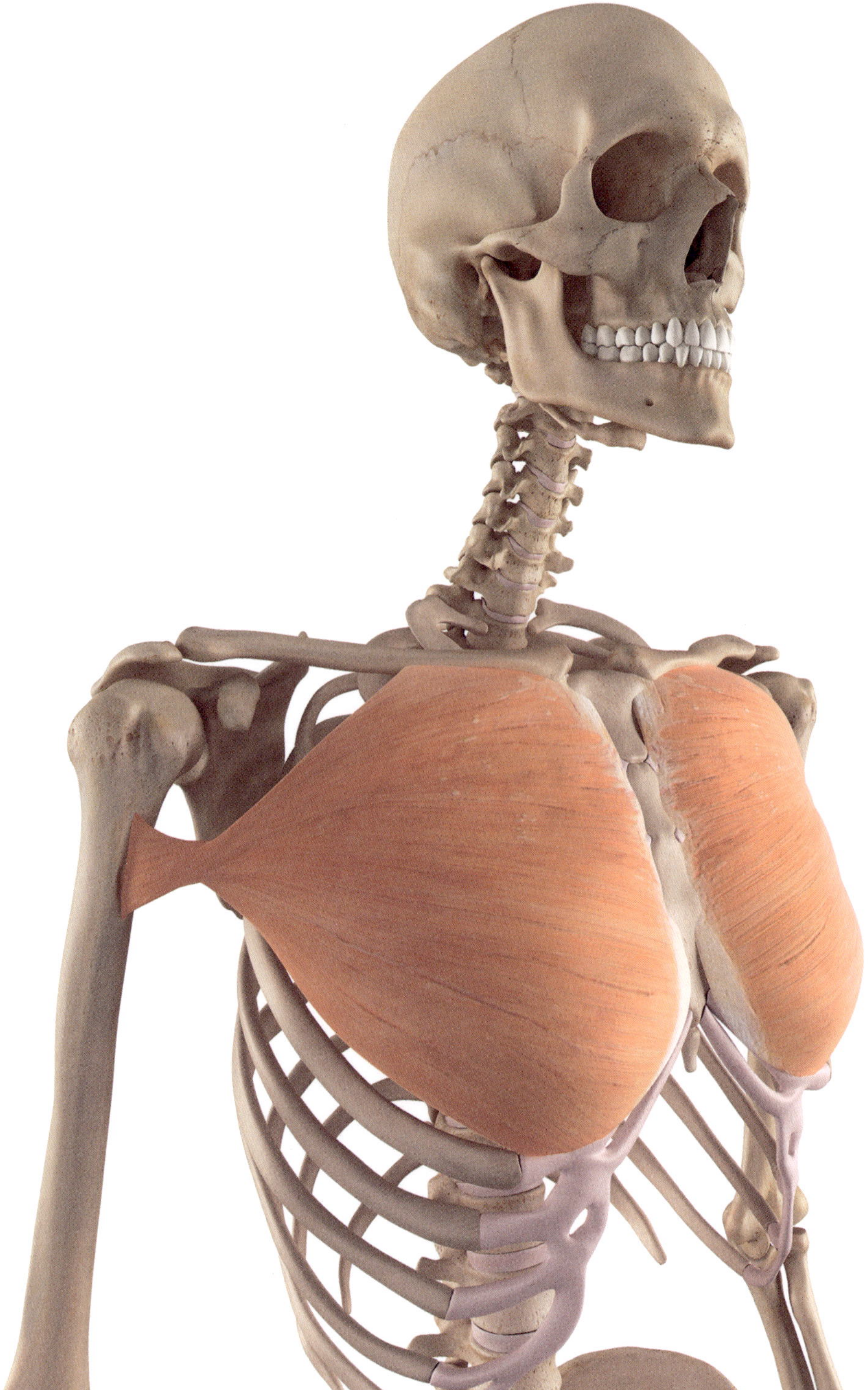

4

BRIEF NOTES ON ANATOMY

You might be wondering why there's a section on anatomy in a book about training for climbing. However, understanding how our body is designed will give us a better insight into how it works. One of the objectives of this book is to understand how our body works so we can understand how to design a training plan, why an exercise has to be done in a certain way or why choosing a different exercise could lead to injury.

To simplify the information and make it easier to digest, let's say that most of the time in climbing, the muscles in the upper body are used for *pulling* (the basic action of holding on and pulling up), while the muscles in the lower body are used for *pushing*, or propelling, us up the wall. Between the upper and the lower body lies the core (a firm favourite at the gym), linking these parts of the body and bringing both actions together into one fluid upward motion.

This chapter looks at which muscles and anatomical structures are most important for climbing, keeping the level of detail (and tedium) to a minimum and drawing on information provided by Schünke *et al.* (2005).

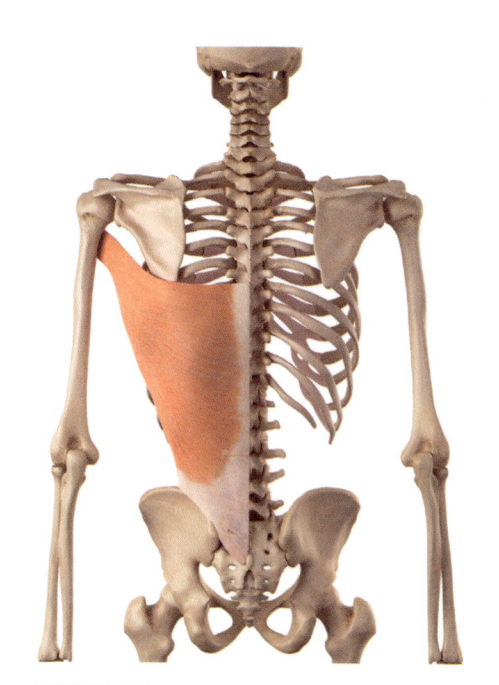

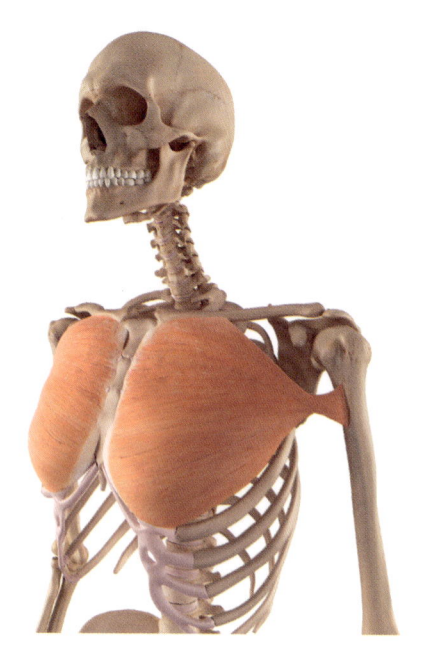

LATISSIMUS DORSI

PECTORALIS MAJOR

UPPER BODY: PULLING MUSCLES

To help understand the anatomy of the upper body, the muscles can be divided into three main groups:
- *Torso muscles:* the latissimus dorsi and the pectoralis major are the main muscles in this group and the most important for climbing. The latissimus dorsi is the number one pulling muscle in climbing, while the pectoralis major, far from being its antagonist, helps to stabilise the glenohumeral joint (shoulder) and to move the arm towards and away from the body.
- *Shoulder girdle:* in addition to the shoulder joint, the arm is also attached to the torso by a group of joints and muscles (a girdle) that connects the humerus to the scapula and the clavicle. It also connects the scapula to the spine and the rib cage, and the clavicle to the sternum. This aside, let's look at the shoulder girdle in a little more depth. By understanding the scope and complexity of this structure, we'll see why its stability is so important. On the one hand, the large latissimus dorsi, pectoralis major, serratus anterior and the anterior deltoid, helped by other smaller

4 BRIEF NOTES ON ANATOMY | **35**

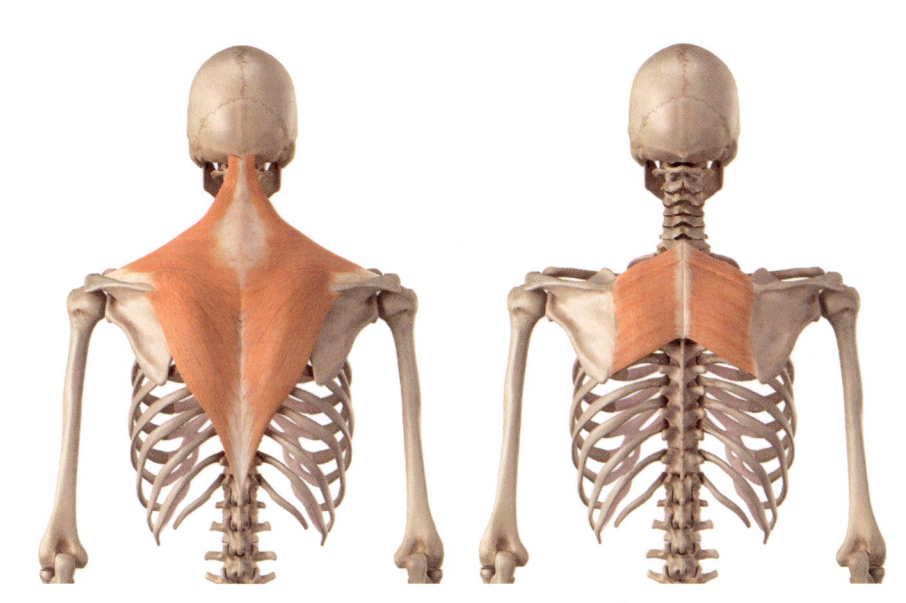

TRAPEZIUS   RHOMBOIDS

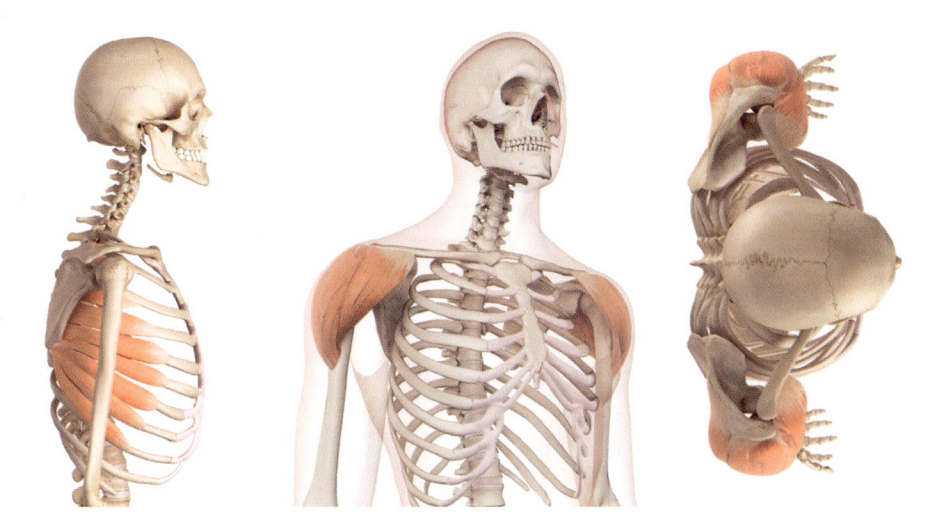

LEFT: SERRATUS ANTERIOR (NOTE THE EXTENSION FROM THE SCAPULA ROUND TO THE RIBS)
CENTRE: DELTOIDS
RIGHT: NOTE THE EXTENSION OF THE DELTOIDS FROM THE CLAVICLE TO THE POSTERIOR PART AT THE SCAPULA

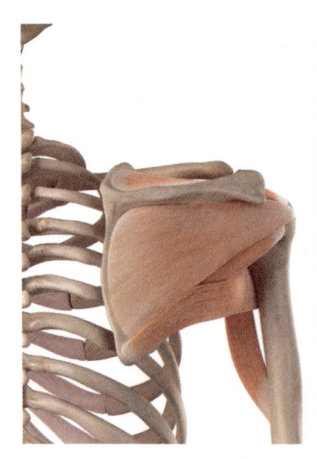

36 | THE SCIENCE OF CLIMBING TRAINING

ROTATOR CUFF 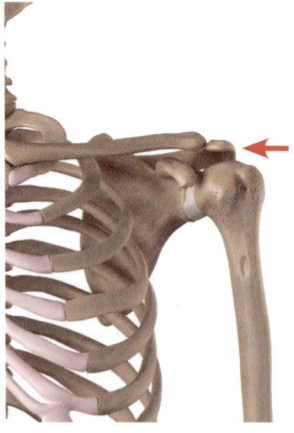   SUBACROMIAL SPACE 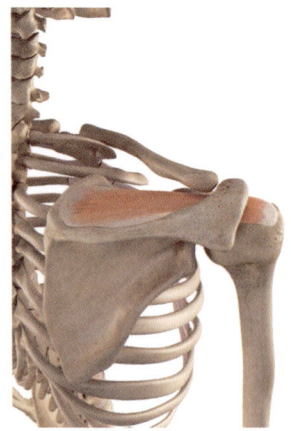   SUPRASPINATUS MUSCLE IN THE SUBACROMIAL SPACE

muscles like the teres major and the subscapularis, are responsible for internal rotation and scapular protraction. In contrast, only the infraspinatus muscle and the teres minor are responsible for external rotation, and only the trapezius and rhomboids are responsible for scapular retraction. As a result, if we don't actively counter the predominant action (internal rotation and scapular protraction), we'll end up not only with rounded shoulders but at a much higher risk of injury.

On the other hand, the socket of the shoulder joint (where the large head of the humerus articulates with the glenoid fossa of the scapula) is so shallow that the glenoid ligament, a fibrocartilaginous structure, is needed to deepen the socket and improve contact. The difference in size between the humeral head and the glenoid fossa makes the shoulder joint incredibly mobile but also very unstable, leading to a high risk of injury. On the subject of injury, the subacromial space also deserves a mention. This space is located between the humerus and the acromion (see image, above), and the supraspinatus tendon runs through it. If the scapula is not properly stabilised (for example, retracted and depressed for deadhangs), this space is compressed and the supraspinatus tendon can become impinged. Bursitis, tendinosis and even tears are some of the nasty injuries that can occur (not to mention long periods of intense rehabilitation and retraining) if we neglect the shoulder girdle and the subacromial space.

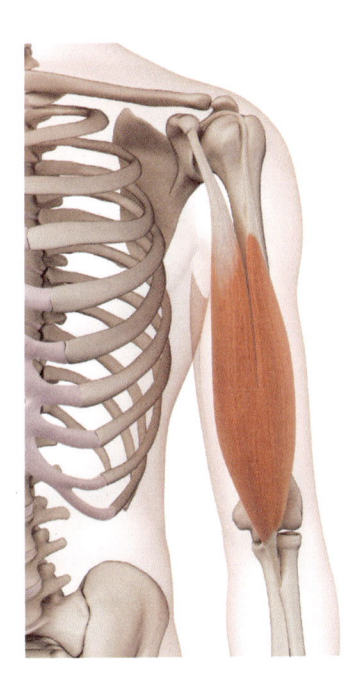

BICEPS BRACHII

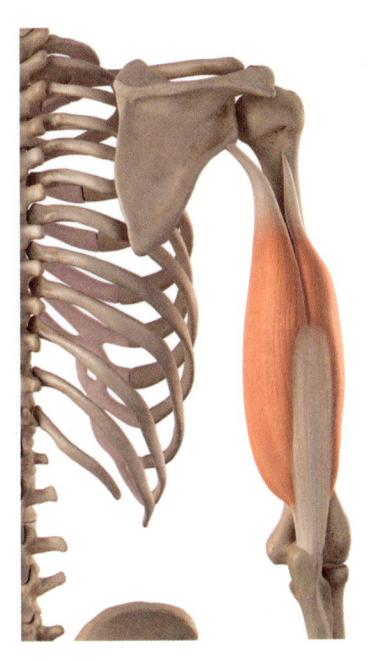

TRICEPS BRACHII (NOTE THE LONG HEAD THAT RISES FROM THE SCAPULA)

- *Upper arm and forearm muscles:* despite being part of the most important limb in climbing, the upper arm doesn't really have that many muscles. It contains the biceps and the brachialis, which are elbow flexors, and the triceps, which is an extensor muscle. The long head of the triceps also helps the latissimus dorsi to move the humerus towards the torso.

    The forearm and the hand, the stars of the show, are a little more complex. There are 19 muscles in the forearm (eight flexors, eight extensors and three radial) and 11 in the hand. In climbing, we need a good degree of balance and synergy between all these muscles and a high level of strength in different grip positions. That said, the flexor digitorum profundus (FDP) is *the* most important muscle in climbing (Philippe et al., 2012). This is because it flexes the interphalangeal joints in digits two to five, which are the fingers used for dragging. In turn, the flexor carpi ulnaris and the palmaris longus muscle are used most with slopers. The extensors help maintain joint stability, and they move the wrist and forearm into the right position for gripping and pulling. As for pinches, the muscles in the hand do most of the work.

38 | THE SCIENCE OF CLIMBING TRAINING

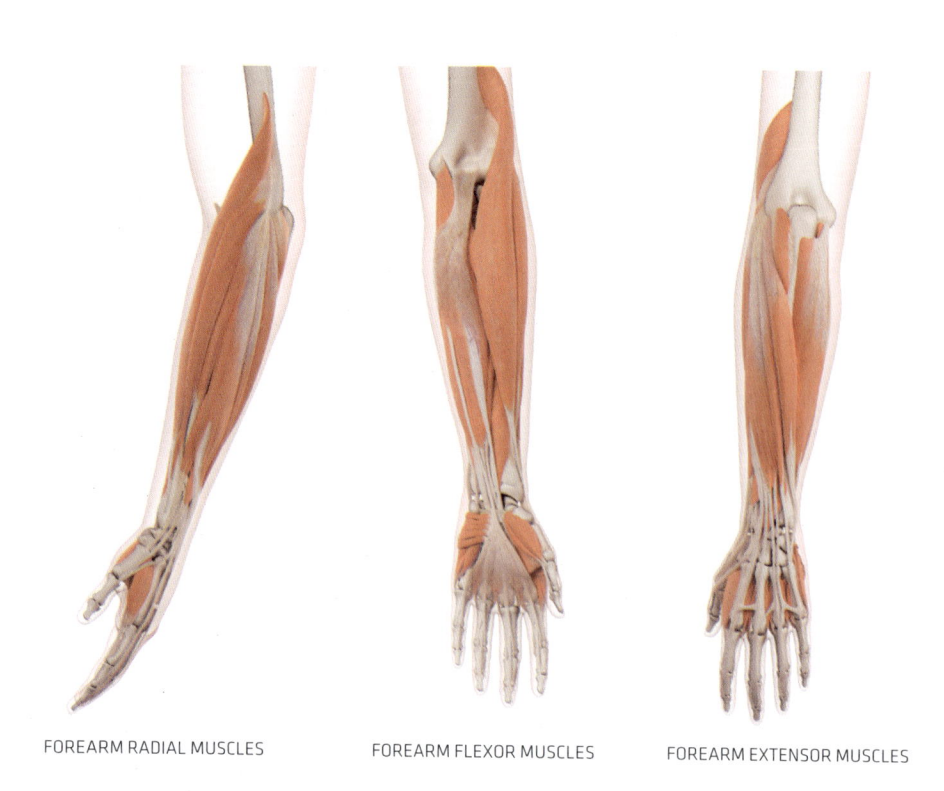

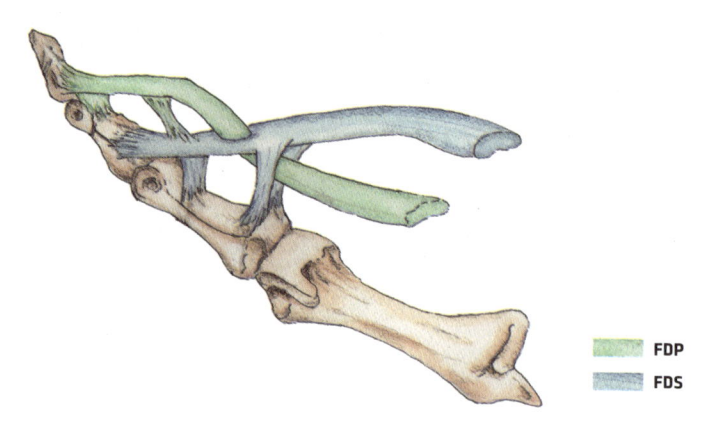

FOREARM RADIAL MUSCLES   FOREARM FLEXOR MUSCLES   FOREARM EXTENSOR MUSCLES

FDP
FDS

INSERTION IN THE FINGER BONES OF THE FLEXOR DIGITORUM SUPERFICIALIS (FDS) AND THE FLEXOR DIGITORUM PROFUNDUS (FDP)

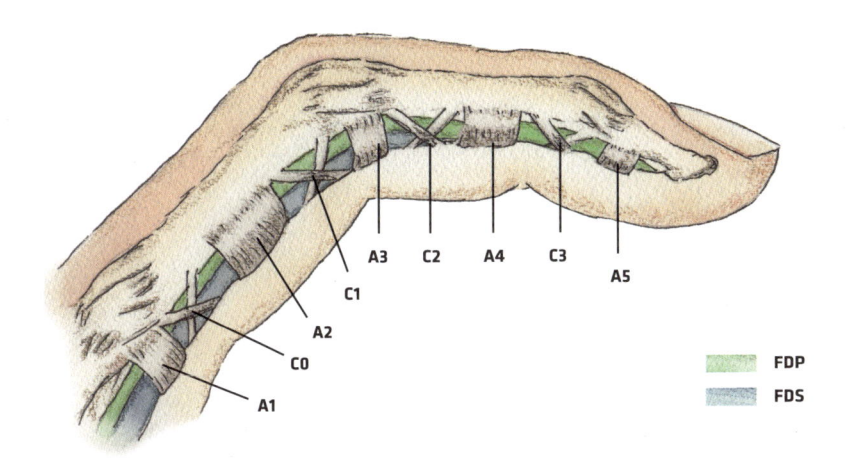

ANNULAR PULLEYS (A) AND CRUCIATE PULLEYS (C), WHICH GUIDE AND SUPPORT THE FDS AND FDP TENDONS

The hand is one of the most complex parts of the human body, biomechanically speaking, due to its broad range of movement and incredible fine motor control. Without detracting from this impressive complexity, we'll just focus on the finger tendons and ligaments (pulleys) since they are most prone to injury, as seen in the section on injury prevention.

CORE: THE CONNECTING CHAIN

The core (centre or nucleus) has a dual function: it transfers force between the upper and the lower body, and it also stabilises and protects the spinal column (remember there's a complex system of nerves that branch off from the spinal canal and that an injury anywhere along the spine could have devastating consequences).

Considering these complex functions, it is no surprise that the core consists of much more than just the abdominal muscles (Boyle, 2017):
- *Scapular muscles:* the rhomboids and the serratus muscles connect the scapulae (and therefore the arms) to the rib cage. They transmit force from the arms to the body and vice versa.
- *Deep core:* focusing on the transverse abdominal muscle and the multifidus muscle. These muscles perform anticipatory postural adjustments, which means they're activated before the rest of the muscles involved in any given movement in order to protect and stabilise the spine.

40 | THE SCIENCE OF CLIMBING TRAINING

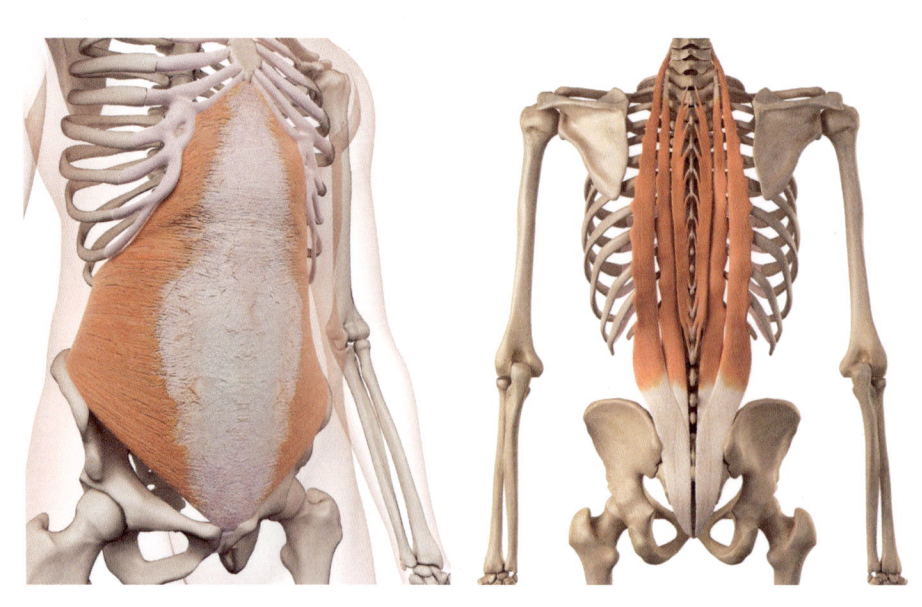

TRANSVERSE ABDOMINAL MUSCLE

PARASPINAL MUSCLES

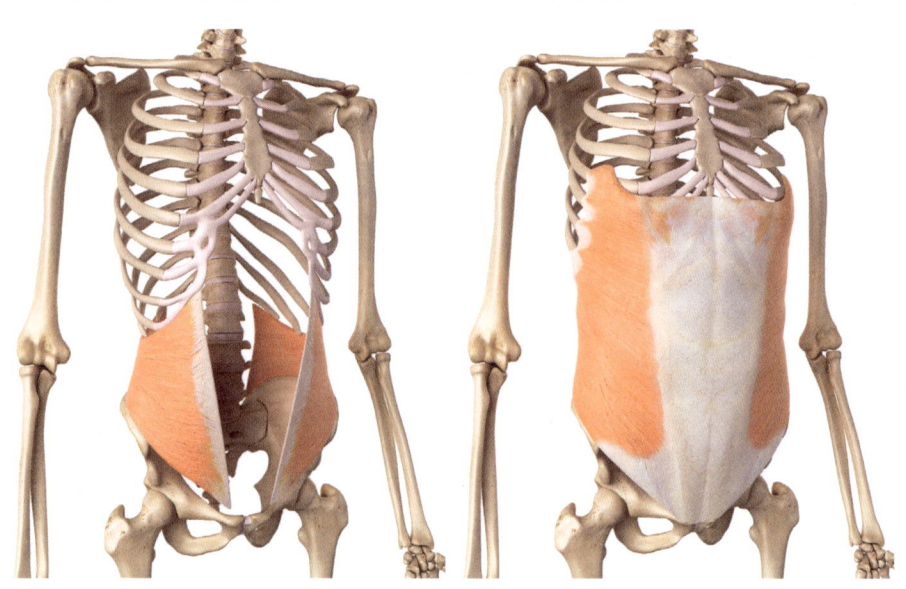

LEFT: INTERNAL OBLIQUE (INSERTION IN THE FASCIA OF THE EXTERNAL OBLIQUE)   RIGHT: EXTERNAL OBLIQUE

4 BRIEF NOTES ON ANATOMY | 41

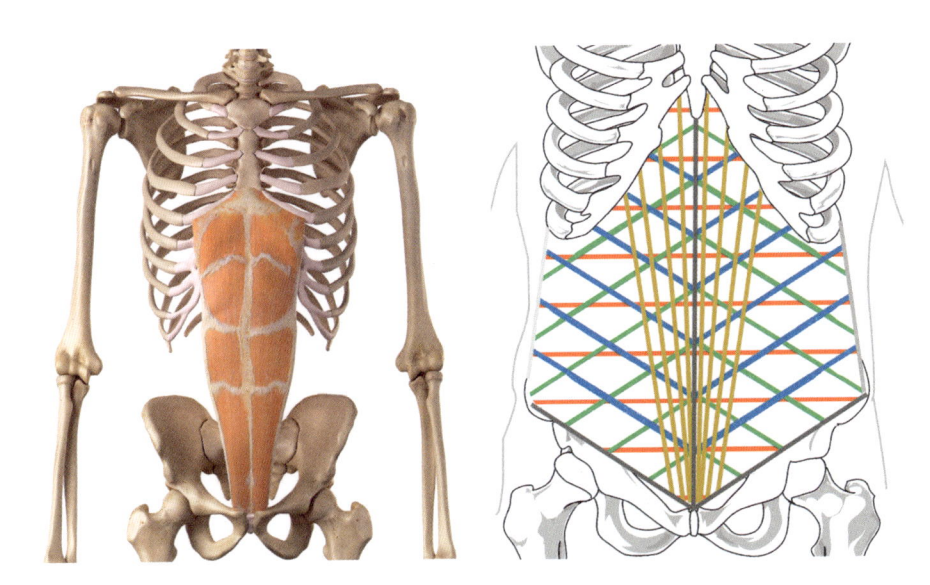

LEFT: RECTUS ABDOMINIS   RIGHT: THE ABDOMINAL 'CORSET' (THE FIBRES OF THE TRANSVERSE ABDOMINAL MUSCLE ARE SHOWN IN ORANGE, THE FIBRES OF THE INTERNAL OBLIQUE IN GREEN, THE FIBRES OF THE EXTERNAL OBLIQUE IN BLUE AND THE FIBRES OF THE RECTUS ABDOMINIS IN YELLOW)

- *Abdomen muscles:* internal and external obliques, rectus abdominis and quadratus lumborum. This complex web of muscles forms a stabilising and protective corset around the lower back. There's a great deal of stress on this part of the body, so it's protected by having a very limited range of movement. The importance of the lower back for a long and healthy life cannot be overstated. The abdomen muscles also play a key role in holding the visceral organs in place. And, as we'll see, there are no 'upper', 'middle' or 'lower' abs. The rectus abdominis is made up of various muscle bellies, which form the different sections of the oh-so-coveted six-pack. It consists of one muscle on the left and one muscle on the right. And the way it looks has little to do with how much we train, as the size and layout of the muscle bellies is genetic.
- *Diaphragm and pelvic floor:* two large dome-like muscles that top and tail the core. The diaphragm is essential for breathing. The pelvic floor holds absolutely everything in place but with the slight 'issue' of having two 'holes' (genital and anal). It's often forgotten about, but poor function can lead to health problems (for example, incontinence or prolapse). What's more, although it may seem irrelevant to climbing performance, it can also lead to incorrect activation of the abdominal corset, resulting in a loss of strength through the central zone.

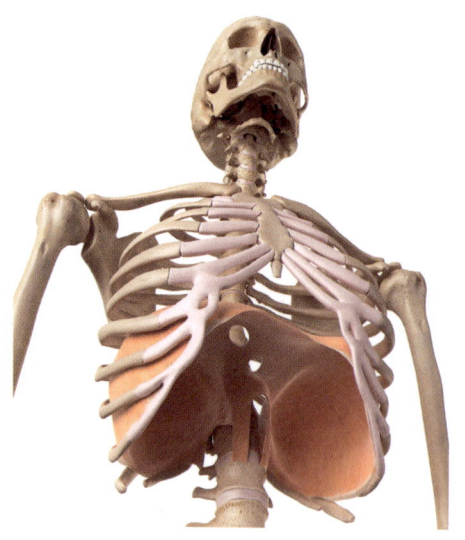

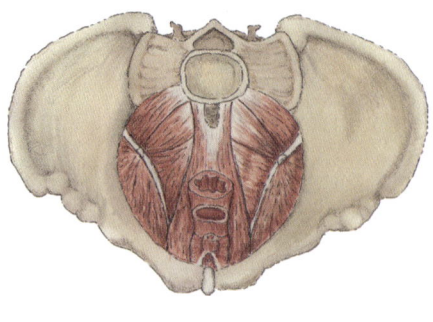

DIAPHRAGM

PELVIC FLOOR (PELVIS VIEWED FROM ABOVE)

- *Psoas:* the psoas connects the lower limbs to the lumbar spine and is one of the key muscles in hip flexion, meaning it helps you lift and place your feet when climbing. It's a really important muscle, both in terms of climbing movement and health of the lumbar region. If, for whatever reason, the psoas can't lift the femur, it will pull the lumbar region forwards. This exaggerates the natural curve in the lower back and puts pressure on the lumbar spine. The rectus abdominis stabilises the psoas and stops this from happening. The majority of supposed 'core' exercises, such as sit-ups or leg raises, are based on this biomechanical principle. They mainly work the

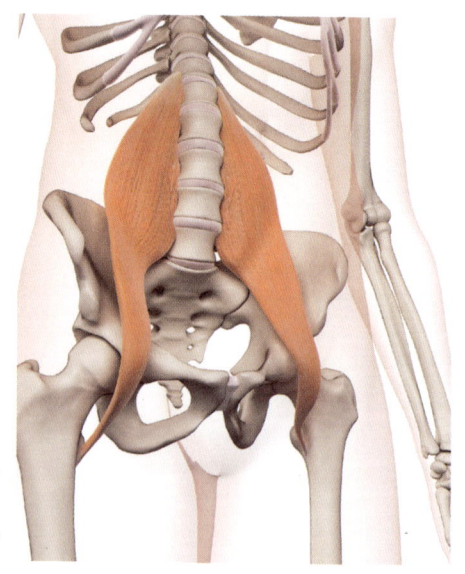

PSOAS

iliopsoas muscle and, indirectly, the rectus abdominis as it tries to stabilise the iliopsoas. If the rectus abdominis isn't strong enough to do this, you'll end up with a nasty injury to the lumbar region.

LOWER BODY: PUSHING MUSCLES

The lower body is the driving force behind both horizontal (floor-based) and vertical (wall-based) propulsion. It has three key joints: the coxofemoral joint (hip), the knee and the ankle.
- *Hip muscles:* like the shoulder joint, the hip joint is amazingly complex, but it's less mobile and therefore much more stable. We'll focus here on the gluteus muscles around the hip joint. The gluteus maximus is the most powerful muscle in the human body and the primary hip extensor. When we've got a really high foot, it's what gives us the strength to weight it and stand up. The gluteus medius and minimus are mainly leg abductor muscles (they lift the leg away from the body), and they also help stabilise the hip joint. The gluteus maximus and the tensor fasciae latae, which is a small muscle at the front of the hip, mark the origin of the

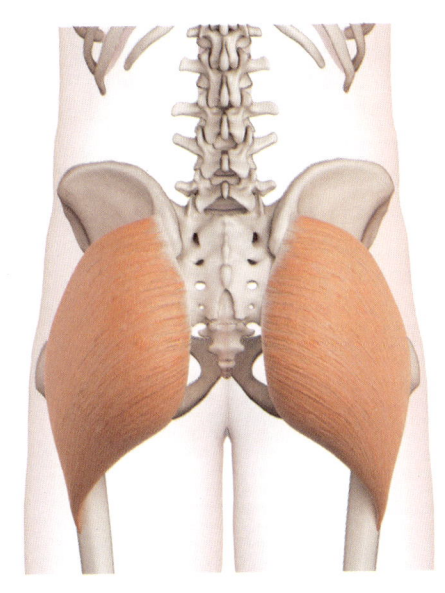

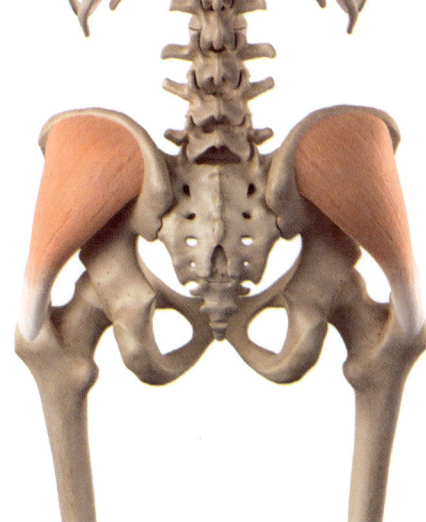

GLUTEUS MAXIMUS   GLUTEUS MEDIUS

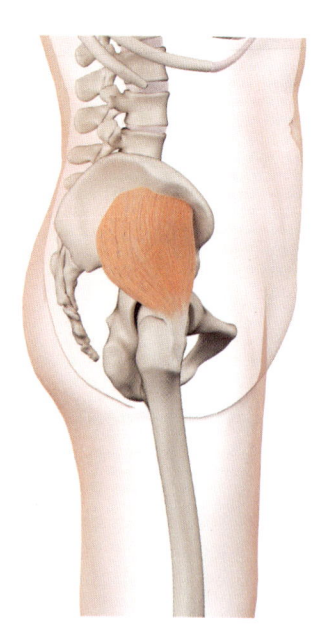

GLUTEUS MINIMUS

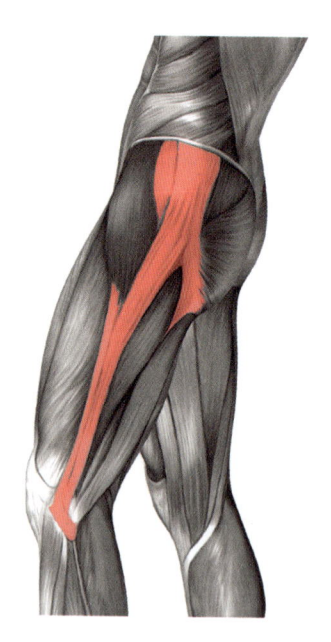

ILIOTIBIAL BAND (IN RED)

iliotibial band. This is a thick band of fascia that runs down the side of the thigh to below the knee, helping to transfer force to the lower leg. One of the heads of the quadriceps (the rectus femoris muscle) also originates in the pelvis, meaning that, in addition to its role in knee extension, it works in synergy with the psoas in hip flexion and leg elevation. This is why in exercises like sit-ups, we feel the burn in our quads (when we thought we were working our 'abs').

- *Thigh muscles:* to simplify things as much as possible, we'll only look at the quadriceps as a knee extensor and the biceps femoris as a flexor muscle (sending our apologies to the rest of the thigh muscles, like the abductors or the semimembranosus and the semitendinosus). Originating in the head of the fibula, the biceps femoris not only flexes but also externally rotates the knee. This is why you get a more powerful heel hook with your toes pointed outwards, but you could also end up damaging your knee if you pull too hard.
- *Lower leg muscles:* our focus here is on the tibialis anterior, which is located on the lateral side of the tibia and is the main muscle used for toe hooks, and the triceps surae, which is located on the back of the lower leg. The triceps surae consists of the gastrocnemius muscle (which lifts the ankle, allowing us to stand on our tiptoes, and is also responsible for knee flexion) and the soleus (which lifts the ankle when the knee is bent).

4 BRIEF NOTES ON ANATOMY | 45

RECTUS FEMORIS MUSCLE

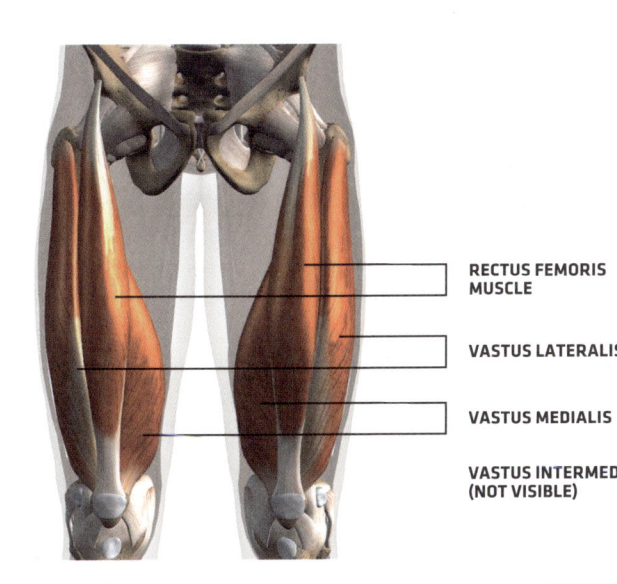

VASTUS LATERALIS

VASTUS MEDIALIS

VASTUS INTERMEDIUS (NOT VISIBLE)

QUADRICEPS (NOTE THE ORIGIN OF THE RECTUS FEMORIS IN THE PELVIS, WHICH IS WHY IT CONTRIBUTES TO HIP FLEXION)

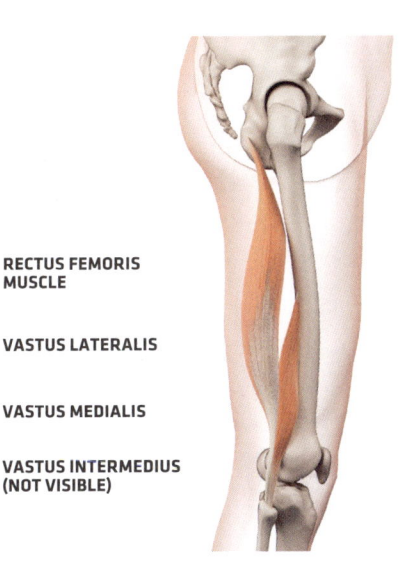

BICEPS FEMORIS (NOTE THE ORIGIN OF THE LONG HEAD IN THE PELVIS, WHICH IS WHY IT CONTRIBUTES TO HIP EXTENSION)

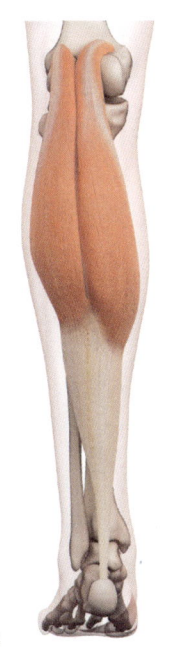

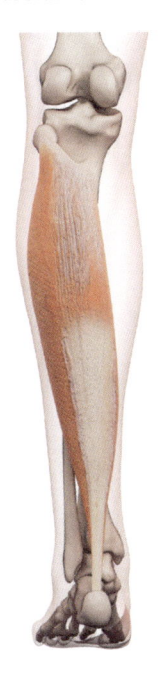

GASTROCNEMIUS

SOLEUS

CONNECTIVE TISSUE: TENDONS AND LIGAMENTS

Although tendons and ligaments are completely different, they are often confused and there is a general misunderstanding of what they are and how they work. A better understanding of tendons and ligaments will help us take better care of them and lower our risk of injury.

Tendons transmit force from muscle to bone, and vice versa. They're mainly composed of collagenous fibres (90 per cent), which are flexible (note: not elastic) and highly stretch-resistant. Tendons are a bit like a static or semi-static rope. Imagine your car is stuck in a ditch. What happens if you try to use a dynamic rope to pull it out? Being dynamic (elastic), the rope just absorbs all the energy of your tugging and pulling. Very little force is transmitted to the car and it doesn't budge. If you instead use a static or semi-static rope, which isn't dynamic but is still flexible because you take good care of it, much more force will be transmitted to the car and you'll be able to pull it out. Tendons work in much the same way. Aside from collagenous fibres, they also contain elastic fibres (0.5 per cent), mucopolysaccharides (0.5 per cent) and water (9 per cent).

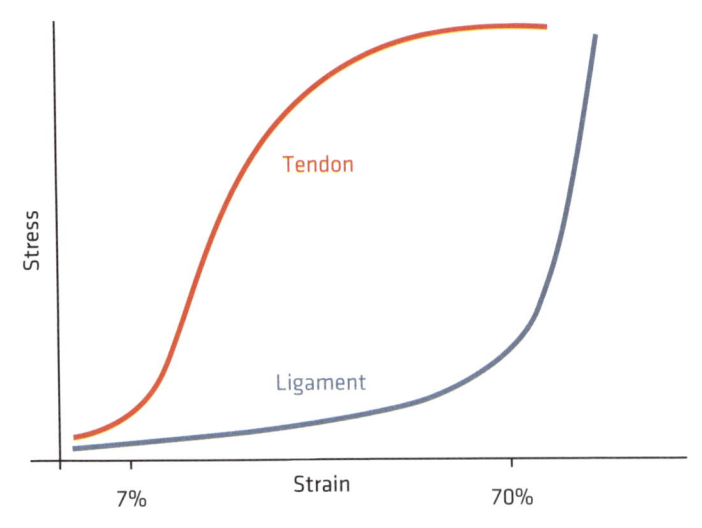

STRESS STRAIN CURVE FOR TENDONS AND LIGAMENTS

As for ligaments, their main function is to reinforce our joints. They limit joint mobility to prevent dislocation. Although they aren't particularly elastic, they have a little more give than tendons.

5

FASCIA, MUSCLE CHAINS AND BIOTENSEGRITY

FASCIAL ANATOMY: SUPERFICIAL FASCIA AND DEEP FASCIA

Fascia: a mysterious substance that permeates the human body. A continuous, interconnected structure with lots of different names. Fascia is connective tissue. It surrounds, encloses, supports and connects each and every element of the human body. Fascia *is* connection. On a microscopic level, it's a liquid tissue (non-Newtonian fluid). Its key functions are to transfer energy and to help other structures glide over each other by reducing excessive wear or friction that could result in injury.

Fascia can be divided into two main groups:
- *Superficial fascia:* this is located beneath the dermis and is made up of loose connective tissue and varying amounts of fat. It's like the thin silvery film on a joint of meat at the butcher.

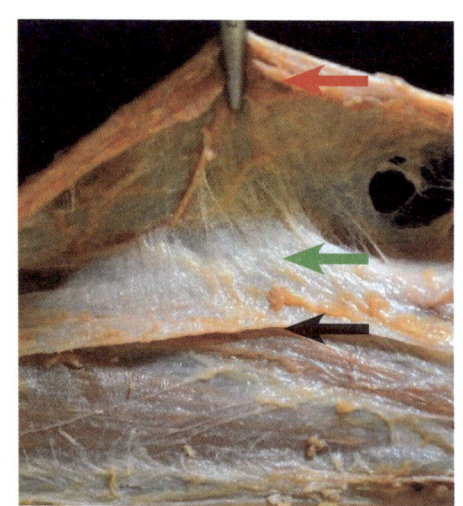

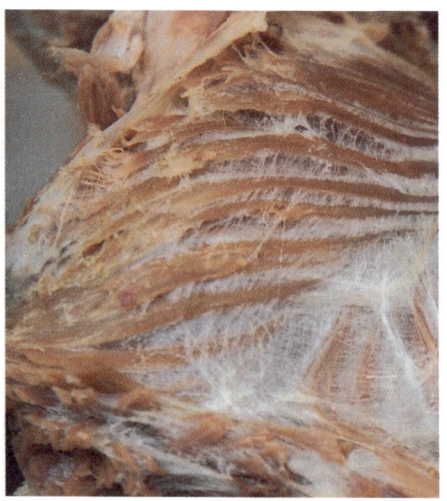

LEFT: SUPERFICIAL FASCIA OF THE FOREARM AROUND THE EXTENSOR MUSCLES. THE RED ARROW INDICATES THE SUPERFICIAL FASCIA; THE GREEN ARROW INDICATES CONNECTIVE TISSUE MADE FROM COLLAGEN; AND THE BLACK ARROW INDICATES THE INTERMUSCULAR SEPTUM (DONES ET AL., 2013)   RIGHT: DEEP FASCIA
PHOTOS: JULIAN BAKER

- *Deep fascia:* this is connected to superficial fascia and is made up of dense connective tissue that surrounds and sections off different structures. It connects absolutely everything in the human body: from the muscles in our feet to the vital organs in the abdomen, the nerves in the cervical spine, and so on, linking everything to everything.

Interestingly, unless the fascia cells (known as fibroblasts) are stimulated directly by way of myofascial release, they are very slow to adapt to movement, unlike our muscles, which respond instantly. But what does this mean and how is it connected to climbing? In practice, it has a big impact on climbing performance. Imagine you've been sitting at a desk for the past eight hours; you then arrive at the wall and start training like mad without warming up or doing any myofascial release. Although your body is already climbing, the fibroblasts in your fascia are still 'sitting down', in the same position they've been in all day. They haven't had time to adapt to this change in movement. Then one day, you'll be climbing away and suddenly feel a strange tightness or strain somewhere for 'no reason at all' …

This is why we should include a good dose of myofascial release in the mobility section of our warm-up, either by flossing, using massage balls or skin rolling (ask your physio to show you how). These techniques target the superficial fascia which, in turn, helps to release the deep fascia. As a result, muscle fibres will glide more smoothly over each other, any tension built up over the day will be reduced and you'll see better quality of movement.

MAIN MUSCLE CHAINS

Many authors (such as Busquet, Kabat and Mézières) have studied different systems of muscle chains and each has developed their own way of explaining the connectivity and function of our muscles, with pros and cons to each model. Personally, I work with the GDS system designed by Denys-Struyf (2008), which describes six different muscle chains (see image on following page):

- *PM:* postero-median chain. The extensor chain that saw us evolve from walking on four limbs to walking on two. It mainly runs down the back of the body.
- *AM:* antero-median chain. The main antagonist chain to the PM muscles. It is a closing and flexion chain and mainly runs down the front of the body.
- *PA and AP, sometimes referred to as PAAP:* postero-anterior and antero-posterior chains. Two complementary chains that can function as a single chain. They contain muscles deep within the body and are responsible for joint adjustment.
- *AL:* antero-lateral chain. A chain that criss-crosses through the entire body and is mainly responsible for closing movements and internal rotation.
- *PL:* postero-lateral chain. A chain that criss-crosses through the entire body and is mainly responsible for opening movements and external rotation.

Why use the GDS system? Denys–Struyf studied these chains and the postural changes caused by overloading the muscles in each chain in bipeds in static positions. These excessive loads modify joint alignment, reducing efficiency and causing significant wear. They also create a tendency to overload certain muscles and increase the risk of certain injuries.

The complex system of GDS muscle chains is a brilliant tool for injury prevention, among many other things. As such, if at all possible, I'd recommend finding a physio or a coach who works with this method. They can do an assessment and show you preventative exercises to address any imbalances within your muscle chains.

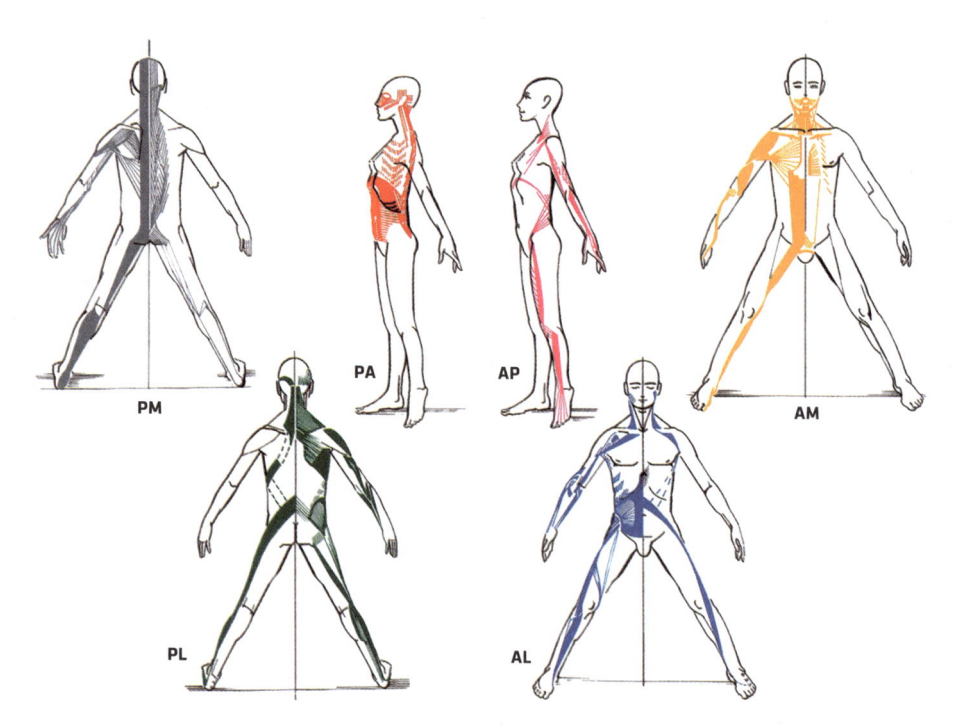

MUSCLE AND JOINT CHAINS ACCORDING TO DENYS-STRUYF

THE BODY AS A BIOTENSEGRITY STRUCTURE

Biotensegrity: another unusual word. Simply put, it describes the human body as a structure in a state of balanced tension. Any change in tension or position needs to be compensated for in another part of the body. The concept complements, expands on and supports the ideas discussed in this chapter.

On a practical level, if an excessive load in the forearm isn't stopped and compensated for in time, it will need to be compensated for elsewhere – for example, in the upper arm, the shoulder or the neck.

Following this rather abstract section, which you might think has nothing to do with training for climbing, I'd urge you to take away one simple idea: the body as a single, interconnected being. It's yours and you're part of it: listen to it and look after it. It isn't something to be trained or punished. If you look after it to the best of your ability, it will allow you to perform to the best of your ability, responding how and when you want it to. And if your body is trying to tell you something, don't ignore it: respect it.

6

BIOENERGETICS AND METABOLISM

FOCUS: ENERGY PRODUCTION

The metabolism is our body's way of producing energy. At the risk of stating the obvious, we need energy to move. Our ability to generate force and resist external stress is completely dependent on our ability to produce energy and to maintain energy production. If you can't run a marathon in under two hours, it's probably not due to a lack of endurance: it's almost certainly because you aren't able to produce the energy needed to run quickly enough and to maintain this level of energy for a whole two hours.

In order to create energy, the human body uses several different metabolic pathways: each with its own advantages, disadvantages and different characteristics. Each pathway draws energy from a substrate or fuel (phosphagens, carbohydrates and fats) to supply the energy needed for any given activity, movement or action. Understanding how energy is produced in each pathway and the consequences of these processes will give a better understanding of the reasons behind different training methods.

The energy-carrying molecule is known as ATP (adenosine triphosphate). When ATP reacts with a class of enzymes known as ATPases, one of its phosphate groups is separated off and the ATP is converted into adenosine diphosphate and inorganic phosphate, releasing a large amount of energy.

THE ATP–PCr SYSTEM

Also known as the phosphagen system or the anaerobic alactic system, this is the main source of energy for very short bursts of activity (10 to 15 seconds or less). Our muscles store small deposits of both ATP and creatine phosphate (PCr), which is another very high-energy molecule that actually produces more energy than ATP. Creatine phosphokinase helps release energy from PCr molecules by separating the creatine from the phosphate. This is a really fast way to produce energy and can be done without any oxygen (anaerobic). It also doesn't produce any lactate. However, these ATP and PCr stores are small and quickly depleted, so the body will switch to a different metabolic pathway if the demand for energy continues. As we'll see in more detail later on, climbing mainly involves intermittent contractions as we grip and release each hold, with just a short period of recovery between holds. As such, the ATP–PCr system supplies most of the energy needed in our forearms when climbing (Bertuzzi et al., 2007).

ANAEROBIC GLYCOLYSIS

Glycolysis is the metabolic pathway that produces energy by breaking down glucose (*lysis* means 'separation' in Greek). Glucose makes up 99 per cent of the sugar in our bloodstream and is produced by digesting carbohydrates and by breaking down glycogen, which is stored in our liver and muscles. To simplify this, imagine glycogen as little bricks made up of several glucose molecules.

A total of 12 reactions are needed to produce energy from glucose, and no oxygen is required as this is an anaerobic pathway. The net return on this process is two molecules of ATP for every molecule of glucose, and the glucose is then broken down into pyruvic acid, which then becomes lactic acid. The lactic acid releases hydrogen ions (H^+) which, when produced in large quantities, acidify the muscle fibres by lowering their pH. When this happens, the muscle fibres lose contractile capacity (Wilmore and Costill, 2007).

Therefore, although this system can produce high doses of energy, it also creates a build-up of waste products that end up inhibiting the production of energy. As such, it isn't an especially efficient system. Let's look at an analogy: imagine putting some wood (glucose) into a wood-burning stove to create heat (energy). When the fire has burnt out, you're left with ash (lactic acid). If you let the ash build up and don't clean it out, at some point the stove will become so full of ash (muscle acidification) that you won't be able to burn any more wood (muscle can't contract).

AEROBIC GLYCOLYSIS

Although glucose can be converted into energy anaerobically, this can also be done aerobically. In the presence of oxygen, glucose is still converted into pyruvic acid but this then becomes Acetyl-CoA, instead of lactic acid. Acetyl-CoA is then used in another complex series of chemical reactions (the Krebs cycle) that produces two additional molecules of ATP (double the energy than in anaerobic glycolysis). In this cycle, the glucose is eventually converted into carbon and hydrogen. The carbon combines with oxygen to form carbon dioxide (CO_2), which is easily removed from the cell into the bloodstream and transported to the lungs to be exhaled. The remaining hydrogen (H^+) is used in another series of reactions (the electron transport chain) and ends up combining with oxygen to form water (H_2O), preventing the build-up of acid in our muscles and generating even more ATP. In total, 38 molecules of ATP can be produced from the oxidation of glucose (Wilmore and Costill, 2007). As such, this system is far more efficient and sustainable than the anaerobic production of energy.

FAT OXIDATION OR LIPOLYSIS

Although aerobic glycolysis sounds like a great way to produce energy, it 'only' produces between 1,200 and 2,000 kilocalories from our blood glucose and liver and muscle glycogen stores. This might be enough for a couple of goes on a boulder problem or just enough for a short, hard route, but it's nowhere near enough for a serious training session or a full day at the crag.

If 1 gram of fat stores 9 kilocalories of energy, a man of average weight, say 70 kilograms, who is in good shape and has a low body fat percentage (without being so low as to affect performance), say 12 per cent body fat, would have a total of 8.4 kilograms of fat, creating an energy reserve of 75,600 kilocalories. Enough energy to run three marathons, climb a bunch of routes and cycle back home ... Quite a difference, right?

It seems that burning fat can provide a much longer-lasting source of energy. However, this metabolic pathway is much more complex than the others discussed in this chapter, so all I'll say here is that the oxidation of fatty acids produces three times more ATP than the oxidation of glucose. What's more, the presence of oxygen means there is no build-up of lactic acid and no acidification of muscle fibres, meaning no loss of contractile capacity (Wilmore and Costill, 2007).

JAVI CANO AT THE CLIMB OPEN BOULDER FESTIVAL

THE ENERGY CONTINUUM

These energy-producing systems don't function independently: they are constantly interacting with each other. It would be illogical, inefficient and even dangerous to fully deplete one of these pathways before moving on to the next. Depending on the duration, intensity of effort, level of training and our individual hormones, one pathway will take precedence over the others but the interaction between them remains constant.

Climbing provides a good example of this interaction between pathways. As we usually need a lot of effort for a short period of time (when we're in contact with a hold), we're mainly using the ATP–PCr system. However, since our PCr (creatine phosphate) stores are practically emptied each time we latch a hold, the system uses the small window of time between holds to produce more energy via the oxidation of fats. This energy won't guarantee that we can keep climbing (we might not have enough power for those microscopic crimps, for example), but it will bind more phosphate to creatine, topping up our PCr stores and providing more high-intensity energy for the next hold.

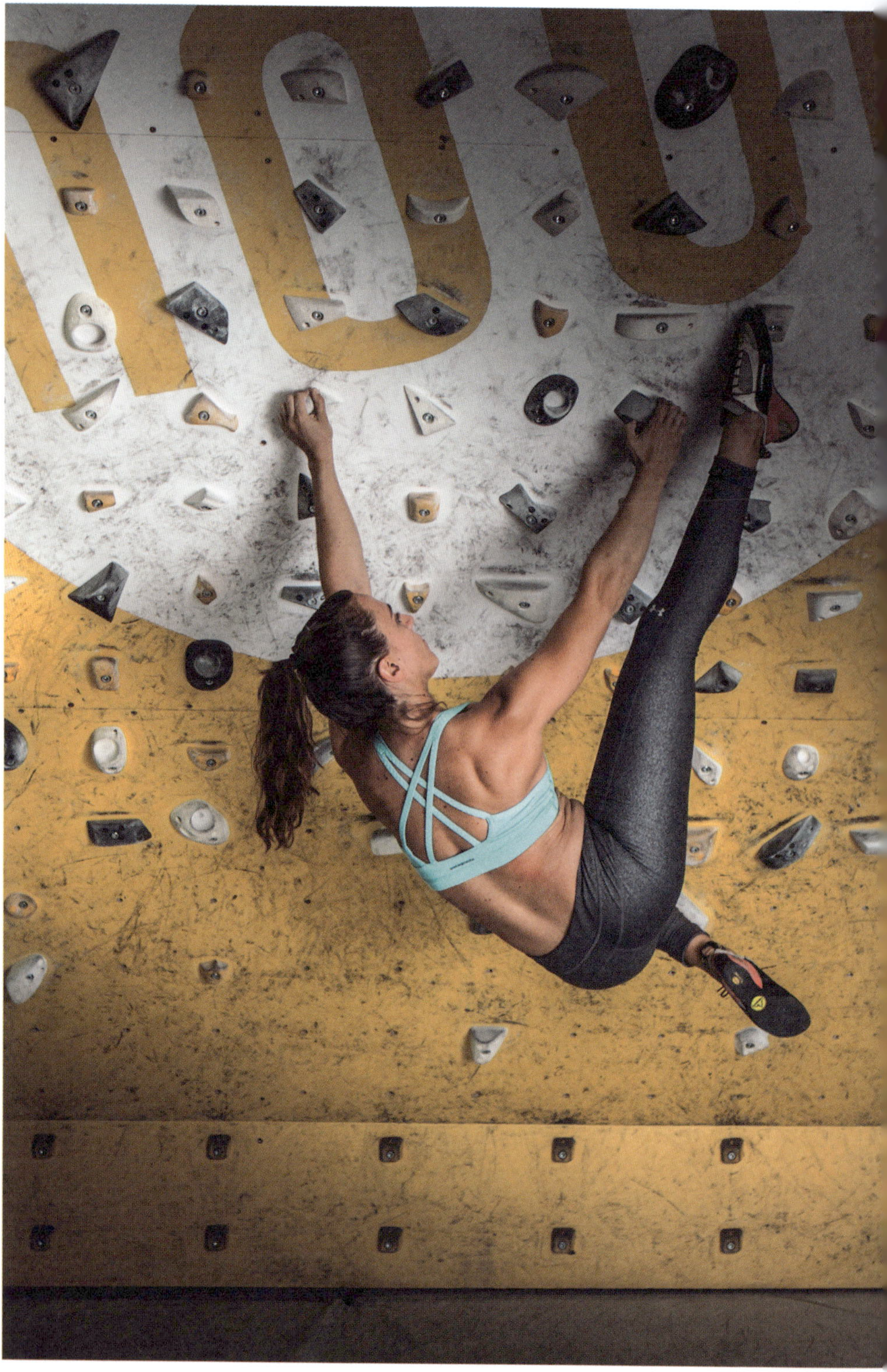

7

ANALYSIS OF THE MAIN PHYSIOLOGICAL FACTORS IN CLIMBING PERFORMANCE

When it comes to training and performance, comparing bouldering to sport climbing is like comparing ping-pong to tennis. There are rackets, a ball and a net in both, but they're completely different sports. And it's the same in climbing: the demands of each type of climbing, and therefore the physiological profiles of each type of climber, are quite different. That said, with a well-designed training programme, the benefits of training specifically for one discipline can be transferred to other disciplines.

THE OLD PARADIGM OF PERFORMANCE: INTENSITY AND ENERGY SYSTEMS ACCORDING TO NUMBER OF MOVES

Sports physiology explores how the body responds to different stimulation in sport, laying the foundations for the development of sports training. For decades, there have been countless studies on all types of responses (metabolic, cardiovascular, and so on) in 'established' or 'popular' sports such as cycling, swimming and rowing. However, quality research into climbing has only really begun to emerge in recent years.

Until very recently, climbing has been likened to athletics, and this is still the case outside of competition and in popular culture. As such, the physiological demands and training methods of one have been applied to the other. A four-move boulder problem that takes 13 seconds to climb is compared to the 100 metres, so that's the anaerobic alactic system. A 20-move route that takes about a minute to climb is compared to the 400 metres, so that's anaerobic lactic. A 100-move route that takes 30 minutes to climb is compared to the 10K, so aerobic ... and so on. The dominance of one metabolic pathway over the others is based on the duration of activity and the number of moves, just like in athletics. And whatever training methods are used in athletics (for example, levels of intensity or intervals) are used in climbing as well. Epic fail.

Cyclic sports (like cycling) are based on repetitive movements that involve the concentric contraction of large muscle groups to produce a unified systematic response. Continuing with the example of cycling: the heart pumps lots of blood to the leg muscles, and the lungs help the metabolism to expel large amounts of CO_2 (a by-product of the aerobic energy system). When the glycogen stored in our muscles runs out, the liver provides its glycogen stores so that the cyclist can keep pedalling. The whole body works in unison to supply energy to the legs. If the legs can't keep producing energy, the cyclist will stop pedalling, even if their pecs or lats aren't fatigued.

In climbing, the main limiting factor is our forearm muscles. Failure to produce (and keep producing) enough force to keep our fingers in contact with a hold is the main reason we fall off (Vigouroux and Quaine, 2006). Our forearm muscles are much smaller than the legs of our cyclist. A small link in the chain, a bottleneck, is what limits performance. Our body's response to the energy demand of a small group of muscles is incomparable to the way in which it responds to the needs of the large muscle groups.

What's more, climbing involves intermittent isometric contractions at different intensities. In fact, it's practically impossible to calculate the intensity or force with which we grip a hold (even if it's fitted with a dynamometer), because even on the same hold, the amount of force will vary depending on body position (Michailov, 2014). This points to a model with very different needs and characteristics to cyclic sports.

A study on changes in lactate levels during the 400-metre sprint found lactate levels of around 17 mmol/L (Hirvonen *et al.*, 1992), and anaerobic strength (Wingate) tests on BMX bikers found lactate concentrations of 29 mmol/L (Zabala *et al.*, 2011). However, in sport climbers and boulderers, on a national and international level, in lab testing and official competitions, studies have found much lower concentrations of 5 to 7 mmol/L (Gáspari *et al.*, 2015; La Torre *et al.*, 2009; Billat *et al.*, 1995; Schöffl *et al.*, 2006). As lactate is simply a waste product of anaerobic glycolysis (so higher levels of lactate indicate greater predominance of this metabolic pathway in energy production), these findings show that anaerobic lactic metabolism is far from the predominant energy system in climbing.

Therefore, it makes little sense to approach forearm training, and training for climbing in general, as if we were runners or cyclists.

NEW FINDINGS ABOUT LIMITING FACTORS IN CLIMBING PERFORMANCE: ROUTES AND BOULDERING

So, what are the limiting factors in climbing performance? To answer this question, we should first distinguish between two different levels: general (factors that affect the whole body), and local (the crucial link: the forearm).

Let's begin at the general level. Broadly speaking, novices or intermediate climbers will be most affected by these factors (in elite climbers, these factors are optimised) and without a well-designed training plan they will have little to no control over these factors. As seen in the diagram overleaf, there are three main factors that influence our ability as climbers: physical factors, strength-to-weight ratio and injuries.

- *Physical factors:* factors that determine how we're able to move when climbing.
    » *Strength:* inevitably, strength is one of the factors that will either help or hinder our movement on the wall. While an elite climber can do pull-ups with lots of added weight or with just one arm, a novice might struggle to do even one regular pull-up. Likewise, the strength to stabilise our joints and core, in addition to overall balance, is crucial for certain moves like stopping a barn door. And, of course, the ability to push down and stand up (propulsion) on key footholds is crucial on any boulder problem or route.
    » *Mobility:* as discussed in chapter 3, poor mobility will limit the positions we can get into on the wall, how far into certain positions we can get and how difficult it will be to move out of them.

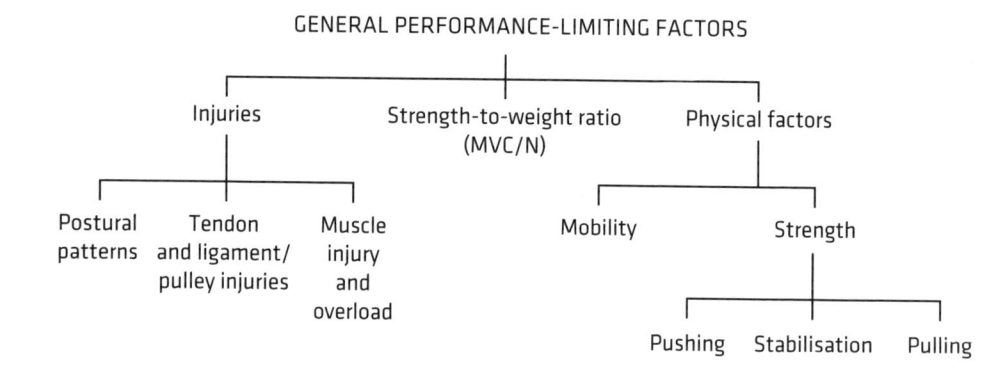

GENERAL PERFORMANCE-LIMITING FACTORS

- Injuries
  - Postural patterns
  - Tendon and ligament/pulley injuries
  - Muscle injury and overload
- Strength-to-weight ratio (MVC/N)
- Physical factors
  - Mobility
  - Strength
    - Pushing
    - Stabilisation
    - Pulling

- *Strength-to-weight ratio:* as we can see from just looking at elite climbers and according to numerous studies including a PhD thesis by Couceiro (2010), on an anthropometric level, top-level climbers are not that heavy and, importantly, have a very low body fat percentage. Despite being the best energy store in the human body, fat is not contractile, so rather than helping us to climb it actually weighs us down, meaning it takes more effort and energy to get up the wall. It's not the total weight of a climber that's important, but rather their 'useful weight'. The more soft tissue we have that is useful/contractile/able to generate force, and the less additional weight, the better our strength-to-weight ratio. For example: take a 67-kilogram climber who can do a pull-up with 45 kilograms of added weight. In total, they're lifting 112 kilograms. Their strength-to-weight ratio is 1.67 kilograms per kilogram of body weight. That is, every kilogram of their body is able to generate enough force to lift 1.67 kilograms. Now take an 80-kilogram climber who can't do any unassisted pull-ups. They need the equivalent of 10 kilograms of help to do one pull-up. Their strength-to-weight ratio is 0.875 kilograms per kilogram of body weight. That is, every kilogram of their body is able to generate enough force to lift 0.875 kilograms, almost half that of the 67-kilogram climber. In scientific terms, this is known as (MVC/N): the force produced in a maximum voluntary contraction relative to the weight of the climber in newtons. Studies performed by Fryer *et al.* (2015b, 2015c) show that elite climbers have a much higher strength-to-weight ratio than advanced climbers, intermediate climbers and non-climbers.
- *Injuries:* regardless of how strong, lean or mobile we are, if we don't follow a well-designed and individualised training plan, we're putting ourselves at an exponential risk of getting injured and even having to give up climbing. Injury prevention covers a broad range of areas, such as the protection of soft tissue (mainly tendons and

pulleys) through gradual progression and adaptation to training. It also covers the correction of postural adaptations or deformations caused by excessive tension in certain muscle groups. And finally, it includes agonist/antagonist muscle balance and the optimal (not excessive) loading of different muscle groups.

At this general level, we see the importance of the body as a whole (fingers of steel are of little use if you can't do a single pull-up or if you're nursing a shoulder injury). Now let's look at the latest research into the key limiting factor in climbing: the forearm.

- *Strength:* once again, strength takes centre stage. There are two factors that determine the importance of strength:
  » *Maximum grip strength:* Schöffl *et al.* (2006), Magiera *et al.* (2013), Ozimek *et al.* (2016) and López-Rivera (2009) suggest that maximum grip strength is one of the key deciding factors of climbing performance. And, as mentioned earlier, an inability to produce and/or keep producing the necessary force to remain on a handhold is the main reason for a failed ascent or fall (Vigouroux and Quaine, 2006). In turn, Fryer *et al.* (2017) found that boulderers have much higher MVC than sport climbers (so if you're a boulderer, you need to focus on finger strength training). Mermier *et al.* (2000) performed a comparative study on men and women and found that, considering strength relative to mass, men have much better grip strength than women. In addition, Ozimek *et al.* (2017) compared elite climbers (F8b/8c) with advanced climbers (F7c+/8a) and found that, for a three-second max-weight hang, the elite group could hang with 14 per cent more weight than the advanced group.
  » *RFD (rate of force development):* according to Fanchini *et al.* (2013), RFD is the deciding factor of performance in boulderers, as their RFD was found to be 36.73 per cent higher than in sport climbers. Laffaye *et al.* (2016) saw similar findings comparing boulderers to sport climbers. RFD is the amount of force developed per unit of time. In other words, it's how fast you can develop force. For climbing, the standard unit of time is 200 milliseconds. It's a bit like calculating acceleration: how much force you can produce in 200 milliseconds. This concept is closely linked to (but not the same as) explosive strength and the ability to do dynamic and explosive moves. It is also a crucial factor in contact strength. For example: imagine a climber doing a dynamic move to a sloper. To hold the sloper, they'll need to apply 200 newtons of force. Their MVC is 280 newtons so they should be able to stick the move. However, they have a very low RFD and can only generate 170 newtons when they hit the sloper, meaning they can't keep hold of it and they fall off. Levernier and Laffaye (2019) found

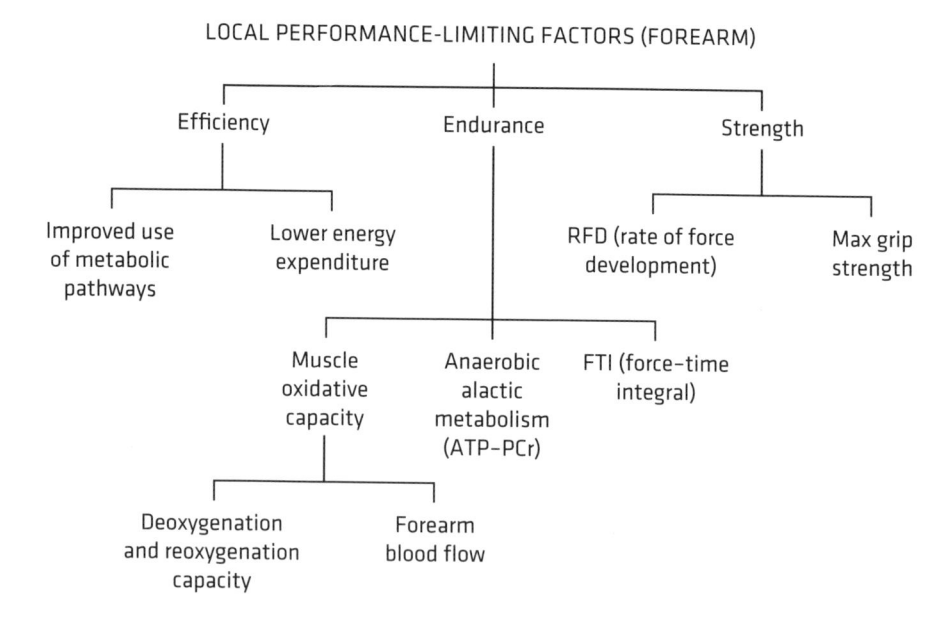

```
                    LOCAL PERFORMANCE-LIMITING FACTORS (FOREARM)
         ┌──────────────────────────┼──────────────────────────┐
      Efficiency                 Endurance                   Strength
         │                          │                           │
    ┌────┴─────┐                    │                    ┌──────┴──────┐
Improved use   Lower energy                           RFD (rate of force   Max grip
of metabolic   expenditure                            development)        strength
pathways
                    ┌───────────────┼───────────────┐
                 Muscle          Anaerobic      FTI (force-time
                 oxidative       alactic         integral)
                 capacity        metabolism
                                 (ATP-PCr)
              ┌──────┴──────┐
         Deoxygenation    Forearm
         and reoxygenation blood flow
         capacity
```

that RFD$_{200ms}$ is a variable that can distinguish a climber's level of ability. As such, the ability to generate large amounts of force as quickly as possible, like making rapid and strong contact with a hold, is essential to reach a high level of performance.

- *Endurance:* the main physical quality that differentiates between sport climbers and boulderers (Fryer *et al.*, 2017) and the biggest limiting factor when it comes to sending a route (Michailov, 2014). The ability to maintain a muscle contraction or a series of contractions to exhaustion is what sets apart an elite climber from an advanced climber (Saul *et al.*, 2019). Interestingly, Philippe *et al.* (2012) compared time to exhaustion in male and female climbers for intermittent isometric contractions. Female climbers showed longer time to exhaustion, even at a lower climbing grade (both redpoint and on sight) than their male counterparts, although no concrete physiological explanation was found for this result. Endurance is determined by three things:
    » *Force–time integral (FTI):* a variable that shows the amount of force which can be maintained over a certain length of time (intermittent or continuous). It is calculated using the formula *0.4 x duration of the contraction (s) x force (N)* and is

measured in newtons per second (Fryer *et al.*, 2015b). More advanced climbers can do harder moves (moves that require more force) for longer. For example: picture a route with 25 moves. Each move requires 200 newtons of force. Let's assume that all climbers who attempt this route take three seconds to do each move. A novice climber can do five moves so their FTI will be 1,200 N·s. An intermediate climber can do 12 moves so their FTI will be 2,880 N·s. And an elite climber who can climb the whole route will have an FTI of 6,000 N·s. This variable is therefore directly proportional to elite, intermediate and novice levels and gives significantly different results for each group (Fryer *et al.*, 2015b). In order to measure FTI, you'd need to attach a dynamometer to a hold and perform a test to exhaustion (intermittent or continuous). The device will then provide a reading.

» *Anaerobic alactic metabolism:* as surprising as it may seem, the main pathway responsible for providing ATP to the forearms is the anaerobic alactic pathway and not anaerobic glycolysis (Bertuzzi *et al.*, 2007). Isometric contractions (duration of contact with each hold) during the crux section of a climb usually last for no more than 10 to 12 seconds (López-Rivera, 2014d), meaning that we are mainly using anaerobic alactic metabolism during this time. As the contractions are intermittent, with a (short) period of recovery between each hold, the aerobic system will try to replenish as much creatine phosphate as possible during this time to provide enough energy for the next move. We'll look at this in greater depth later on.

» *Muscle oxidative capacity:* the true crux of the matter. This refers to the ability to replenish energy. After a systematic review of over 350 studies, Saul *et al.* (2019) concluded that the oxidative capacity of the flexor digitorum profundus (FDP) is directly proportional to a climber's maximum redpoint grade. Oxidative capacity is dependent on:

> › *Forearm blood flow:* continuous high-intensity contractions, coupled with relatively negligible recovery between these contractions, can progressively limit blood flow to the forearm muscles. This, in turn, limits oxygen supply, the replenishment of energy reserves (Michailov, 2014; Staszkiewicz *et al.*, 2018) and the ability to flush out metabolic waste (Vigouroux and Quaine, 2006). However, in adaptation to training, more advanced climbers have developed wider arteries that increase blood flow to the forearm muscles (Fryer *et al.*, 2015a). They've also demonstrated a degree of vasodilation (widening of the blood vessels) during recovery, and their muscles, when contracting, exert less pressure on the arteries (metaboreflex), ensuring as much blood as possible gets to the muscles (Macleod *et al.*, 2007; Fryer *et al.*, 2015b; Thompson *et al.*, 2015; Green and Stannard, 2010). Another adaptation found to increase blood flow in elite climbers is known as capillary angiogenesis. This is the creation of new capillaries (blood vessels) that supply even more blood to the different muscle fibres (Macleod *et al.*, 2007; Philippe *et al.*, 2012; Fryer *et al.*, 2015a). Increased blood flow during recovery is directly linked to a higher FTI (Fryer *et al.*, 2015b), and elite climbers reoxygenate muscle 83 per cent faster than intermediate climbers (Fryer *et al.*, 2015a).

> › *Deoxygenation and reoxygenation capacity:* the biggest determining factor of a muscle's oxidative capacity and, as such, of forearm endurance (Fryer *et al.*, 2016). Elite climbers are much better at getting the oxygen carried in the bloodstream to their muscles (reoxygenation) and at removing oxygen from their muscles (deoxygenation), in both intermittent and continuous contractions. This means they can both use more and replenish more PCr stores to produce more energy (Fryer *et al.*, 2015a; Fryer *et al.*, 2015b; Fryer *et al.*, 2015c; Fryer *et al.*, 2017; Michailov, 2014; Green and Stannard,

2010; Philippe, *et al.*, 2012). In addition, greater deoxygenation during contractions and greater reoxygenation during recovery results in a higher FTI (Fryer *et al.*, 2015b). The deoxygenation and reoxygenation capacity of our muscles can be measured using NIRS (near infrared spectroscopy). There are several types of wearable NIRS devices but they're currently only designed for cyclic sports and not for climbing. Maybe in the future, we'll be able to use one a bit like a runner uses a heart rate monitor.

- *Efficiency:* efficiency can be defined as using less energy to perform the same action or task. Zigzagging between two points is effective, insofar as you leave one point and arrive at the other. However, going in a straight line is not only effective but also more efficient: using less energy to perform the same task. Bertuzzi *et al.* (2007) suggest that for climbers, economy of movement is more important than a good metabolism. Efficiency is linked to technique, visualisation, good footwork, motor abilities and skills, psychological factors, and so on (Fryer *et al.*, 2016). Only continued and extensive practice, experience, and mileage on both plastic and rock will lead to better economy of movement. Efficiency in climbing can be measured through:
  » *Lower energy expenditure:* Baláš *et al.* (2014b) compared energy expenditure in novice climbers and climbers who had climbed up to F8b. Both groups climbed a circuit of 15 moves, six times in a row; first at 90 degrees (vertical) and another five times immediately afterwards at 105 degrees (overhanging). The circuit was graded at around IV using the UIAA grading system (so, French grade 4a). The elite climbers used up to a fifth less energy than the novice climbers, as a result of better economy of movement. Another study by Baláš *et al.* (2014a) compared the FTI produced by the loading of footholds in novice and intermediate climbers, linking this data to the energy expenditure in each group. Climbers who put more weight through their feet (producing a higher FTI) had up to 11 per cent lower energy expenditure and 14 per cent lower heart rate.
  » *Improved use of metabolic pathways:* acidosis, which causes a build-up of lactate in the forearm muscles, has been proven to cause fatigue (Philippe *et al.*, 2012). In a systematic review of over 350 studies, Saul *et al.* (2019) confirmed that elite climbers have lower concentrations of lactate than recreational climbers. This suggests that elite climbers are able to produce more energy via anaerobic alactic and aerobic pathways, enough for the hardest sections of a climb, without having to switch to the anaerobic lactic pathway, unlike climbers with a lower level of ability.

PART II

OPTIMISATION OF TRAINING

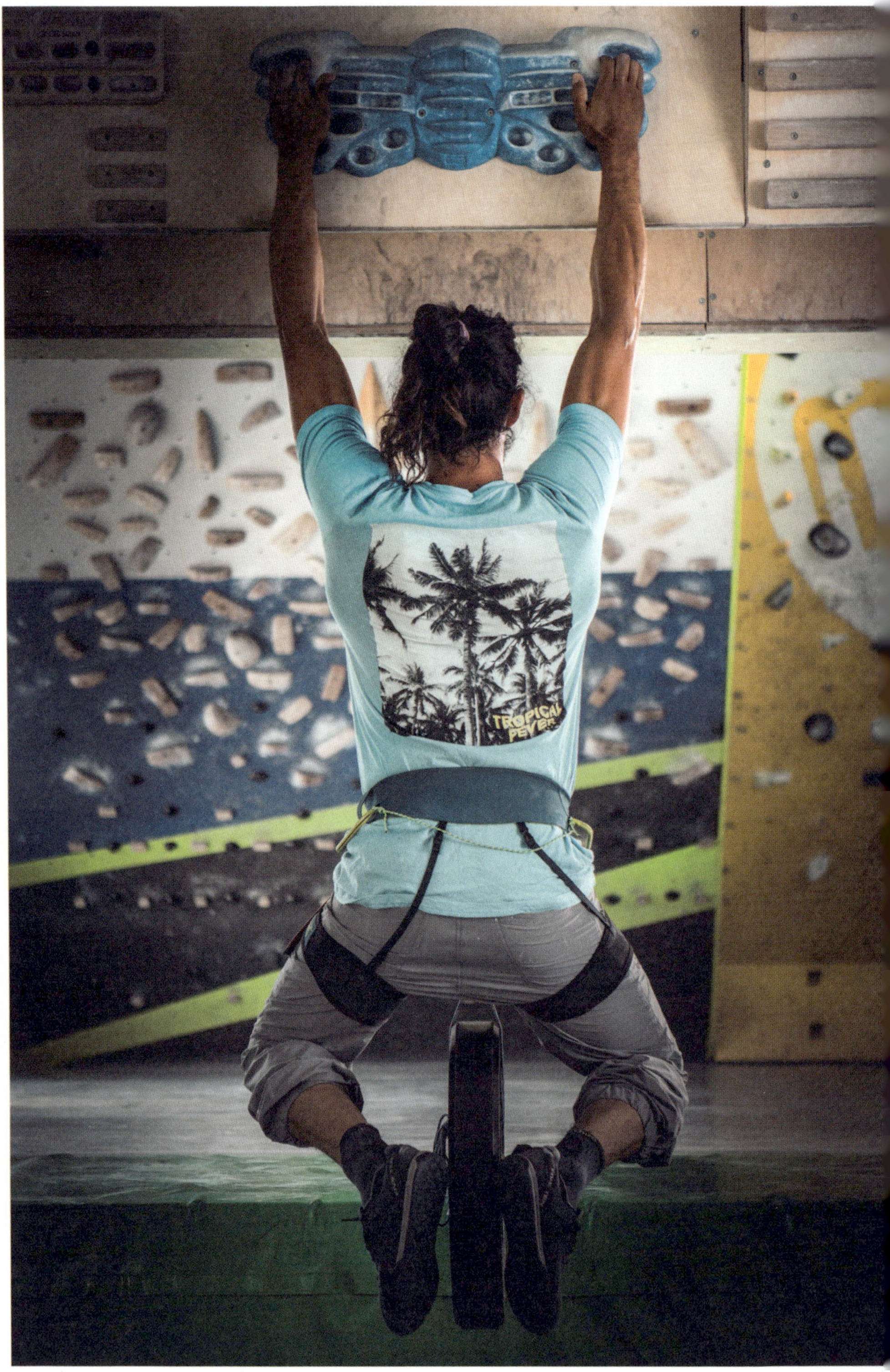
TROPICAL
FEVER

8

WHAT CAN I OPTIMISE IN MY TRAINING SESSIONS?

DEFINITION OF TRAINING GOALS

'If you don't know where you're going, any road will get you there.' This saying highlights the importance of knowing what you're training for. The definition of training goals is the first step to knowing what you should train. Are you preparing for the winter season? The sport climbing season? Is your project a big wall? A boulder problem?

In practice, and except at the most elite levels, the majority of climbers do a bit of all types of climbing (although they usually have a preferred discipline), and they either project individual routes or tick off lots of different routes, progressing climb by climb. Not planning this progression or selection of climbs can mean that if at the end of the season you decide to try a certain route, you won't have done the right type of training for a successful ascent.

How can I set my training goals? I know that this can be quite hard to do, and we don't always know in advance what we might want to climb. The following example shows one way to structure your goals to help assess, on various levels, where you're at and what you need to work on, so you can design your goals for the season:

- *End goal:* what you want to climb by the end of the season. For example: *Rabadá-Navarro*, a classic multi-pitch in the Picos de Europa in Spain: 750 metres, 21 pitches, F6c+. A very long limestone route with the hardest pitches at the beginning and a well-known traverse halfway up. You'd train very differently for this route if the hardest pitches were right at the top or if it were a granite corner or slab.
- *General goal:* for success on your chosen route, you need to plan your training so that you're ready and able to climb it by the end of the season. If your route has two F6c and F6c+ pitches and the rest are between F6a+ and F4, you should aim to be redpointing at least F6c+/7a, onsighting at least F6b+/6c and F6a should feel like continuity training.
- *Intermediate goals:* these are routes or exercises that you'd do at set points in the season to train for specific features of your chosen route. For example, what characterises the difficulty of the crux pitches on your route? Is it a certain type of move or hold (crimps, friction-dependent moves, two-finger pockets, sustained climbing with no rests)? Are there any other parts that you might struggle with (do you need to work on traversing, for example)?
- *Specific goals:* these are a further breakdown of our intermediate goals. They could include things like not cutting loose on overhangs, getting stronger on two-finger pockets, foot swaps, and so on.

Now you know where you want to be, the next question is where are you starting from? Your starting point, together with how much time you have, will determine how you go about achieving your goals.

To properly plan your training, you need to objectively measure what it is that you need to improve. And as we all know: if you can't measure it, you can't improve it. As such, you need to ask yourself three questions: What do I want to measure? How do I measure it (we need to know the reliability of the methods we're going to use)? Is it relevant to what I want to achieve? For example, it's no good measuring how fast you can dribble a basketball, regardless of how reliable your methods are, if it has absolutely nothing to do with your goals. Let's look at some examples:

- Example A
  What do I want to measure? Finger strength.
  How do I measure it? Using a dynamometer or a deadhang test.
  Is it relevant? Dynamometry is a scientifically proven way to measure the concentric strength of the hand flexor muscles but is this type of contraction really relevant to climbing? Or is isometric strength, measured by doing a deadhang test, more relevant?
- Example B
  What do I want to measure? Pulling strength.
  How do I measure it? By working out how many pull-ups I can do.
  Is it relevant? We know that climbers need a basic level of pulling strength, but is there any correlation between the amount of pull-ups I can do and the grade I can climb?

In addition to analysing specific details, we should also look at performance in a broader sense. Let's look at finger strength again: imagine a climber who really struggles with short, crimpy overhanging routes. They think their problem is finger strength and start training to fix this. After a while, they can hang a 14-millimetre edge for 57 seconds, which, according to López-Rivera (2014d), corresponds to a high level of finger strength. However, when they get back on the same routes, they keep falling off, just like before. If they've got better at what they thought was holding them back, what's going wrong? This is where we need to look at the bigger picture. Maybe their fingers were strong enough for these routes and the limiting factor was a lack of core strength to keep their feet on the wall. Maybe poor mobility meant they couldn't get into the best positions to use the crimps. Maybe they were getting too pumped too soon and the problem was with short-duration endurance.

Proper analysis of your starting point means you can select the best route to achieving your goals and have the best chance of success.

Now you know where you're starting from, let's get moving!

GENERAL WARM-UP. JOINT MOBILISATION. COORDINATION-BASED CARDIO. INCREASING ROM. MUSCLE ACTIVATION

We all know from gym classes or PE lessons that warming up is very important. But animals don't warm up before going hunting, so why should we warm up before climbing or sport? For better or worse, the human body works differently to other animals. We're hugely affected by body temperature (our metabolism is simply a chain of chemical reactions, which work much better with a bit of heat). For a more scientific explanation, the findings of a meta-analysis performed by Fradkin *et al.* (2010) speak for themselves: a proper warm-up affects 79 per cent of performance-related factors and can improve performance by up to 20 per cent.

Returning to the earlier topic of fascia (chapter 5): a good warm-up will increase the viscosity of deep fascia, improving the sliding of muscle fibrils and the transmission of information, force and muscle movement. It also helps achieve the right degree of fascia stiffness.

Now here's the question we've all been waiting for: do we really know how to warm up for climbing?

As this book is all about training, we'll mainly focus on warming up for training at an indoor wall. The foot of the crag isn't always the best place to warm up, so just try to recreate as much of your indoor warm-up as you can. If this isn't possible, aim to start climbing or moving with the principles and ideas of your warm-up in mind.

To begin, there are three basic aims of a good warm-up:
- To increase body temperature, proprioceptive sensitivity and central stability.
- To refine movement patterns and mental focus for the session.
- To avoid any muscular, psychological or metabolic fatigue that would interfere with the aims of the session.

A good warm-up can be divided into two parts: a general warm-up and a specific warm-up. A general warm-up prepares the body for movement (to make sure you do this, keep your trainers on when you get to the wall and only switch to climbing shoes when you're ready to climb). A specific warm-up does the same but with climbing-specific motor skills and movement.

A good general warm-up begins with joint mobilisation. You could start at the ankles and work up to the head and arms, or vice versa. The aim is to move your joints in all possible directions, while keeping the muscles gently engaged. This will loosen up the joints, get them into the best possible position, improve mobility and stimulate the flow of synovial fluid.

With your joints now prepared for the session, it's time to raise your body temperature in the simplest possible way: with a little bit of cardio. Four to five minutes are enough. Running, high knees, star jumps, exercise bike, skipping, and so on. Keep the intensity at 40 to 50 per cent so you don't get tired. If you can, try to add some coordination work (for example, star jumps raising a different arm with each jump, or high knees circling your right arm on every third raise of your left knee … use your imagination!). This will help to refine movement patterns, to improve general coordination and to focus your attention on your training.

Now you need to increase the functionality and stability of your joints in all possible positions and angles. We're talking mobility again, just like in chapter 3. There are several different options for improving ROM during your warm-up:

a) *Stretching:* as we already know, it doesn't make much sense to do any passive or static stretching (which triggers the autogenic inhibition reflex). Instead, you should be doing active or dynamic stretching, holding each stretch for less than eight seconds to avoid activating the autogenic inhibition reflex. The number of reps/contractions/bounces is up to you. Go with what you need, how your body responds and how you're feeling that day. Some days, six to eight reps are enough, and others you might need up to 15.

b) *Foam rollers, massage sticks, balls … :* around 8 to 10 passes are enough to inhibit the transmission of nociceptive signals to and from the brain and you'll see an improvement in ROM. Where should you do this? Focus on areas with the least ROM, wherever you feel the most tightness or stiffness. Think about where you might need better ROM, for example, calves, hamstrings, glutes, hip abductors, psoas, between the scapulae. If you have a GDS muscle chain assessment, I'd recommend focusing on your causal and reactive chains (see images on the next page).

c) For areas where your ROM is particularly limited (for example, if you can't properly rotate your shoulder or it hurts when you do, or if your hip abductors need some attention), you could use local vibration combined with isometric contractions held for five seconds each. Five contractions might be enough or you might need more, depending on how you feel and your individual needs. Don't overdo it, though: you're aiming for activation, not fatigue!

74 | THE SCIENCE OF CLIMBING TRAINING

FOAM ROLLING CALVES

FOAM ROLLING HAMSTRINGS

FOAM ROLLING GLUTES

FOAM ROLLING BETWEEN SCAPULAE

FOAM ROLLING HIP FLEXORS

FOAM ROLLING ABDUCTORS

Now you can move on to muscle activation. Start with general or multi-joint exercises such as dips, pull-ups, TRX rows, squats and lunges. Then switch to more targeted or single-joint exercises, working the biceps, triceps, and so on, which you can do using resistance bands. Remember to adjust the intensity of these exercises to ensure activation, not fatigue. There are two muscle groups that deserve a special mention here: the hamstrings and the rotator cuff. We often forget to specifically activate the hamstrings, but a nasty shooting pain mid heel hook will soon remind us that they don't like being left out. As for the rotator cuff, you may have seen climbers grab their resistance bands and vigorously work the external rotator muscles 'to prevent injury'. However, warming up and strength exercises for injury prevention are two very different things. When the rotator cuff is fatigued, it's less able to secure the humerus in the glenoid cavity (Chopp et al., 2010), causing joint instability and therefore increasing the risk of injury.

CORE ACTIVATION

Core strength is fundamental in climbing, and the need for core training goes without saying. It's essential for any climber looking for even the most basic level of performance and injury prevention.

Is the warm-up the right time to focus on core? It is, but with the caveat already used in this section: you need to activate, not work or fatigue, the core. You can do this through isolated exercises (such as plank, Pallof press or ab roll-outs) or through climbing exercises that require a little extra core activation (Tic Tac Toe, Feet forwards or Get'em!). But which is better: isolated exercises or climbing exercises? My recommendation is simple: do a few isolated exercises to activate the muscles, followed by some functional exercises that include actual climbing moves where you need to use your core.

At the end of this chapter, you'll find a section on physical conditioning that contains lots of different exercises, including the following core exercises that you could use in your warm-up:

- Plank
- Pallof press
- Ab roll-outs or TRX roll-outs
- Farmer walk
- Cat-cow
- Glute bridge
- Kneeling superman

SPECIFIC WALL-BASED EXERCISES

TRAVERSING. INTRODUCING THE SESSION'S TARGET TECHNIQUE

The specific warm-up is what most of us skip to at the start of a session. We get straight on the wall, do some traversing, easy climbing, and so on.

The aim here is to activate climbing-specific patterns of movement, activating your muscles for the movements inherent to climbing. So let's really make the most of this part of the warm-up. What are you planning to train today? Campus boarding? Crimpy problems? Endurance? Tailoring your specific warm-up to the focus of your session is a much more efficient way to train. If you're going to train problems with big moves, campusing or dynos, it doesn't make sense to warm up on small crimps and balancey moves, or to avoid having to pull. It would be much more efficient to do traverses, problems or moves that gradually activate the main pulling muscles and to work hand–eye coordination on increasingly difficult dynamic moves. This targeted activation of the most relevant movement patterns and muscle fibres will help you get the most out of your training session.

WALL-BASED CORE WORK, RESISTANCE BAND EXERCISES AND BODY TENSION

The next step is specific core activation through exercises integrated into climbing movement. Again, remember that the aim is to activate, not strengthen. Matros *et al.* (2013) suggest the following exercises:

- *Tic Tac Toe:* hang from a hold, ideally on an overhanging wall, and tap the furthest possible hold to your right-hand side with your right foot at knee height (remember that you need to move your hips to properly activate the core) and return to centre. Then tap a hold at hip height and return to centre, and finally tap a hold at head height and return to centre. Link this final move into beginning the exercise on your left-hand side with your left foot but this time in reverse order (head height and centre, hip height and centre, knee height and centre).
- *Diagonal:* on a very overhanging wall, or better still a roof, hang for 10 to 15 seconds using just one hand and the opposite foot. The further apart the holds, the harder the exercise.
- *Get'em!:* like Diagonal, you'll need a steep overhang or a roof. Jump up and grab a hold above your head. Swing your feet towards the wall and try to touch (and stay on!) the furthest possible foothold. To increase the intensity, try a running jump to create extra momentum as you jump and swing.

78 | THE SCIENCE OF CLIMBING TRAINING

DIAGONAL

HANG AROUND 1

GET'EM! 1

HANG AROUND 2

GET'EM! 2

HANG AROUND 3

8 WHAT CAN I OPTIMISE IN MY TRAINING SESSIONS? | **79**

TRAVERSING WITH A RESISTANCE BAND AROUND THE HIPS

TRAVERSING WITH A RESISTANCE BAND AROUND THE FOOT

- *Hang around* or *Cut loose:* on an overhang or a roof, choose a problem or a traverse of medium difficulty. After each move, cut loose with both feet and put them back on again.
- *Feet forwards:* in this exercise, touch the next handhold with your foot before getting it with your hand. Repeat on each move. The steeper the climb, the easier the exercise (see images on next page).
- *Traversing with a resistance band around the foot or hips:* in pairs, one climber traverses while the other pulls on a resistance band looped around the climber's hips or foot.
- *Body tension boulder problems* (see images on page 81)*:* on this type of problem, both your hands and feet should be a long way from your centre of gravity, meaning you need a lot of full body tension to not fall off. Another way to recruit full body tension is through an exercise called Freeze:
  » Find a problem with no dynamic moves and 'freeze' in position for two to three seconds after each move. This exercise not only works core strength but also develops lock-off strength, technique and movement efficiency.

80 | THE SCIENCE OF CLIMBING TRAINING

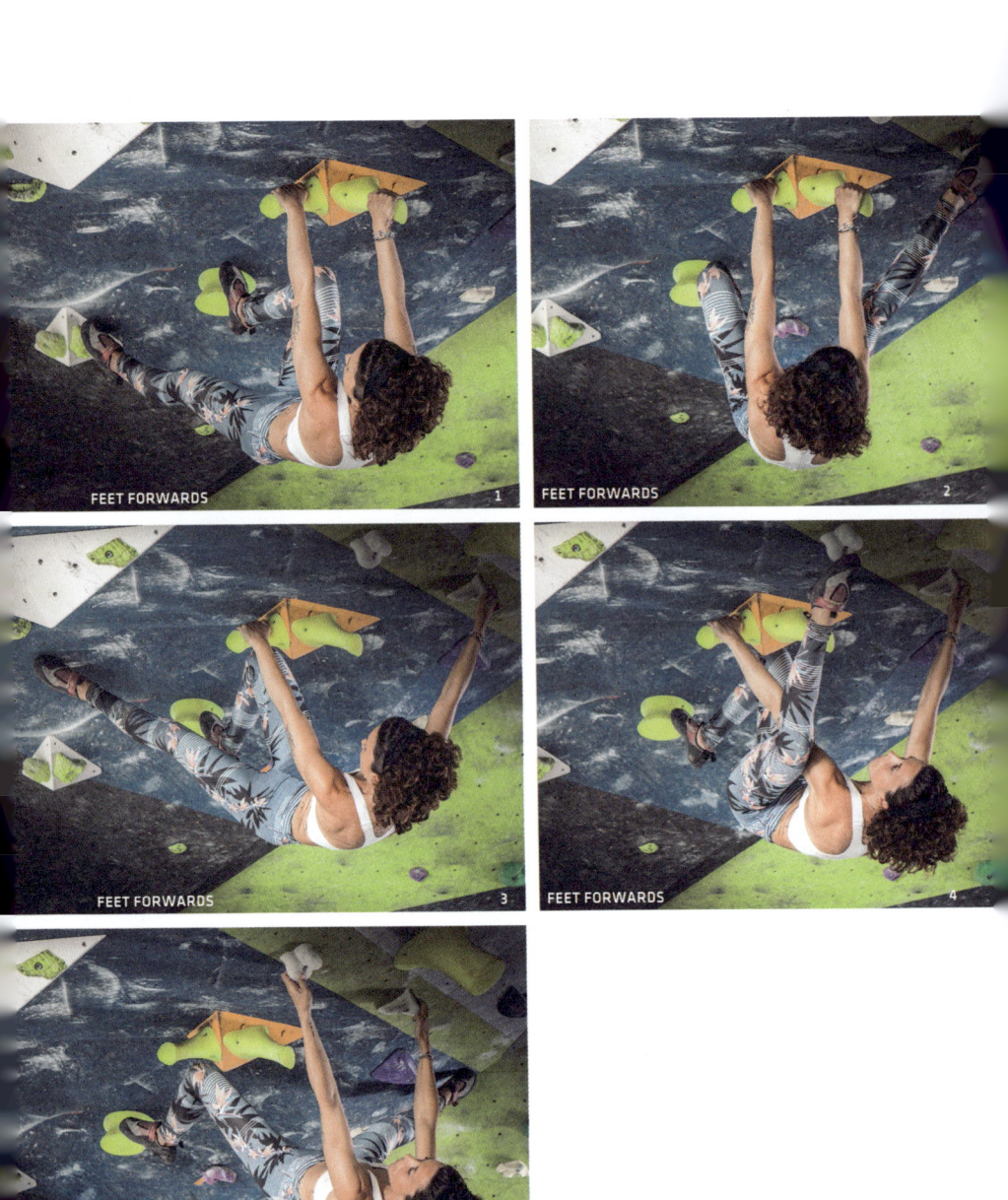

FEET FORWARDS 1

FEET FORWARDS 2

FEET FORWARDS 3

FEET FORWARDS 4

FEET FORWARDS 5

BODY TENSION PROBLEMS 1

BODY TENSION PROBLEMS 2

ENHANCING PERFORMANCE: POST-ACTIVATION POTENTIATION

Post-activation potentiation (PAP) can lead to a high degree of neural stimulation and result in better motor neuron recruitment, greater firing rate and improved interaction of actin and myosin muscle fibres (Marchante, 2015). In other words, it not only warms up your muscles, but gives the nervous system that touch of maximum activation to maximise your training performance.

It involves doing exercises specific to your training session (for example, if you're going to train hard crimpy problems, you'd use deadhangs for your PAP) at a very high intensity but without causing fatigue. PAP training can be applied to both dynamic exercises (such as weighted pull-ups, jumping pull-ups, jumping dips and box jumps) and isometric exercises (such as max weight hangs on a large edge, minimum edge hangs or weighted lock-offs at different angles).

How does PAP work? The first thing to know is that PAP only works for very advanced climbers as it targets fast-twitch muscle fibres (it won't have any effect if you are a beginner). The following points are essential for effective PAP training:

- *Intensity:* you have to be working at maximum intensity – higher than 85 per cent of your 1RM, your max weight hang on a large edge or the smallest edge you can hang.
- *Number of sets:* depending on ability, you could do between one and five sets, resting for around three minutes between each set.
- *Repetitions and time under tension:* anything over five repetitions, or isometric contractions for longer than five seconds are likely to cause fatigue. For optimal results, do no more than three to four repetitions and hold isometric contractions for no longer than three seconds.

After PAP training, you'll need to rest for 7 to 12 minutes before continuing with your session. However, don't just stand still during this time as you might cool down and lose all the work you've done warming up. Make the most of this time to keep moving on the wall or to focus on your weaknesses.

A good warm-up will take up a lot of your training session. So, you might be tempted to spend more time training and less time warming up. However, following the advice and philosophy of this book ('don't train more: train better'), you'll see that an effective training session can be much shorter than you might think. And as the saying goes: it's best to keep it short and sweet.

CLIMBING-SPECIFIC TRAINING NEEDS

Before revealing the 'recipe for success', which many readers will be looking for from this book, I'd like to define some useful terminology.

Methods are the processes that define an exercise, the means that are used and the applicable training load. For example, we could use the velocity-based training method when doing pull-ups to train pulling strength.

Means are the equipment or apparatus used to implement a training method. For example, the campus board is a means (not a method) of training power. And there are several means of training endurance: an outdoor route, an indoor route or a MoonBoard.

Training volume refers to the total amount of training activity, measured in time, distance covered, total number of moves, and so on.

Intensity is the qualitative measure of the training load: the more work per unit of time (for example, metres climbed in one minute, or weight lifted in one rep), the higher the intensity. It's determined not only by mechanical effort, but by energy used in the nervous system and psychological load.

Lastly, *training density* is the amount of work time versus the amount of recovery time: for example, one minute of work × two minutes of rest; two days of training × one day of rest …

MAXIMUM STRENGTH TRAINING

As mentioned in previous chapters, maximum strength is the maximum amount of force that can be applied in a specific action or exercise. It's vitally important in any sport and especially in climbing, where there are three areas where performance is dependent on maximum strength:

- *Maximum grip strength:* as in any other sport, climbers need to do isolated training exercises, where all elements can be controlled without the multiple/additional stimuli of actual climbing. This allows us to apply as much force as possible and is why deadhangs are used to improve maximum grip strength. However, for the strength gained in these exercises to be useful, it needs to be transferred to climbing, and this is where bouldering comes in.
- *Maximum pulling strength:* the maximum amount we can pull (and hold) with our arms. A good level of pulling strength helps with very physical moves, lock-offs, overhangs, and so on. We can train pulling strength by doing weighted pull-ups, lock-offs and heel hooks.
- *Maximum pushing strength:* often in climbing, despite being in the right position, we're not able to 'use our feet' to weight them properly and push with our legs to do the move. This also applies to pushing strength in our arms on mantels where we don't have the strength to push our way through the move. This is why we need to train pushing strength by doing deadlifts, squats, pistol squats (one-legged squats), bench presses and dips.

At the risk of sounding like a broken record, maximum strength training is so important in climbing because:

- *It reduces the risk of injury:* as we saw in chapter 2, strength training is the most efficient type of training for injury prevention, and training at over 80 per cent of 1RM results in greater strength gains. It also makes a lot of sense from a structural perspective: if you can do a weighted hang on a 10-millimetre edge, pulling on a 16-millimetre edge is going to be much easier on your tendons than if you can barely hang a 14-millimetre edge. Once again, maximum strength increases submaximal strength; think back to our analogy of the 70-horsepower car and the 500-horsepower Ferrari. Greater levels of maximum strength mean less stress on your tendons.
- *It improves performance:* the stronger you are, the harder you can climb: You can use smaller handholds and footholds, apply more force through these holds, pull harder, do bigger moves, keep your feet on more often and get them back on much easier … What's more, the further away you are on each move from maximum effort, the easier each move will feel, so your endurance will also improve.

Is there a risk of injury when training maximum strength? The answer is YES. Max strength training exposes muscles and tendons to a huge amount of mechanical strain. The injuries that could occur include:
- Torn muscle belly: the least likely to happen.
- Tear at the muscle/tendon junction or tendon/bone junction.

But this is why you should work progressively. You should never dive straight into weighted deadhangs or squats at 90 per cent of your 1RM. Training is all about process, adaptation and progression. In any case, the following guidelines can significantly reduce the risk of injury in maximum strength training.

For general strength exercises (Benito, 2008):
a) A minimum of 18 months (consecutive, not spread over 10 years) of strength training is recommended before training at between your 1RM and your 3RM (three-repetition maximum: the maximum amount with which you can perform three repetitions).
b) With less experience, it's better to do higher reps and lower weights (three to five repetitions).
c) Always do multi-joint exercises: squats, pull-ups, deadlifts, bench press, and so on. Attempting a 1RM bicep curl is like begging for a ruptured tendon.
d) Always use proper equipment: make sure there's a mechanism or a spotter in place in case you can't complete a lift. Power racks or Smith machines are perfect for training with heavy weights.

For climbing-specific exercises (deadhangs):
a) A minimum of two years of uninterrupted training (two to three sessions a week) is recommended (López-Rivera, 2018a).
b) With less experience, strength should be built by climbing (López-Rivera, 2018a) or by hanging on a pull-up bar or on a minimum 24-millimetre edge/three-pad hold (Hörst, 2006/2004).

MAXIMUM GRIP STRENGTH. DEADHANGS. EVIDENCE AND PROTOCOLS. ADAPTATION FOR DIFFERENT LEVELS OF TRAINING

Edge size	Time (seconds)	Level
14mm	0–30	Low
	30–50	Medium
	50+	High

Proposed maximum strength assessment for deadhangs (López-Rivera, 2014d)

We've finally reached the part you've all been waiting for: how to train, what to do ... the magic formula. The first thing to consider is which is the most efficient: weighted deadhangs on a large edge, or deadhangs on the smallest possible edge with no added weight. Thanks to high-quality research, notably Eva López-Rivera's PhD thesis (2014d), we can answer this with proven scientific evidence.

Participants in the study conducted by López-Rivera did two different tests:
1. *Strength test:* hang on a 15-millimetre edge for five seconds with as much added weight as possible.
2. *Endurance test:* hang on an 11-millimetre edge for as long as possible with no added weight.

The participants were then divided into two groups:
- *Group A:* this group started with four weeks of 10-second max-weight hangs on an 18-millimetre edge. They rested for two weeks and then did four weeks of 10-second minimum-edge hangs (hanging on the smallest possible edge with no added weight).
- *Group B:* this group did the same but in reverse order. They started with four weeks of 10-second minimum-edge hangs. They rested for two weeks and then did four weeks of 10-second max-weight hangs on an 18-millimetre edge.

The study found that:
1. Compared to initial levels, the greatest changes in strength and endurance occurred after four weeks of training in both groups.
2. There was a significant positive correlation between improved grip strength and grip endurance, adjusting for body weight.
3. The most efficient way to improve grip strength and endurance is to first train max-weight hangs on a large edge and then train minimum-edge hangs.

López-Rivera (2018b) proposes the following protocol for max-weight hangs on a large edge:
- 3–5 max-weight hangs × 8–20mm × 5–15 seconds (1–5): 3–5 minutes

In other words, do three to five max-weight deadhangs on an edge between 8 and 20 millimetres deep, hanging for five to fifteen seconds, at an effort level (EL) of one to five seconds, resting between hangs for three to five minutes. This formula gives a range of combinations for different abilities, allowing for controlled progression.

For minimum edge hangs, López-Rivera (2018b) proposes:
- 3–5 hangs on minimum edge × 5–15 seconds (1–5): 3–5 minutes

In other words, do three to five deadhangs on the smallest edge that you can hold for five to fifteen seconds, at an EL of one to five seconds, resting between hangs for three to five minutes.

The effort level (EL) in the López-Rivera protocols represents the difference between the number of seconds you hang for and the maximum number of seconds you *could* hang for. That is, it's your margin before failure or the number of seconds held in reserve. As a way of measuring intensity based on personal perception, it's perfect for adapting intensity to any individual or level of ability. Other authors express effort level as: number of reps done (maximum number of reps possible). For example: 5(10). This is also referred to as level of intensity or perceived effort.

Another leading voice in training for climbing, Eric Hörst, proposes the following protocols (2016):
- Training on a large edge (14–20mm) with maximum added weight:
    Two sets (where one set = five hangs × 10 seconds on an edge you can barely hold for 13 seconds at maximum effort x three minutes of rest between hangs) with five minutes of rest between sets.

CORRECT ALIGNMENT FOR DEADHANGS.

- Training on a minimum edge with no added weight:
    Two sets (where one set = five hangs × 12 seconds on an edge you can barely hold for 15 seconds at maximum effort x three minutes of rest between hangs) with five minutes of rest between sets.

The following climbers **should not do max weight or minimum edge protocols** and will need to use other training methods to build maximum strength without injuring themselves (López-Rivera, 2011):
- Climbers with less than two years' experience of systematic training.
- Climbers under 16 years old.
- Climbers with a medium level of strength: able to hang with straight arms for over 15 seconds on a 24-millimetre edge, under 35 seconds on a 20-millimetre edge and under 10 seconds on a 10-millimetre edge.

Hörst (2006/2004) suggests the following alternatives for these climbers:
- Hanging on a pull-up bar until they can hang for one to two minutes.
- Deadhangs on a 24-millimetre edge or three-pad hold on a fingerboard (i.e. a good hold).

Now let's take a look at correct technique for deadhangs (Smith and Blumenthal, 2016):
1. Always ensure good scapular retraction (shoulder blades back and down away from the ears, neck long).
2. Arms should be fully extended, elbows soft. Elbow crease should be facing towards the ears.
3. Head should be in line with the rest of the body, not straining forwards.
4. Use an open-hand grip position (recommended) or half crimp, but never full crimp (thumb over fingers).
5. Don't overextend your wrist. The metacarpal bones (knuckles) should be in line with the shoulder, with no rotation through the wrist.

Are assisted hangs a good idea? The answer, like practically everything to do with training, is, 'it depends':
- If you need to take weight off because the edge that you're using is too small, then obviously the answer is NO. If you aren't strong enough to hang the edge, this will cause excessive strain on your tendons and ligaments with too great a risk of injury.
- If you're taking weight off because you're doing one-finger or two-finger hangs and you want to reduce the strain on your tendons, ligaments, etc., then the answer could be yes. However, you need to think critically and be sure that you're not training beyond your limits. It may well be better to build maximum strength in these fingers by climbing on rock or plastic.
- One good reason for taking weight off is to progress to one-arm hangs. With one-arm hangs, aside from doubling the load on the active hand, the shoulder joint is far more vulnerable and needs protecting from both vertical forces (through scapular retraction) and rotational forces (using the pectoral muscles, rotator cuff and the muscles surrounding the elbow joint). Holding on to a rope with the assisting hand means you can progressively increase the load on the active hand, while also preventing rotation through the shoulder joint. A second option is to use a resistance band, which provides less assistance. A third option is to use a pulley system, which gives selective and precise control over the amount of weight you take off. However, this system won't stop the shoulder from rotating. As a final recommendation, even if you can hang a 10-millimetre edge, you should start

doing one-arm hangs on a three-pad hold. This will progressively build the strength needed to stabilise the shoulder joint while not overloading the elbow joint.

MAXIMUM PULLING STRENGTH. PULL-UPS. VELOCITY-BASED STRENGTH TRAINING. MAXIMUM INTENSITY METHODS AND CALCULATING YOUR RM

Pull-ups are the climbing exercise par excellence. Although the ability to do endless pull-ups isn't synonymous with climbing really hard, it's undeniable that you're going to need to pull with your arms on certain moves. And, as we've said many times in this book, the greater your maximum strength, the easier it is to make a move – in this case, pulling yourself up with your arms.

Research carried out by Dr González-Badillo and his team has led to the development of velocity-based training (VBT). This research found a 0.96 to 0.99 correlation (r^2) between the mean propulsive velocity (MPV) at which someone can lift a certain weight and the relative intensity that this entails. That is, a nearly 100 per cent reliable method of using velocity to measure intensity. But what does this mean? It means that if we measure the speed at which we can lift a certain weight (in this case, our body weight, with or without added weight), we can work out the exact intensity at which we're working.

Sounds good so far. In relation to building strength, this type of training is the ultimate expression of my training philosophy, 'don't train more: train better'. To build maximum strength through myofibrillar hypertrophy, stimulating neural pathways to maximise recruitment of muscle fibres, we know you need to be working at maximum intensity (80 to 85 per cent of 1RM). We can use a range of devices (T-Force, VITRUVE, Beast Sensor, Push Band, Velowin) to measure MPV for pull-ups. And we can use the following table to calculate intensity based on our MPV:

Intensity %	MPV
50	1.11m/s
55	1.02m/s
60	0.93m/s
65	0.84m/s
70	0.75m/s
75	0.66m/s

Intensity %	MPV
80	0.57m/s
85	0.48m/s
90	0.39m/s
95	0.30m/s
100	0.21m/s

Muñoz-López *et al.* (2017)

Begin by measuring how fast you can do the upward pull of a pull-up (concentric phase) and add extra weight until your MPV coincides with the intensity at which you want to work. Remember that you need to be pulling as fast as you possibly can.

Once you know the amount of weight to add, you can start training. Another key benefit of VBT is that it allows you to objectively quantify and reduce fatigue. But why is it so important to reduce fatigue? The aim of training is to train at maximum intensity for the maximum amount of time, but the more fatigued we get, the harder it is to maintain maximum intensity. If you reach a level of fatigue in one session that stops you from giving 100 per cent in the next, you're missing an opportunity to improve. In other words, you need to train at maximum intensity for just the right amount of time so you don't get too tired and can give it your all in the next session. If your MPV dips (i.e. your pull-up is slower) after a certain number of reps or sets, it means that you're finding it harder than you should to lift the same load and that, although you're working at maximum effort, your neuromuscular system just isn't able to produce the same amount of strength. As discussed in the section on training to failure (page 13), a 40 per cent reduction in MPV compared to your first rep brings you dangerously close to failure, leading to excessive fatigue and consequences that are simply not compatible with efficient training. It's all about training as little as possible for the greatest possible results. As soon as you're not training at maximum intensity you should stop, as you won't get the results that you're working so hard to achieve. In strength training, there should be a loss of no more than 15 to 20 per cent compared to your first rep. This coincides with approximately half the maximum number of reps you could do with the same load, for example an effort level of 2(4). Therefore, if your MPV at the start of a set is 15 to 20 per cent lower than your initial MPV, it's time to stop doing pull-ups and move on to something else.

What are the actual benefits of VBT compared to more 'traditional' methods? VBT provides a precise method for adjusting the intensity of training, which is a difficult thing to get right for two reasons:

- On the one hand, the external load (the weight lifted over a set number of reps) needs to increase over the course of your mesocycle. For example, you measure your RM on day one and you can do one rep with 40 kilograms of added weight. Then you train for four weeks at 90 per cent of your RM, which is 36 kilograms of added weight. If the training is effective and you get stronger, your RM should have improved by the fourth week. As such, 36 kilograms will correspond to a lower intensity than before, meaning you'll no longer be working at 90 per cent as planned. So, what's the solution? Calculate your RM each week and adjust the added weight accordingly? However, your RM can vary a lot from one day to the next, so a weekly calculation isn't that helpful. What about measuring RM on a daily basis?

This would create too much fatigue and detract from your actual training, as well as creating an unnecessary risk of injury.
- On the other hand, and yet closely related to the previous point, your internal load also varies from day to day: you don't always get the same amount of sleep, your eating habits change, stress at work can affect you differently at different times, your motivation isn't always the same, and so on. All these variables can have a huge effect on your ability to generate force and will therefore also affect RM.

With velocity-based training, you can measure the speed of your pull-up in real time, meaning you can calculate the exact intensity you're working at to lift a specific load. You can also adjust the external load depending on your internal load, meaning you can prevent any undue fatigue. What's more, these calculations are based on objective data and offer near 100 per cent reliability. But is this going a little overboard?

And, of course, what if you don't have a VBT device? Unfortunately, these devices aren't cheap (varying between £250 and £4,000) but you could still use the maximum strength methods developed by González-Badillo and Gorostiaga-Ayestarán (2002) before the VBT system. In any case, I would recommend using these VBT principles as a guide:
- Maximum intensity method I (**for advanced climbers**)
  » 4–6 sets × 1–2 reps × 95–100% 1RM × 3–5 minutes of rest between sets
- Maximum intensity method II (**for novice climbers, focus on avoiding muscle failure**)
  » 4–5 sets × 3–5 reps × 85–90% 1RM × 3–5 minutes of rest between sets

To accurately calculate your RM without actually doing a RM, you could use the Brzycki formula. This formula is 99 per cent accurate with a weight that can be lifted 7 to 10 times (Nascimento et al., 2007).
- 1RM = weight lifted/(1.0278 - (0.0278 × number of reps))

For example, if you weigh 72 kilograms and can do eight full pull-ups (chin above the bar, arms fully extended and scapular retraction maintained) with 18 kilograms of added weight and fail on the ninth pull-up, your 1RM calculation would be:

(72 + 18)/(1.0278 - (0.0278 × 8)) = 111.75 kilograms

And so to work at your 1RM, you would need to add 39.75 kilograms (111.75 – 72 kilograms).*

What if you can't do a pull-up? It's fairly common to see novice climbers using resistance bands to do assisted pull-ups, but this isn't such a good idea for two reasons:
1. The band gives the most assistance when it's most stretched (at the start of the movement) and takes gradually less weight as it returns to its original length (during the upward pull). Therefore, it could give more help than you actually need at the start of the pull-up and not enough in the middle or at the end.
2. Doing lots of reps with lighter or submaximal weights is not the best way to gain strength.

The eccentric method (just lowering down from the bar) is the most efficient way to work towards a full pull-up. Eccentric contractions generate more force than concentric ones, and more force is exactly what is needed. Standing on a step, bench or chair, position your chin over the bar as if you've just done a pull-up and lift your feet off. Now try as hard as you can to stay in this position. Keep fighting to stay up, even as you start lowering down, as you need to keep the brain signalling to the muscles to pull up. González-Badillo and Gorostiaga-Ayestarán (2002) suggest the following protocol:
- 4–5 sets × 1–6 reps × 100–140% 1RM × 3–5 minutes of rest between sets

---

* To calculate the weight lifted in the Brzycki formula, use body weight only for pull-ups. If the formula is used to calculate RM for any other exercise, use weight lifted only.

As for intensity, if you can't do a pull-up, it suggests that your own body weight is over 100 per cent of your RM as it's a weight that you're not able to lift. If you can comfortably do six reps of eccentric pull-ups but you still can't do the upward pull without assistance, instead of resorting to resistance bands, continue with the eccentric method but start adding weight. How much weight? Add as much as possible providing you can still control the movement, aren't training to failure or lowering down too fast (it should take three to nine seconds to lower down properly).

At the opposite end of the spectrum, very strong climbers may want to progress to one-arm pull-ups. Del Castillo (2019) recommends being able to do 20 pull-ups before starting to train for one-arm pull-ups. Alternatively, PowerExplosive (2013) suggests being able to do between one and three weighted pull-ups with 65 per cent of your body weight. PowerExplosive also warns that pull-ups are very demanding on your biceps so you should focus on strengthening your biceps if they aren't as strong as your lats, forearms, and so on, to reduce the risk of injury. According to Del Castillo (2019), you should start with some form of static support (such as a towel) for your free arm, progressing to elastic support and finally to holding the wrist and then the shoulder of the pulling arm. You can also use the eccentric method, although to begin with you might need someone to support and stabilise you.

You may be wondering what the best grip position is for pull-ups (narrow, wide, neutral, pronated, supinated, and so on). The answer is simple: the aim is to improve maximum strength, so choose the grip where you feel you can generate the most force. That said, a study on scapular biomechanics by Prinold and Bull (2016) found that supinated pull-ups (chin-ups) and wide grip pull-ups can compress the subacromial space, leading to greater risk of subacromial impingement (pinching the supraspinatus tendon). As such, if you have any problems with your shoulders, it's best to go for a narrower grip.

As for proper technique for pull-ups, optimal range of movement and other considerations such as transfer to climbing, the section on physical conditioning 'Strength training to maximise performance. Methods and techniques for upper body, core and lower body exercises' gives a detailed description that should answer all your questions (page 119).

MAXIMUM ISOMETRIC STRENGTH. LOCK-OFFS

Unfortunately, the VBT method can't be used to train lock-off strength, as lock-offs are an isometric exercise and so there's no velocity to measure.

It's important to stress that isometric training only increases strength at the exact angle you're training at. For example, if you train lock-offs at 90 degrees, your lock-off strength will only improve at 90 degrees, not at 89 or 91 degrees. As such, you need to include as many different angles and positions as possible and choose positions that are most transferable to climbing. (In my opinion, a two-handed supinated lock-off with your chin over the bar isn't really that useful as you'd be hard pressed to find that position in climbing.)

González-Badillo and Gorostiaga-Ayestarán (2002) also suggest two methods for training maximum isometric strength:
- Isometric RM method:
    5 sets × 2 reps (contraction – rest – contraction) × 3–6 seconds per contraction × load 100 per cent 1RM × 3 minutes of rest between sets
- Isometric fatigue method (load closer to 60 per cent 1RM for beginners and closer to 90 per cent for more advanced climbers):
    3–5 sets × 1 rep × 12–20 seconds × load 60–90 per cent 1RM × 3 minutes of rest between sets

Interestingly, a study by Schaefer and Bittmann (2017) compared how long subjects could resist an external force to how long they could push against the same force (both isometric actions), working at 80 per cent of their MVC. The subjects could push against the external force for over twice as long as they could resist. Take note!

RECOVERY TIME DURING AND BETWEEN SESSIONS

In terms of recovery, whether between reps, sets or training sessions, there are two types of fatigue to bear in mind: metabolic fatigue and central nervous system fatigue.

Metabolic fatigue reduces creatine phosphate (PCr) stores by 60 to 70 per cent. As we're doing so few reps per set, we're barely using anaerobic or aerobic glycolysis to produce energy, so we'll not look at the depletion of glucose stores. There's an 84 per cent recovery of phosphagen after two minutes, 89 per cent after four minutes and 97 per cent after eight minutes (Billat, 2002). This is why it's so important to rest for three to five minutes between sets in any type of maximum strength training (hangs, pull-ups, lock-offs, and so on), even if you don't feel like you've done that much or you don't feel that tired.

Central nervous system fatigue affects the function of neurotransmitters (mainly acetylcholine), which play a key role in transporting electrical energy through the nervous system to the motor neurons and on to the muscles, where it's converted into mechanical energy. That is, they help transform electrical signals into muscle contractions (Wilmore and Costill, 2007). After maximum strength training, which causes central nervous system fatigue, you'll need between 24 and 48 hours' rest to make sure you can train efficiently in your next session (Zatsiorsky, 1995).

With deadhangs, López-Rivera (2018c) suggests two sessions per week, with 48 to 72 hours between each session for the best results.

POWER AND RFD TRAINING

Before looking at how to train power, it's important to understand what power is. In physics, the following definition is used:

Power = Force × Velocity

Being dependent on two factors, if one factor has a low value, the end result (power) will be lower than if both factors are of a high value. Therefore, power depends on a climber's level of strength. Greater strength means greater power. If you don't train maximum strength, you'll have less power. Easy. Simple. Concise. As for speed, this is determined by:
  a) the amount of type II fibres in your muscles (which can be altered slightly via neural adaptation to max strength training but is largely genetic and therefore out of your control); and
  b) the volitional action of lifting a weight/doing a move at maximum speed, although this is conditioned by a).

Some coaches recommend slow pull-ups (both the upward/concentric phase and the downward/eccentric phase). However, a study by Earp *et al.* (2016) on the effects of lifting a load at different speeds found:
- Greater muscle activation and greater RFD (rate of force development) at maximum speed.
- Greater tendon compression at the start and the end of the movement.
- Greater tendon degradation/damage at slower speeds.

These results show that working at maximum speed not only improves performance but also helps prevent tendon injury.

In relation to improving RFD, in addition to their work on movement at maximum voluntary concentric speed, Levernier and Laffaye (2019) studied 14 climbers on the French national team who climbed at an elite level, competed in world-ranking competitions and climbed above F8b. The study measured maximum grip strength and RFD in open-hand, half-crimp and full-crimp positions. The climbers were split into two groups and both trained for four weeks. The control group followed a normal bouldering training programme, while the experimental group did one-arm hangs (120-degree lock-offs), three times a week, on an edge of their choice between 6 and 25 millimetres deep, on which they could hang for six seconds before failure (falling off).

Number of sets: 2	
Number of hangs per set: 6	
Rest between sets: 3 minutes	
Open-hand left	Length of hang: 4–6 seconds
Half-crimp left	Length of hang: 4–6 seconds
Half-crimp left	Length of hang: 4–6 seconds
Open-hand right	Length of hang: 4–6 seconds
Half-crimp right	Length of hang: 4–6 seconds
Half-crimp right	Length of hang: 4–6 seconds

The results showed no gains in maximum grip strength but considerable improvement in RFD_{200ms}, which increased by 32 per cent in the open-hand position, 27.5 per cent in half crimp and 28 per cent in full crimp, despite not even training in this position.

The authors believe that these incredible results (bearing in mind that even the smallest gains are a huge achievement for elite climbers) were down to neural adaptation, an increased number of electrical impulses transmitted from motor neurons to muscle fibres, which occurs at the start of a muscle contraction and is decisive in the first 100 to 200 milliseconds.

CAMPUS BOARD TRAINING

The campus board was invented in 1988 by legendary climber Wolfgang Güllich to build the power he needed to climb *Action Directe*, the world's first F9a.

Campus board training is therefore a tool for developing a specific quality: power and RFD. Using it for anything else or using it incorrectly will at best lead to inefficient training and at worst to an unacceptably high risk of injury.

To generate power when campusing, you need both strength (to hold on to the rungs/holds) and speed (to move from one rung to the next). So, if you're not moving at speed (we've all seen a beginner or someone who's very fatigued fighting to do one more move, constantly readjusting their grip), there's no power, and if there's no power then you're not using the campus board efficiently.

If you can't do each move at maximum speed, you should consider whether this type of training is really that suitable. For example:

- If you have to readjust your grip on each move (a sign that you aren't able to hold the rungs), you need to work on maximum finger strength instead by using larger rungs and doing more deadhanging.

- If you can't move from one rung to the next (a sign that you aren't able to lift your own body weight), you need to work on maximum pulling strength by doing pull-ups. Using either velocity-based training or the maximum intensity methods, try training until you can do at least the same number of pull-ups as there are rungs on your campus board.

Without sufficient strength or speed, the pulleys and tendons in your fingers (which aren't prepared for such levels of stress) will be exposed to exponentially more time under tension, and the risk of injury will skyrocket. Training should improve performance and prevent injury, so if what you're doing is likely to injure you instead, you're probably doing something wrong!

If you have the grip strength and pulling strength to use the campus board safely but you lack the coordination to campus properly, I'd recommend campusing with feet on while you learn the movement.

A practical recommendation for increasing power and RFD would be to do half the maximum possible number of moves (for example, EL 5(10)) or to stop as soon as you're moving 15 to 20 per cent slower than the first rep of the set (González-Badillo and Rivas, 2002, within Balsalobre-Fernández and Jiménez-Reyes, 2014). First set: start campusing up the board. Even if you don't make it to the top, end your set as soon as you start to slow down (even if you've only done one or two moves). If you get to the top of the board without slowing down, drop off and do another lap. Repeat until you start to slow down. With this method, you could have a set of 10 moves, 6 moves, 7 moves, 4 moves, or so on.

How many sets should you do? Six? Ten? Two? How many moves per set? The answer is simple: it depends on the individual. When planning this type of training, remember that the campus board is a tool which has been designed to train power and RFD. Therefore, as soon as your speed drops, you're no longer working power. If you keep going when you can't move fast enough, you'll create unnecessary fatigue, make it harder to achieve your training goals and increase your risk of injury. In short: a tremendously inefficient, illogical way to train.

If you're going to campus back down, remember that any type of eccentric muscle movement produces greater force than concentric movements. What's more, this eccentric movement will produce even greater force due to the acceleration caused by gravity. As such, I strongly recommend using an open-grip position as your tendons and pulleys will have to bear whatever extra force your muscles are unable to absorb or dissipate. Again, it comes down to common sense and an honest, critical approach. Ask yourself: are my muscles and soft tissue really ready for the stress of campusing back down? If I campus down instead of dropping off, will I be able to campus back up again with enough speed? And will this take too much out of me, meaning I won't be able to go as fast in the next set (cutting short my training for power)?

8 WHAT CAN I OPTIMISE IN MY TRAINING SESSIONS? | **99**

BUMPS 1

BUMPS 2

BUMPS 3

BUMPS 4

BUMPS 5

Campus board training is a perfect example of the 'no pain, more gain' mantra or my personal training philosophy: 'don't train more: train better'.

As for campusing with added weight, you should ask yourself two questions:

1. Will I be able to maintain a high degree of power and RFD? Campusing with added weight means you'll need to apply more force, but if you lose speed then you lose power, in which case the extra weight is counterproductive. You should only add weight if you can maintain the same speed and it's not going to jeopardise RFD.
2. Can my tendons cope with this added weight? I've said it a lot, but the aim of this book is to encourage the most efficient way of training. A training-related injury could stop you from training or climbing for quite some time, which would obviously have a big impact on efficiency. The possibility of injury should never, under any circumstances, enter into your training programme.

I'd recommend the following progression of campus board exercises, listed from least to most powerful (Matros et al., 2013):

- *Bumps:* with two hands on the starting rung, bump one hand up rung by rung without moving the bottom hand. This is a great exercise for learning how to train RFD on the campus board.
- *Matching ladders:* with two hands on the starting rung, campus up the board matching hands on each rung. Alternate the leading hand if you want to work symmetrically or lead with the same hand if you want to work one side first and then the other.
- *Standard ladders:* with two hands on the starting rung, campus one hand on even rungs and one hand on odd rungs. This makes the moves slightly bigger than with matching ladders, upping the intensity of the exercise (requiring more power). See images on following pages.
- *Skipping rungs:* as with ladders, you can do this with or without matching. Not matching hands requires considerably more strength and speed.
- *Maximum extension:* the power exercise par excellence. From your starting rung, campus to the furthest possible rung. Depending on the size of the campus board and your level of power, you can then repeat with the other hand, campusing as far as you can without matching hands.

8 WHAT CAN I OPTIMISE IN MY TRAINING SESSIONS? | **101**

MATCHING LADDERS 1
MATCHING LADDERS 2
MATCHING LADDERS 3
MATCHING LADDERS 4
MATCHING LADDERS 5

THE SCIENCE OF CLIMBING TRAINING

STANDARD LADDERS 1
STANDARD LADDERS 2
STANDARD LADDERS 3

SKIPPING RUNGS (WITHOUT MATCHING) 1
SKIPPING RUNGS (WITHOUT MATCHING) 2
SKIPPING RUNGS (WITHOUT MATCHING) 3

8 WHAT CAN I OPTIMISE IN MY TRAINING SESSIONS? | 103

MAXIMUM EXTENSION 1

MAXIMUM EXTENSION 2

MAXIMUM EXTENSION 3

MAXIMUM EXTENSION 4

104 | THE SCIENCE OF CLIMBING TRAINING

DOUBLE DYNOS 1

DOUBLE DYNOS 2

DOUBLE DYNOS 3

With the trailing/lower arm, you could try the following progression to increase range, power and speed (providing you can still maintain RFD and therefore continue the exercise): start by locking off at shoulder height, then progress to a deeper lock-off at rib height, waist, hip, and so on. Extremely strong climbers could even lock off with the arm fully extended below, much like a muscle-up.

- *Double dynos:* campus with both hands at the same time, either rung by rung or skipping rungs (depending on ability). This exercise requires not only a huge amount of power but also really good motor skills and hand–eye coordination.

At what point should I let go to go for the next rung? To answer this question, let's look at some basic physics: when an object is launched vertically into the air, it will gradually slow down, due to gravitational pull, until its velocity is equal to zero. At this point, it changes direction and starts falling back down. The object has a constant or uniform rate of acceleration. Any exercise on the campus board starts with a pulling motion (a pull-up).

A pull-up starts with the arms fully extended and ends when the hands are in line with the shoulders. The movement starts with the application of force, followed by an inevitable loss of velocity at the end of the pull. In other words, from zero velocity (a static hang), you'd apply a maximum amount of force, experience a gradual loss of velocity and at the end of the movement you'd return to zero velocity. It is at this point of zero velocity when you should let go with your leading hand and go for the next rung. Why? Because each time you campus, you lead with either your left or your right hand, and the direction of travel is slightly different on each side. As such, you need to change direction with each move and the point of zero velocity is when you need the least amount of force to do this. What's more, the body is weightless at this point as gravity still hasn't begun to exert any downward force. In summary: go for the next rung at the high point of your pull (hands in line with shoulders) before gravity kicks in and starts pulling you back down.

RECOVERY TIME DURING AND BETWEEN SESSIONS

As with maximum strength training, to train efficiently, it's important to keep fatigue to a minimum to ensure the right level of intensity and the greatest possible production of force and speed.

Once again, there should be no more than a 15 to 20 per cent velocity loss between reps, which is the same as doing half the maximum number of moves that you're able to do. However, as less force is required (since in most cases you're 'only' working with your own body weight and not adding extra weight), the intensity is maintained by doing more repetitions than in maximum strength training. This causes a higher degree of mechanical fatigue, resulting in higher levels of hydrogen and ammonium.

The amount of rest between sets and training sessions is very similar to the recommended rest for maximum strength training: three to five minutes between sets to replenish PCr stores, and a minimum of 24 hours between sessions for central nervous system recovery. Due to the higher degree of mechanical fatigue, I'd recommend resting for 7 to 10 minutes after campus board training before moving on to other types of training (bouldering/routes).

INTEGRATED STRENGTH, POWER AND RFD TRAINING: BOULDERING

Bouldering, aside from being a sport in its own right, is a brilliant way to train for other types of climbing as, generally speaking, it requires greater strength, power and RFD. What's more, boulderers show a greater degree of neural adaptation to building strength, power and RFD (Fryer *et al.*, 2017).

Boulderers also have a higher percentage of type II muscle fibres (stronger and more explosive) than sport climbers, who have more type I fibres (less explosive but more resistant to fatigue) (Laffaye *et al*., 2016). This gives an interesting insight into compensatory hypertrophy or the selective conversion of type IIx fibres into type II or type I depending on our performance needs (Benito, 2008). For a sport climber with a good level of endurance but poor maximum strength, power and/or RFD, bouldering will encourage the conversion of type IIx fibres into type II fibres, improving these qualities via neural adaptation and helping the climber to address these weaknesses.

Since the aim of bouldering as a form of training is to increase strength, power and RFD, it's important to remember that:

- *Regarding intensity:* you should be training on maximum intensity problems; the limiting factor shouldn't be the number of moves but the explosiveness of the moves (big, dynamic) and the amount of strength (pushing, pulling, lock-off and grip) required to do them. Be wary of very small edges, shallow pockets or monos and remember that injury is not an option!
- *Regarding recovery:* you should always rest for three to five minutes between attempts or problems to ensure the best possible recovery. Working at maximum intensity each time you pull on is essential for neural adaptation.

ENDURANCE TRAINING

As discussed in previous chapters, a good level of endurance in the forearm flexor muscles, specifically the flexor digitorum profundus (FDP), is a defining quality among sport climbers.

Remember that endurance is simply the ability to maintain the production of force. And the more fatigued we become, the harder it is to produce force. This highlights the undeniable link between endurance and efficiency.

We know that a high volume of low-intensity training is essential for aerobic endurance sports (such as rowing, cycling, athletics, cross-country skiing), and it's the same for climbing: hours and hours of indoor and outdoor climbing is essential to build greater efficiency and endurance. In other words, training a couple of days a week at the wall and going to the crag once a month might keep you in shape, but it won't be enough to help you really push your grade.

Therefore, your endurance training should focus both on improving efficiency by doing a high volume of climbing, and on improving the defining aspects of endurance: force–time integral (FTI), PCr stores and the oxidative capacity of your muscles.

What is the best way to target these factors in order to improve them? Scientific research shows that:
- Strength training, high-intensity intermittent endurance training and low- to moderate-intensity continuous endurance training improve capillary ratio and density (Alomari *et al.*, 2010, within Philippe *et al.*, 2012).
- Improved capillary density has a direct impact on increased blood flow and greater muscle reoxygenation (Robbins *et al.*, 2009; Jensen *et al.*, 2004; Green *et al.*, 1999; McCall *et al.*, 1996; Henriksson, 1992; and Klausen *et al.*, 1981; within Philippe *et al.*, 2012).
- Faster reoxygenation means faster replenishment of PCr stores (McMahon and Jenkins, 2002; and Tomlin and Wenger, 2001; within Philippe *et al.*, 2012).

As with maximum strength and power, endurance training can be divided into isolated training (mainly intermittent deadhangs, aka repeaters) and integrated training (different methods of wall-based endurance training). However, the aim of both forms of training is to improve recovery (specifically the recovery of PCr stores). Remember that, in climbing, aerobic/oxidative metabolism supports anaerobic alactic metabolism by producing energy not so we can continue climbing but to bind more phosphate to creatine and provide that burst of energy needed to latch the next hold. As such, optimising all factors that contribute to the aerobic energy system, in order to produce more creatine phosphate and replenish our PCr stores, should be the primary aim of endurance training.

PHYSIOLOGICAL EFFECTS OF DIFFERENT INTENSITIES

As discussed in previous chapters, the efficiency of the oxidative system (the oxidative capacity of any given muscle) is determined by the blood flow to our muscles and the muscles' ability to use their oxygen stores (deoxygenation) and then replenish them with fresh oxygen (reoxygenation). This section will look at how we can optimise these three factors.

The different intensities at which we train or climb have different sets of demands and also effects on our body. Understanding what determines climbing performance and how these determining factors work (a key aim of this book) is essential for knowing which training method to use, depending on what impact you want to have or what you want to improve.

In very simple terms, training can be classified according to:
- Intensity: low, medium or high
- Form: continuous or intermittent

Different combinations of these two factors will have different physiological effects.

Low-intensity, high-volume training enhances blood flow to the targeted muscles, which increases capillarisation (encouraging angiogenesis, the creation of new blood vessels) by approximately 20 per cent (Mujika, 2012) and improves the reoxygenation capacity of muscle fibres (Baechle and Earle, 2000; López-Rivera, 2014b). In good news, the creation of new blood vessels begins after just one to two weeks of training (Mujika, 2012). In addition to increasing the number of capillaries and, therefore, improving the capillary–muscle fibre ratio, low-intensity, high-volume exercise not only has a direct impact on blood flow but also on muscle fibre. It encourages the creation of new mitochondria in muscle fibre (mitochondrial biogenesis) (Mujika, 2012; House and Johnston, 2014), meaning that each fibre is able to oxidise more fatty acids and produce more energy. However, this process is a little slower than angiogenesis and begins after around six weeks of training (Mujika, 2012). To create new mitochondria, there must be no muscle acidification, meaning no hydrogen produced by lactic acid (House and Johnston, 2014). Interestingly, the absence of metabolic waste, a key feature of low-intensity training, also raises the excitation threshold of the sympathetic nervous system. Certain metabolites (H^+, lactic acid, K^+, arachidonic acid, adenosine and diprotonated phosphate) stimulate the sympathetic nerve endings, causing the constriction of blood vessels. However, Mostoufi-Moab *et al.* (1998) found that in non-exhaustive exercise (working at 25 per cent of MVC), these metabolites didn't stimulate the sympathetic nerve endings in the forearm muscles but instead raised the intensity threshold at which these metaboreceptors are activated. In simpler terms, low-intensity training means you'll be able to climb at a higher intensity without constricting the blood vessels in your forearms, meaning you get better blood flow at higher intensities.

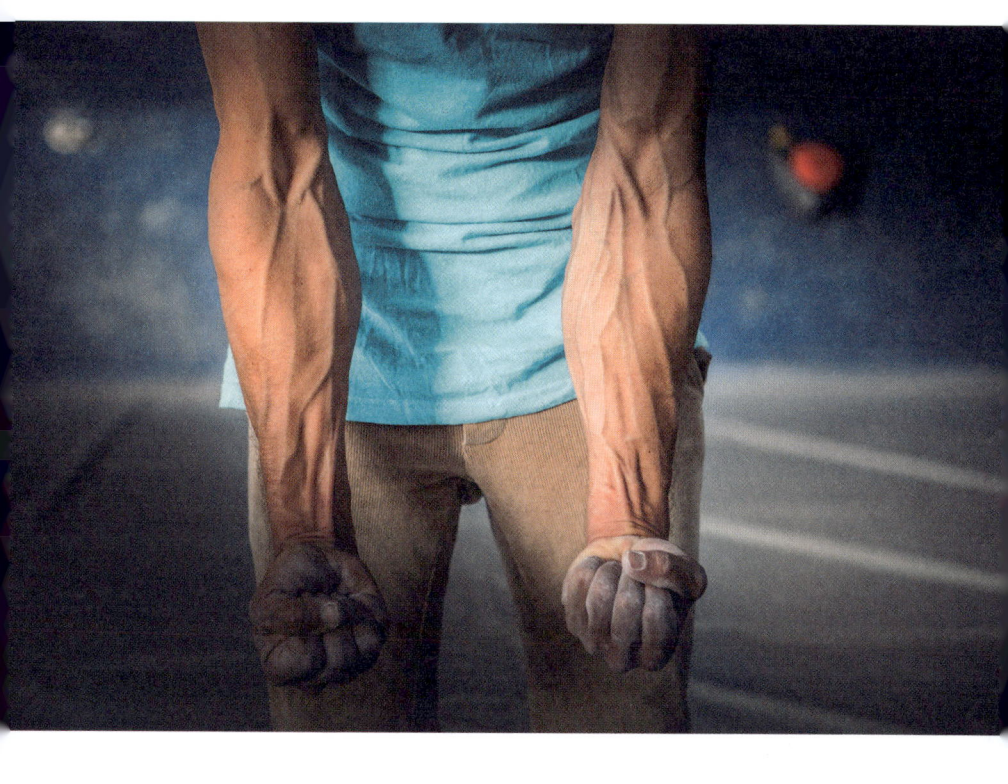

At higher intensities, the body starts to favour anaerobic glycolysis over the pairing of anaerobic alactic and aerobic metabolism. But how necessary is it to train or to stimulate this metabolic pathway/anaerobic glycolysis?

A systematic review by Saul *et al.* (2019) of over 350 studies confirmed that the steeper the overhang, the higher the concentration of lactic acid in the blood. That is, if you climb overhanging routes or problems, anaerobic glycolysis will be important to you. But how much lactic acid are we talking? Billat *et al.* (1995) found that after climbing routes graded around F7b, climbers had concentrations of between 4.3 and 5.7 mmol/L in their blood. Similarly, Schöffl *et al.* (2006) found concentrations of 5.0 ± 1.3 mmol/L after a Treadwall test (a rotating training board with variable speeds and angles; like a treadmill but for climbing). So, the answer is ... not very much. Training this metabolic pathway could be useful in preparation for certain sequences or difficult sections on a climb, but that's about it. What's more, you'd also need to be training your ability to flush out metabolic waste while resting. This ability has been linked to a high force–time integral (FTI) (Fryer *et al.*, 2015b), which is a strong indicator of climbing performance. In other words, climbing until your forearms feel like they're going to burst, when you're totally pumped and you can't even close your fingers around a hold, makes little sense if you want to improve performance. There will be such a build-up of metabolic waste by this point that it will only lead to reduced blood flow to the forearm muscles (due to a build-up of pressure and metaboreceptor stimulation); acidification of muscle cells (making muscle contractions more difficult); and the onset of muscle failure (increasing the risk of injury, increasing the amount of time you need to recover, reducing RFD) – that is to say, the exact opposite of the things you need in climbing.

INCREASING FOREARM BLOOD FLOW. CONTINUOUS, LONG-INTERVAL AND INTERMITTENT METHODS. BLOOD FLOW RESTRICTION TRAINING (BFR)

As we've seen, increasing forearm blood flow is really beneficial when it comes to climbing performance. And to increase it, we need to be training high volume and low intensity. In climbing, intensity is determined by the percentage of maximum strength needed to remain on a handhold and by how long we're holding on for. Then there are additional factors, such as what we're doing with our feet, whether we're clipping, the angle of the wall, and so on, which will vary for each individual climb (López-Rivera, 2014b).

We know that to encourage muscle capillarisation, we need to be training at a low intensity. To be exact, this means under 25 per cent of our maximum grip strength. Why? Because blood flow is greatest at 10 to 25 per cent of our MVC; there's no increase in blood flow at 25 to 40 per cent and blood flow starts to reduce at 40 per cent and over (Barnes, 1980; Byström and Kilbom, 1990; within López-Rivera, 2014b). In addition, some authors consider 25 per cent MVC as the upper limit of aerobic metabolism (Fallentin *et al.*, 1993;

Byström, 1994; Kimura *et al.*, 2006; within López-Rivera, 2014b). Finally, the more intense the contraction, the greater the intramuscular pressure, which can occlude the blood vessels. The occlusion of forearm blood vessels begins at 30 per cent MVC, with total occlusion at 50 to 70 per cent MVC (Barcroft and Miller, 1939; Barnes, 1980; Sjøgaard *et al.*, 1998; within López-Rivera, 2014b).

How can you work out the percentage of MVC that you're using? An isometric contraction at 10 per cent MVC can be maintained for one hour; a contraction at 12 per cent MVC can be maintained for around 40 minutes; continuous and intermittent contractions at 25 per cent MVC (10-second contraction/two-second rest) can be maintained for six to eight minutes; and contractions at around 30 per cent MVC can be maintained for about two to four minutes (Rohmert 1960; Byström, 1994; Allison *et al.*, 2004; Frey and Avin, 2010; within López-Rivera, 2014b).

According to López-Rivera (2014b), you can feel whether you're working at a low intensity by checking for the following key signs:
- *Forearms:* slight pump and moderate activation, avoiding extreme tightness or pump. Some widening of the blood vessels (heat, flushed skin, more visible veins). Progressive feeling of 'emptiness' and mild pain (between one and two on a subjective one-to-five scale of pump/pain, where five would be the maximum).
- *General signs:* slight increase in heart rate and breathing, light perspiration and a progressive awareness, especially towards the end, that you're moving more slowly.

Now we know the best training intensity to encourage capillarisation and to maximise the efficiency of the oxidative energy system, let's take a look at the following protocols proposed by López-Rivera (2014c):
- *Continuous method:* 5 to 45 minutes of continuous climbing, staying on the wall the whole time.
- *Long-interval method:* two to eight sets of 4 to 20 minutes of continuous climbing, resting for between 45 seconds and three minutes between sets, with a total of 8 to 60 minutes of climbing.
- *Intermittent method:* this method is perfect for less advanced climbers who might struggle with the continuous or long-interval methods. Begin by choosing a period of time (for example, eight minutes). Start your timer when you get on the wall. Climb until you reach a level of intensity of over two out of five, then stop climbing and pause your timer. Take as much time as you need to recover, then get back on the wall and restart the timer. Repeat until you've completed the chosen period of time (eight minutes).

What's the recommended volume of climbing? López-Rivera (2014c) suggests aiming to maintain the key physical signs mentioned above for the following periods of time:
- From 8 to 12 minutes for beginners.
- From 15 to 30 minutes for intermediate climbers.
- Over 40 minutes for advanced climbers.
- Up to 60 minutes or more for very advanced training or training for multi-pitch routes.

Another strategy to consider, borrowed from the world of strength training, is the use of vascular occlusion, blood flow restriction (BFR) or KAATSU training (the original commercial name). In this method, a cuff, band, strap or tourniquet is used to apply pressure at higher than normal systolic levels (above 120mmHg (millimetres of mercury, the measure of blood pressure)). The cuff is attached at armpit height or above/below the elbow, depending on the target area (whole arm or forearm).

What are the benefits of vascular occlusion? Low-intensity strength training (20 to 40 per cent 1RM) with vascular occlusion has been scientifically proven to give similar results (mainly through sarcoplasmic hypertrophy and therefore not via neural adaptation) to regular high-intensity training (70 to 85 per cent 1RM) (Peña et al., 2013). It's also highly beneficial in injury rehabilitation as you can recover high levels of strength without putting excessive strain on your tendons.

What's more, the effects of BFR training on endurance are also pretty impressive:
- Counts et al. (2016) found a 62 per cent improvement in muscular endurance in the elbow flexor muscles after eight weeks of training with 40 per cent arterial occlusion.
- Amani-Shalamzari et al. (2019) and Taylor et al., (2016) found that BFR training led to increased capillary density.
- A very interesting study by Jeffries et al. (2018) analysed the effects of preconditioning with BFR on the lower body. For seven consecutive days, while at rest, participants underwent four 5-minute sets of occlusion at 220mmHg on the upper thigh. Seventy-two hours after the seventh day, the participants performed a plantar flexion isometric contraction test (contract for 2.5 seconds, rest for 2.5 seconds) for two minutes at 40 per cent MVC and then at 60 per cent MVC. The study found that muscle reoxygenation was 33 per cent faster at 40 per cent MVC and 43 per cent faster at 60 per cent MVC. These spectacular results suggest that even if we miss a week of climbing for whatever reason (such as travel or work), it's possible to not only maintain but also improve muscle oxidative capacity.
- Biazon et al. (2019) studied the effects of high-intensity strength training and training at both high and low intensities with BFR. The greatest benefits in terms of deoxygenation were found at low intensities with blood flow restriction.

8 WHAT CAN I OPTIMISE IN MY TRAINING SESSIONS? | 113

- Horiuchi and Okita (2012) found a significant increase in the secretion of vascular endothelial growth factor (VEGF), which is responsible for angiogenesis (growth of new blood vessels), after using BFR. This is because the production of VEGF is stimulated by hypoxia (a lack of oxygen). What's more, the bioavailability of nitric oxide, a powerful vasodilator that guarantees blood flow to the muscle, increases after the secretion of VEGF. It all sounds pretty good, right?

One of the defining features of BFR is that it promotes the recruitment of type II muscle fibres during low-intensity training. This could be due to the localised hypoxia caused by BFR which, in turn, puts greater demand on the anaerobic lactic energy system to ensure the resynthesis of ATP (Domínguez, 2015).

A basic protocol for BFR training could be summarised as follows (adapted from Peña et al., 2013):

- Frequency of training: two to three times a week.
- Fifteen moves or more per set, aiming for muscle failure.
- Three to five sets per session.
- Resting for 30 to 60 seconds between sets, maintaining BFR.
- Intensity: low to moderate (20 to 40 per cent). Avoid very small holds or holds that put a lot of strain on the tendons; the aim is mechanical function not muscle tension.
- Total time under occlusion: 10 to 15 minutes.

If you're concerned about the safety of this method, the risk of blood clots or other nasty side effects, Manini and Clark (2009) analysed over 30,000 BFR training sessions and found the most common side effects were bruising (13.1 per cent), numbness (1.3 per cent) and slight dizziness (0.3 per cent), while more serious side effects, such as blood clots, only occurred in 0.06 per cent of cases. That said, I wouldn't recommend BFR to anyone at an increased risk of cardiovascular disease.

IMPROVING RECOVERY. HIGH-INTENSITY INTERVAL METHODS. ACTIVE WALL-BASED RECOVERY. INTERMITTENT DEADHANGS

At this stage, it goes without saying that efficient recovery is really important, especially for sport climbers. The question to ask is: how can I improve my recovery? What can I do to recover better?

After a difficult section of climbing, I'm sure many of us would shake out on the next available jug. I hate to say it, but Green and Stannard (2010) have demonstrated that shaking out has no bearing on recovery. They found that in the event of full vascular occlusion, a trained climber becomes comparable to an untrained climber. Moral of the story: you've got to train to avoid getting totally pumped on crux moves, to visualise them and climb them as efficiently as possible, or you'll never be able to climb a whole route at your grade.

A study by Valenzuela et al. (2015) sheds some light on how to improve recovery. Participants in their study had three attempts on an indoor F6c route. They had two minutes for each attempt and two minutes to rest between attempts. The study compared the effects of walking and of easy traversing as a means of active recovery. On the one hand, there was no significant difference in blood lactate levels until the final attempt, when levels were lower in climbers who did easy traversing between attempts. On the other hand, loss of hand strength was practically identical for both types of recovery. So, what's the benefit of more active recovery? On their last attempt, the climbers who did easy traversing to actively recover made it higher up the route than the climbers who just did walking.

These findings are especially useful for planning high-intensity interval training. If you want to get better at recovering while on a route, so you can do the crux moves and recover afterwards, it might be better to ditch the typical 4x4 protocol (four sets of four problems in a row at maximum intensity), resting for three minutes between sets, sitting down (or face down!) on the mats, which leaves you totally pumped and drained for the rest of the session. Instead, you could try some low-intensity climbing interspersed with problems of varying lengths at a high or very high intensity, without getting to the point of total vascular occlusion – the point of no return. For example:

- Two minutes of traversing + a four-move problem at very high intensity + one minute of traversing + an eight-move problem at high intensity + two minutes of traversing + a four-move problem at very high intensity + three minutes of traversing.
- A six-move problem at very high intensity + traversing until you feel less pumped + a 10-move problem at high intensity + traversing until you feel less pumped + a four-move problem + traversing until you feel less pumped.

These high-intensity problems or intervals, imitating the crux sections of a route, build strength, power and RFD while mainly using the anaerobic lactic energy system. If we can ensure that these intervals don't leave us 'out of the game', that we don't completely block the blood flow to our muscles, the traverses will help improve our ability to flush out metabolic waste and to reoxygenate our muscle fibres, giving us the best possible chance of getting through the next bit of hard climbing, just like on a route.

Although finding good rests on a route is second nature for more experienced climbers, most beginners never even consider that before getting completely pumped, they could (or might even need to) recover on the route without resting on the rope.

Active recovery is something we need to learn and train. To learn how to recover actively on the wall, I suggest the following progression:

- Start climbing on a non-overhanging wall and when you notice a slight pump in your forearms and long before the point of failure (remember, getting totally pumped is no good if you want to climb well afterwards), stop on a good hold (ideally a three-pad hold or a jug which you can get your whole hand around) and take one

REST POSITION (ALTERNATING HANDS)

REST POSITION (ALTERNATING HANDS)

hand off for a few seconds. Swap hands when the hand you're holding on with starts to fatigue. You could start by swapping hands four to five times on a non-overhanging wall, resting each hand for a minimum of 3 to 10 seconds. When you feel you've recovered, leave the resting hold and carry on climbing. Learning to control your breathing when resting is also an essential part of recovery.

- Start climbing on an overhanging wall (upping the intensity) and when you notice a slight pump or fatigue in your forearms, find a good hold or jug on a vertical wall and take one hand off for a few seconds, and then swap to the other. When you feel you've recovered, go back to climbing on the overhanging wall.
- Climb on an overhanging wall and recover on the overhanging wall.

For less-experienced climbers, increasing recovery time will be a real challenge.

For climbers who can already rest and recover while on a route, doing intermittent deadhangs (also known as repeaters) on a fingerboard is the most efficient way to improve recovery. There are numerous protocols, some easy and some hard, some more logical or reliable than others, some that are specific to certain fingerboards and others that will work with any fingerboard. The key is to make sure you can complete the full volume of training for the entire protocol.

Medernach et al. (2015) compared the effects of training intermittent deadhangs and training bouldering, in competitors in this discipline. Three 150-minute sessions a week at a density of 1:2 (one day on, two days off) produced a very significant increase in grip endurance on crimps, pinches and slopers in the group that performed intermittent deadhangs compared to the group that just did bouldering.

In turn, López-Rivera and González-Badillo (2019) compared the effects of three different deadhang protocols on endurance. They studied 26 F7c+/8a climbers training for six days a week (not just doing deadhangs).

- The MaxHangs group did eight weeks of max-weight deadhangs on a large edge. The training protocol was three to five sets of 10-second hangs (potential hang time of 13 seconds), with three minutes of rest. This protocol tested the effect of maximum strength training on endurance.
- The IntHangs group did eight weeks of intermittent deadhangs on an edge just big enough to complete the protocol. The aim was to fail or be close to failing on the last hang of the last set. The climbers could change the size of the edge if necessary. In the first training session, they began on an edge that they could only just hang for 30 seconds. The training protocol was three to five sets of four 10-second hangs, resting for five seconds between hangs and for one minute between sets.
- The mixed group (Max_IntHangs) did four weeks of the MaxHangs protocol and four weeks of the IntHangs protocol.

The test to measure endurance was time to failure on an 11-millimetre edge with no added weight. The results showed that:

- Hang-time in the MaxHangs group increased by 34.1 per cent (corroborating everything written in chapter 2 about the benefits of max strength training on endurance).
- Hang-time in the IntHangs group increased by an impressive 45 per cent.
- Interestingly, endurance in the Max_IntHangs group increased by only 1 per cent, which is a statistically negligible amount. According to the authors, this surprising result could be due to excessive fatigue from combining both methods in such a

short period of time, a possible ceiling effect (this group had the best results in the initial test, so they could have already been closer to their physiological limit) and the fact that this group recorded the most falls, which would have affected the data.

Having seen the positive effects of intermittent deadhangs on endurance, let's look at different training proposals, methods and protocols.

The intermittent deadhang protocol proposed by López-Rivera (2017):
- 3–5 sets × 4–5 hangs × 10 seconds: 5 seconds/1 minute
  In other words: three to five sets of four to five 10-second hangs, resting for five seconds (micro-rest) between each hang and for one minute between sets.

The logic behind this protocol:
- Regarding hang time: eight to ten seconds is the time needed for a high-intensity contraction.
- Regarding rest between hangs: in crux sections of a route, there's one to five seconds between holds, clipping takes an average of three seconds, and three and five seconds is the amount of time needed for oxidation.
- Regarding rest between sets: one minute isn't long enough to recover strength between sets, forcing us to work on endurance.

The intermittent deadhang protocol proposed by Anderson and Anderson (2014):
- 9 sets × 6 hangs × 10 seconds: 5 seconds/3 minutes

This is one of several protocols given in their training guide. It should be done after warming up on the wall for 30 to 40 minutes. Each set should be done on a different hold on the fingerboard. They suggest 10 seconds on/5 seconds off for beginners and 7 seconds on/3 seconds off for more advanced climbers. They also suggest resting for 70 hours between sessions and doing cycles of six to nine sessions before changing to a different type of training.

The intermittent deadhang protocol proposed by Hörst (2016):
- 2–5 sets × 3 hangs × 7 seconds: 53 seconds/5 minutes

This protocol combines maximum strength and endurance training. Add the same amount of weight as for a max-weight 10-second hang, although in the protocol you only hang for seven seconds. Hörst recommends using an edge no smaller than 14 millimetres, and the perceived intensity of each hang should be 9 to 9.5 out of 10; that is, maximum intensity just shy of failure.

PHYSICAL CONDITIONING FOR CLIMBING

Physical conditioning, or fitness as it's commonly referred to, is essential for improving performance and preventing injury in any sport. Hörst (2006/2004) suggests the following breakdown of time spent on each type of training:
- *Beginner:* 70 per cent climbing, 25 per cent general physical conditioning, 5 per cent strength-building exercises specific to climbing.
- *Intermediate:* 60 per cent climbing, 35 per cent strength-building exercises specific to climbing, 5 per cent general physical conditioning.
- *Elite/high performance:* 35 per cent climbing, 60 per cent strength-building exercises specific to climbing, 5 per cent general physical conditioning.

Spending too much time and energy on physical conditioning is a common mistake, especially among novice climbers. What's more, it is often overly and unnecessarily strenuous, which can be a direct route to overloading key muscles and, in all likelihood, an unwelcome injury. Remember: 'don't train more: train better'.

One of the key messages of this book is that physical conditioning, especially in relation to strength, shouldn't cause a level of fatigue that limits or prevents us from climbing (which is what we actually want to be doing).

STRENGTH TRAINING TO MAXIMISE PERFORMANCE. METHODS AND TECHNIQUES FOR UPPER BODY, CORE AND LOWER BODY EXERCISES

At this point, I think we can agree that maximum strength training (low reps, high loads, max speed) is essential to improve climbing performance. However, some exercises are more important than others (they more directly transfer to climbing) and they shouldn't all be done at the same intensity (upper body pulling strength, which we can train by doing pull-ups, will always have a greater impact on performance than lower body pushing strength, which we can train by doing deadlifts). Although we've already touched on this, the gold standard for strength training is the VBT method, but not everyone has access to a VBT device. As such, the percentage of intra-set loss of speed can be used to calculate the intensity of training expressed as an effort level (EL) – number of reps(maximum number of reps possible), for example 5(10) – and a percentage of your 1RM (adapted from González-Badillo *et al.*, 2017):
- *Beginner (fewer than two seasons of training):*
    - » Loss of speed: 10–20 per cent
    - » EL: 8(20) to 6(12)
    - » Percentage of your 1RM: 55–70 per cent

- *Intermediate (more than two seasons of training):*
  - » Loss of speed: 10–25 per cent
  - » EL: 8(18) to 4–5(7–8)
  - » Percentage of your 1RM: 57–80 per cent
- *Advanced:*
  - » Loss of speed: 15–25 per cent
  - » EL: 8(16) to 1–3(2–4)
  - » Percentage of your 1RM: 60–90 per cent

Remember that since the aim is to build *useful* strength – strength that is of real and not just aesthetic benefit – our total volume of training or the number of sets that we do should be based on our ability to maintain speed and effort level as opposed to sticking to any fixed number or volume.

Upper body exercises:
- *Bench press:* the upper body pushing exercise par excellence. Although the bench press is usually thought of as a pectoral exercise, as with any exercise and especially multi-joint exercises, it involves a much wider range of muscles. The exercise consists of lying flat on a bench and pushing a bar above your chest.

    The antagonist or target muscles include the pectoralis major, anterior deltoid and triceps, while the pectoralis minor, rhomboids, trapezius, latissimus dorsi and even the biceps act in synergy with these muscles to stabilise the scapula and the shoulder joint (Rippetoe, 2011). The involvement of each muscle varies a lot depending on technique

PUSH-UP PLUS 1

PUSH-UP PLUS 2

PUSH-UP PLUS 3

and the weight being lifted. For example, with weights of around 40 per cent 1RM, the split is 40 per cent pectoral muscles, 40 per cent shoulder muscles and 20 per cent triceps; whereas at 90 to 95 per cent 1RM, it's 29.5 per cent pectoral muscles, 40.5 per cent shoulder muscles and 30 per cent triceps (Marchante, 2015).

To do a bench press, lie with your back on a weight bench and with your eyes level with the bar. Your feet should be firmly grounded on the floor at a comfortable distance apart, roughly the same as for a squat, and your shins should be perpendicular to the floor. Your back should be straight, meaning there should be a natural curve at the base of the spine. Don't try to lift your legs and/or support the lower back as flattening this natural curve will weaken the lower back and make it harder for the intervertebral discs to absorb the load. The upper back shouldn't be totally flat either, as the scapulae need to be retracted to protect the shoulders (PowerExplosive, 2015). As for grip position, the narrower you go, the more you target the triceps over the pectoral muscles. The ideal distance is shoulder width plus a palm's width on each side: this will keep the forearms perpendicular to the floor throughout the lift. Once you're in position, take hold of the bar, stabilise and bring it down to lightly rest on the chest. Then lift the bar in a 'J-shaped' motion, pushing up and slightly towards the face (Marchante, 2015). The main difference between using a bar and free weights is stability. Free weights have a lot more movement than a bar held in position by both hands, meaning you'll need to use lighter weights as a lot of your strength will go into stabilising the lift with free weights.

DIPS PLUS 1

DIPS PLUS 2

- *Push-up plus:* push-ups are an excellent alternative if you don't have the equipment to do a bench press. Place your hands slightly wider than shoulder-width apart, with fingers pointing forwards. Your shoulders should be externally rotated and down away from your ears. It's really important to fully engage your core throughout this exercise to prevent over-extending the lower back and endangering the spine. Begin in a plank position and, with your body in a straight line, lower down until your chest touches the floor, without losing body tension or resting your weight on the floor. To add the 'plus', push back up until your arms are straight and continue pushing up to protract the scapula (the opposite of retraction), rounding out through the shoulders and the upper back. This small additional movement really activates the serratus anterior, which helps stabilise the scapula.
- *Dips plus:* dips are incredibly transferable to climbing, especially for mantels. With this exercise, the further forwards your chest, the more you'll activate the pectoral muscles, while a more upright position will target the triceps. Your hands should be far apart

MILITARY PRESS 1

MILITARY PRESS 2

MILITARY PRESS — DON'T STRAIN YOUR HEAD FORWARDS.

MILITARY PRESS — AVOID BEHIND-THE-NECK PRESS TO PROTECT YOUR SHOULDERS.

enough for the wrist and elbow to be perfectly aligned, from a front-on view, for the whole movement. Lower until your shoulders dip just below elbow height. If you've got the mobility, you can go lower but it should never be painful (Marchante, 2015). It's best to do dips on a stable surface so you can apply as much force as possible. You can also do them on rings (as in the photos) but this will significantly increase the demand on the shoulder-stabilising muscles. As with push-ups, you can add the 'plus' to target the serratus anterior.

- *Military press:* also known as overhead press. In this exercise, you start with the bar in line with your collar bones and lift it above your head. As the military press is performed standing up, it requires full body tension, creating a chain of muscles that transfers force from your feet all the way up to your hands (Marchante, 2015; Rippetoe, 2011). As such, it's a good way to work on transferring force from the lower to the upper body, while actively engaging the core and the arms. To do a military press, lightly rest the bar on your collar bones with your elbows perpendicular to the floor. Push upwards until your arms are straight and the bar is above your head. Make sure you don't strain your head forwards; if you can't keep the bar in line with your body due to poor shoulder mobility, you'll need to address this first (try flossing before this exercise if your range of motion is limited). Also be aware of pushing your hips forwards or curving your lower back: your body should be in a straight, stable position with knees slightly bent and a neutral pelvis and spine. To complete the lift, carefully lower the bar back to your collar bones. As for the behind-the-neck press (starting and/or finishing with the bar behind your head), unless you're looking for a nasty shoulder impingement (Michener et al., 2003), I'd recommend avoiding this exercise as the slight extra activation of the anterior deltoid in no way outweighs the really high risk of injury.

- *Pull-ups:* an exercise that all climbers do, but not all climbers do right. You should always begin by retracting the scapulae to avoid compressing the subacromial space. Then think about pulling the bar to your chest, not your body to the bar, working through the full range of movement for this exercise. This means hanging with straight arms, pulling until your chin is above the bar and lowering all the way back down to straight arms, maintaining scapular retraction throughout. Starting or finishing with bent arms or not getting your chin above the bar will creating sticking points, where you'll fail to develop any strength (Marchante, 2015). As a result, you'll notice a real weakness in these positions when climbing. In terms of grip width, a study by Prinold and Bull (2016) found that very wide pull-ups limit scapular mobility, reducing stability and compressing the subacromial space. In terms of grip position, a pronated grip (palms facing away from you – what's commonly known as a pull-up) gives less mechanical advantage but greater recruitment of the brachioradialis, trapezius and latissimus dorsi (Dickie et al., 2017). What's more, a pronated grip has the greatest transfer to climbing. Interestingly, you get better activation of the biceps, brachioradialis and pectoralis major with a neutral grip (palms facing each other) than with a supinated grip (palms facing back towards you – commonly known as a chin-up). And the only advantage of a supinated grip over a neutral grip is slightly greater activation of the latissimus dorsi (Dickie et al., 2017).
- *Barbell row:* barbell rows, with the hands at varying widths apart and mainly using a pronated grip position, are excellent for strengthening the latissimus dorsi, trapezius, teres major, infraspinatus and posterior deltoid muscles (Marchante, 2015). As such, while this lift activates the latissimus dorsi and the internal rotator muscles, it also activates many of the muscles used to stabilise the scapulae. To begin, stand with your back flat and parallel to the floor. Knees should be slightly bent and arms should hang perpendicular to the floor. Grip the bar and pull it up towards you to touch the lower

8 WHAT CAN I OPTIMISE IN MY TRAINING SESSIONS? | 125

ABOVE: MAINTAIN SCAPULAR RETRACTION

chest/upper abdomen, before lowering back down in a controlled manner (see images on the next page). As you lift the bar, retract your scapulae, keep your shoulders down away from the ears and your elbows tucked in. The wider apart your hands, the greater the demand for scapular stabilisation. If you switch to a supinated or neutral grip, this will increase activation of the biceps.

- *Face pull:* this exercise really targets the posterior deltoids and the muscles involved in external shoulder rotation. Begin by holding a resistance band or a pulley at between chest and head height. Pull the band towards your face, separating your hands as you pull back. Keep your elbows bent and arms parallel to the floor, a bit like a double-bicep bodybuilding pose (Marchante, 2015). Keep your shoulders down and try to pinch the scapulae together as much as possible at the top of the pull. This is a brilliant exercise for scapular stability and injury prevention.

BARBELL ROW 1

BARBELL ROW 2

BARBELL ROW WIDE GRIP 3

Core exercises:
Core training is a delicate subject. Firstly, what's advertised (mainly by the fitness industry) as core training is rarely the best way to activate the core: countless balancing acts on unstable surfaces, where the limiting factor is more likely to be the ankle, knee or hip; all sorts of acrobatics; and absolutely any type of TRX exercise, whether it activates the abdomen or not. In a systematic review of multi-joint exercises, both Rogan *et al.* (2014)

FACE PULL 1 | FACE PULL 2

and Martuscello *et al.* (2013) found that squats or deadlifts activated the core much more than traditional exercises like sit-ups, planks, and so on. Logically, if the main function of the core is to stabilise the spine and transfer force between the upper body and the lower body, core training needs to in some way challenge the stability of the lower back or force the transfer of energy from one end of the body to the other. For example, if you're doing squats at 90 per cent of your 1RM, say with 160 kilograms, and your core *isn't* fully engaged, you're probably going to put your back out! That said, in defence of single-joint exercises, they do allow you to feel and activate different parts of your core without the 'distractions' of multi-joint exercises. However, just remember that, according to research, multi-joint or compound movements give greater muscle activation and overall gains.

Isometric exercises will strengthen the stabilising function of the core.
- *Plank:* in this exercise, the core acts like a bridge and the abdominal muscles are the keystone, working to stabilise the lower back. The load on the lower back is similar to when trying to keep your feet on when climbing on an overhang. To perform a plank correctly, on your hands or your forearms, you need to press your heels together (activating the external rotator muscles and the deep hip muscles), activate your quads and squeeze your glutes. The pelvis should be neutral, although if you lack strength and/or motor control, a posterior pelvic tilt (keeping the pelvis rotated back and down) will maximise activation of the rectus abdominis and help maintain a flat and neutral spine. It's also important to draw your navel in, activating the transverse abdominis, and to push down through your hands or forearms to separate the scapulae and activate the serratus anterior. Keep your head in line with your body and your neck in a neutral position (PowerExplosive, 2016). In addition, the spine should be long and neutral (see

PLANK

PLANK: LOW INTENSITY

PLANK: LOW INTENSITY

PLANK: HIGH INTENSITY

PLANK: HIGH INTENSITY

PALLOF PRESS

top image on the opposite page) to properly activate the multifidus muscle. You can reduce the intensity by placing your hands on a stable, raised surface (a block or step), your knees on the floor or your feet out wide for a more stable base (see central images).

To increase the intensity, you can remove points of contact (raising a hand or a foot, or the opposite hand and foot at the same time – bottom left image), place your hands or feet on an exercise ball or an unstable surface, or ask a friend to push you from the hips in different directions or to pull on a resistance band looped around your ankle (bottom right image).

- *Pallof press:* in this exercise, the oblique abdominal muscles stabilise the spine by preventing rotation. In climbing, this is similar to the anti-rotational force needed to stop a barn door swing. Your feet should be no more than hip-width apart, so with roughly the width (not the length!) of one foot between them. The closer together your feet, the harder the exercise. Keep your knees soft, with a slight bend, and the pelvis neutral, maintaining the natural curve of the lower back. Squeeze the scapulae together and drop your shoulders, keeping your head properly aligned (not strained forwards) and the spine long and neutral. In this position, hold on to a resistance band at chest height. Ask a friend to to stand to one side and pull the band tight (or you can anchor it to the wall), then extend your arms out in front of you. This creates a bigger lever and greater demand on the core. The aim of the exercise is to resist the rotational pull of the band and remain in the same forward-facing position (see images). To increase the intensity, you could make a smaller base (with feet close together), change the angle of the band or create intermittent tension.

ABDOMINAL CRUNCH

If these exercises are done correctly, in addition to stabilising the lower back, you will have correctly aligned the spine and moved the shoulder girdle into the best possible position. This effectively teaches the body that in the event of similar external forces, it is the *core* which should absorb these forces while also transferring them to other parts of the body. These positions don't need to be held for very long. In fact, holding a plank for a whole minute has very little transfer to climbing or any other sport: can you think of a move where you're under full body tension, without moving, for a whole minute? Logically, long-hold isometric exercises don't make a lot of sense. Instead, it's better to do them for no more than 12 to 15 seconds and to increase the intensity of the exercise instead (adding unstable surfaces, changes in tension at different angles, and so on), returning once again to the idea that greater maximum strength equals greater submaximal strength (PowerExplosive, 2016).

In turn, dynamic core exercises strengthen both the stabilising function of the core and the transfer of force. However, some of the most popular dynamic exercises come with a significant risk of injury. Let's look at some examples:

- *Abdominal crunch:* an incredibly popular exercise, advertised and performed all over the world. While it may not be the most harmful, it's definitely one of the worst options for improving core strength. Simply put, it has very little transfer not only to climbing or any other sport, but to any aspect of daily life. Can you think of a sport that mimics this movement? The adverse effects of the abdominal crunch are well documented: increased pressure on the nucleus pulposus (the gel-like centre of the intervertebral discs) (Arshad *et al.*, 2016), which pushes the discs backwards and compresses the spinal canal (Davies, 2008); increased intra-abdominal pressure, which has an adverse effect on the pelvic floor; increased ligament stress and tension in the longus colli muscle, which alters the natural curve of the cervical spine (Davies, 2008); and increased pull on the psoas, which compresses and compromises the intervertebral discs in the lumbar spine (Grenier and McGill, 2007; Muscolino, 2014). These combined effects could easily result in a hernia, prolapse or urinary incontinence, so clearly abdominal crunches are not an option for strengthening the core. This goes for both the most concentrated version, where you only raise the scapulae off the floor to target the 'upper abs' (a training fallacy, see chapter 4) and the classic sit-up (which mainly works the iliopsoas, not the rectus abdominis), which we've probably all done in a PE class, strength test or gym assessment.

8 WHAT CAN I OPTIMISE IN MY TRAINING SESSIONS? | 131

RUSSIAN TWIST

- *Russian twist:* this trendy exercise is great 'cross training' and very 'functional' because it uses a kettlebell (note the irony here!). In reality, it alters the natural curve of the spine, puts pressure on the psoas, compromises the lower back, creates scapular instability and is usually performed with very little control. What's more, over 50 years ago, Kapandji had already linked the combination of spinal flexion and spinal torsion to shearing of the intervertebral discs in his renowned book *The Physiology of the Joints*. In short, this is a textbook hernia-inducing exercise.

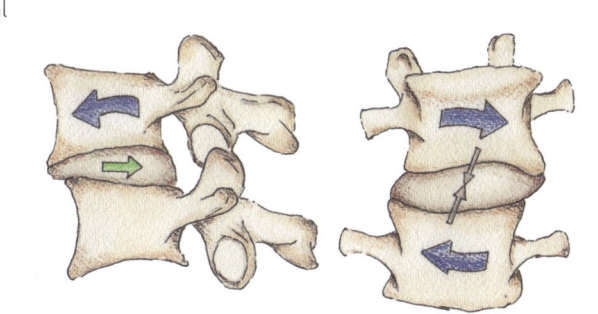

GRAPHICS: JAVIER FERNÁNDEZ DE CARA

LOWER BACK EXTENSION

- *Lower back extension:* whether on the floor or using a back-extension bench, I wouldn't advise this exercise either, because it compresses the intervertebral discs, puts pressure on the facet joints between the vertebrae, causes pelvic instability and can lead to ligament inflammation. The glute bridge is a much better alternative as it activates and synchronises the gluteus maximus and the lower back muscles, making it much more transferable to sport and general health.

There are, however, some exercises that, despite their potential for injury, could be beneficial or even necessary for climbers, such as toes to bar, or knees to elbows.

These exercises are risky because hanging from a bar could compress the subacromial space, compromising the supraspinatus tendon. What's more, the main muscle worked in these exercises is the psoas, and with poor motor control, you'll end up overloading the lower back. That said, with a few modifications (maintaining good scapular retraction, engaging the transverse abdominal muscle, engaging the latissimus dorsi as you lift your legs, and lowering with control to prevent hyper-extending the lumbar spine), these exercises have great transfer to climbing.

KNEES TO ELBOWS

TOES TO BAR

Fortunately, there are a number of safe and efficient dynamic exercises which can build core strength.
- *Ab roll-outs (or TRX roll-outs):* the best exercise for activating the rectus abdominis (Calatayud *et al.*, 2017). If you're new to core training, you could start with a kneeling roll-out and a posterior pelvic tilt (keeping the pelvis rotated back and down) to encourage activation and prevent overloading the lower back. The next step would be a kneeling roll-out with the pelvis in a neutral position. If you have a very strong core, you could do a standing roll-out, without using your knees. With any variation, it's important to keep the hips straight (a straight line from shoulders to the point of contact with the floor) and to pivot from the shoulders. Finally, rolling out really far won't give you greater activation if you can't stabilise your lower back. As a guide, if your lower back hurts when you do this exercise, you're rolling too far.

AB ROLL-OUT 1   AB ROLL-OUT 2

- *Front lever:* more advanced climbers may be able to do a front lever, which is a very demanding core exercise. In terms of progression, there are lots of different options, so I'll stick with the same method we used for training pull-ups: the eccentric method. (Like with pull-ups, if you aren't able to do a front level, it's because it's beyond your max strength.) I'll also explain a bit about the physics of levers.

    In a front lever, the fulcrum or pivot point is your shoulders; the effort arm is mainly the rectus abdominis (as well as the transverse abdominis, latissimus dorsi, multifidus and the pectoral muscles … it's a full body tension exercise); and the load arm is your own body. The longer and heavier the load arm, the harder it is on the abdominal muscles. The first step is to hold a front tuck: both knees tucked to your chest with your back parallel to the floor – this brings the hips and the legs as close as possible to the fulcrum. From here, gradually lengthen the load arm by extending one leg. Once you can fully extend one leg with the other tucked against your chest, the next step is to extend both legs in a straddle position (which reduces the total length of the load arm). The final step is to gradually bring your legs together until you can hold a perfect front lever.
- *Farmer's walk:* walking along while holding a heavy weight (sack, free weights, kettlebell) on one or both sides of the body. This exercise works absolutely every part of your core at all different angles as you walk along (you could even do this when you're out shopping by carrying a heavy bag in each hand and moving in different directions and at different speeds).

8 WHAT CAN I OPTIMISE IN MY TRAINING SESSIONS? | 135

FRONT LEVER PROGRESSION 1

FRONT LEVER PROGRESSION 2

FRONT LEVER PROGRESSION 3

FRONT LEVER

FARMER'S WALK

- *Glute bridge:* a much better option than lower back extension. This exercise helps activate the hamstrings, glutes and paraspinal muscles in the lower back and encourages them to work in unison, which is how they're designed to function. Start by lying with your back on the floor, knees bent and feet hip-width apart, then raise your hips until your shoulders, hips and knees are aligned, stopping at this point.
- *Kneeling superman:* this exercise requires good control of the shoulder girdle, abdominal corset, lower back muscles and hip extensors to keep the lower back in a neutral position. A good stability check is to balance a tennis ball on your lower back: if it falls off when you move, you know something isn't quite as stable as it should be. Begin on all fours with knees under hips and hands under shoulders. With a neutral spine and pelvis, extend one arm and the opposite leg, maintaining the natural curve through the lower back, then return to the starting position.

CAT-COW 1

CAT-COW 2

- *Cat-cow:* cat-cow is a popular exercise that's used in all kinds of physical therapy and activities like yoga and Pilates to reprogramme spinal mobility. On all fours, tilt your pelvis forwards, hollowing out the lower back and exaggerating the natural curve of the spine, while retracting the scapulae and lifting the chin. Then do the opposite: bring the chin to the chest, push down through the floor to separate the scapulae, rounding out the upper back, and tilt your pelvis back.

Lower body exercises:
- *Barbell squat:* the multi-joint exercise par excellence, cornerstone of lower body training and great for the rest of the body as well. You could write a whole thesis (or more) on how to do a squat, so I'll try not to get too carried away here. Before we begin, bear in mind that a squat will look and feel different for everyone. For example, the shape of your pelvis, length of your femur and your level of mobility will affect the width of your base (how far apart you have your feet), the angle of your feet (toes forwards or turned out), the depth of your squat (how low you can go), and so on. The most important thing is to be comfortable, learn the correct movement and then start training with an amount of added weight which is appropriate for you. Now, let's analyse the movement from the feet up:

BARBELL SQUAT

BUTT WINK

To maintain stability, you need to create a solid base, so you should never, under any circumstances, lift your heels off the floor. The tibia should be 30 to 35 degrees off vertical. Unless you have any type of knee injury (in which case, you'll need a physiotherapist to advise on the ideal depth or degree of flexion), your knees should go over your toes when squatting. If not, your upper body will compensate by leaning too far forwards, which increases strain on the lower back by up to 1,000 per cent (Fry *et al.* 2003). McKean *et al.* (2010) analysed the biomechanics of the squat in trained participants and found that knees went over toes by approximately 7 centimetres in male participants and 9 centimetres in female participants. Another standard rule, this time for keeping the hips neutral, is that the knees should move directly in line with the toes, neither turning out nor in. Ensuring that the pelvis remains neutral will maintain the natural curve through the lumbar spine and prevent 'butt wink' (a posterior pelvic tilt caused by poor hip mobility when we squat lower than we ought to). This neutral position will ensure correct alignment of the intervertebral discs and lower the risk of injury.

If you don't have the mobility to squat past 90 degrees while keeping a neutral lower back and pelvis, Boyle (2010) suggests using a 2-centimetre heel lift. This reduces tension in the posterior chain and stops the hamstrings from pulling so much on the pelvis and causing butt wink. As for the upper body, the scapulae should be retracted and the barbell should sit on your trapezius, not your neck or your scapulae (Marchante, 2015). The elbows, depending on shoulder mobility, should point down or very slightly

BARBELL SQUAT 1

BARBELL SQUAT 2

backwards. In summary: comfortable stance, knees forwards, hips back, chest up, squat down, stand up.

- *Deadlift:* this exercise really targets the posterior chain through both the upper and the lower body. In fact, some authors class it as leg training and others as back training (Delavier, 2004; Bompa and Cornacchia, 2002). Thanks to the incredible leg strength gained from this exercise, it's also recommended for climbers in the most recent edition of Eric Hörst's book *Training for Climbing*. In contrast to a squat, where you start high, go down (eccentric phase) and come up (concentric phase), in a deadlift you start low, go up (concentric phase) and come down (eccentric phase). To begin, stand with your feet hip-width apart (or however you're most comfortable), with toes pointing forwards. Your hands should be as close together as possible, without forcing the knees to turn in. Position the bar very close to your shins so that it touches when you bend down. Keeping your back perfectly straight, bend at the hips until you're almost parallel to the floor and then bend the knees to reach down and pick up the bar. With a firm grip on the bar, externally rotate your arms (elbows pointing back, biceps forwards), retract your scapulae and push out your chest. Lift the hips slightly to engage the hamstrings and push up through your legs. When you've got the weight above your knees, keep your back straight and hinge at the hips until you're standing up. To lower, keep the bar close to your body and start by hinging at the hips. When you've got the weight below your knees, bend your knees and place the bar back on the floor (Rippetoe, 2011; Nuckols, 2016).

DEADLIFT 1

DEADLIFT 2

DEADLIFT 3

ROMANIAN DEADLIFT 1

ROMANIAN DEADLIFT 2

ROMANIAN DEADLIFT 3

- *Romanian deadlift:* unlike a regular deadlift, this lift starts from an upright position and you don't bend at the knee. Start at the top of a traditional deadlift (arms externally rotated, scapulae retracted, back straight) and slide the bar as far down your legs as you can without bending your knees. Both the tightness of your hamstrings and the straightness of your back will determine how low you can go. Instead of dipping your head, think about pushing your hips back as the bar glides down your legs. Hinge at the hips to return to standing. The closer the bar to your legs as you stand up, the more you'll activate the latissimus dorsi.

- *Nordic curl:* research shows that the Nordic curl is one of the best exercises for injury prevention. Van Dyk *et al.* (2019) performed a systematic review of the Nordic curl. They analysed 8,459 male and female athletes from different sports, aged 18 to 40, and found that athletes who did Nordic curls had a 51 per cent lower injury rate. As an exercise with an incredible eccentric load, it develops high levels of strength in the target muscles which, as we've said before, is the most efficient strategy for injury prevention. Begin by kneeling (ideally on some padding) with the feet firmly anchored to the floor. Keeping a straight line from the head to the knees (without bending at the hips), fall forwards at a slow, constant speed and engage your hamstrings to control the fall.

8 WHAT CAN I OPTIMISE IN MY TRAINING SESSIONS? | 143

MODIFIED RAZOR CURL 1 
MODIFIED RAZOR CURL 2 
MODIFIED RAZOR CURL: HANDS ON CHEST 
MODIFIED RAZOR CURL: HANDS ON HEAD

- *Modified razor curl:* this variation of the razor curl is a combination of the Nordic curl and the Romanian deadlift. In fact, you could say it's a Romanian deadlift on your knees. Start as you would for the Nordic curl, with feet well anchored to the floor, keep your knees bent at 90 degrees and hips in line with the knees. Place your hands by your hips to reduce the load, or on your chest or head to increase the load (instead of adding weight, you're simply moving the 'mass' further away from the pivot point, which increases the load on your hamstrings as more mass has moved away from the pivot point). Lower your torso as much as you can, hinging at the hips and keeping the back completely flat, then come back up to the starting position. If this is too difficult, start by just lowering down, and as you get stronger you can work on coming back up.

BULGARIAN LUNGE 1

BULGARIAN LUNGE 2

- *Bulgarian lunge:* this unilateral exercise really activates the glutes and the quads. From a standing position, support your back foot on a bench or step without hollowing out through the lower back. Hinge forwards slightly so the psoas doesn't compress the intervertebral discs in the lumbar spine. All your weight should be on your front leg – the aim of this exercise is to do a single-leg squat in a way that's biomechanically more similar to a regular squat. Lower your hips as much as possible, moving straight down not forwards (imagine you're going down in a lift). The front knee should drop to just level with the supporting foot. Come back up until the front leg is fully extended.
- *Step-up:* a real test for the hip muscles, targeting both the gluteus maximus (the main muscle worked by this exercise) and the stabilising muscles. With a step in front of you, place one foot on the step. Step up to fully extend the working leg and tap the step lightly with the other foot. Depending on your balance, you could add extra weight with a barbell on your shoulders or by holding weights at chest height or on either side of your body. The higher the step, the more demanding it is on your glutes and the less demanding it is on your quads. This exercise has great transfer to climbing, especially for developing the strength required to weight a really high foothold.
- *Pistol squat:* a variation or progression of the last two exercises. The pistol squat is a single-leg squat. To build up to a pistol squat, I'd strongly recommend starting with a bench behind you. Begin with a single-leg squat down to a seated position on the

STEP-UP WITH BARBELL   1

STEP-UP WITH BARBELL   2

STEP-UP WITH HANDHELD WEIGHT

bench, lowering in a controlled, steady manner. The next step is to work on getting up from the bench. Gradually reduce the height of the bench until you don't need it any more and you can complete both the eccentric (downward) phase and the concentric (upward) phase of this exercise.

- *Calf raises:* stand with the balls of your feet on a step. Then alternate between dorsal flexion (dropping your heels as low as possible) and plantar flexion (raising your heels as high as possible). You can do one foot at a time or both at the same time. Heels together and toes apart will target the inner calf (the medial head), while toes together and heels apart will target the outer calf (the lateral head). Keeping your feet parallel will spread the load evenly across the calf. You can hold a plate, kettlebell or dumbbell in one hand and use the other hand for balance.

PISTOL SQUAT PROGRESSION 1

PISTOL SQUAT PROGRESSION 2

PISTOL SQUAT 1

PISTOL SQUAT 2

8 WHAT CAN I OPTIMISE IN MY TRAINING SESSIONS? | **147**

CALF RAISES

CALF RAISES

- *Soleus:* as seen in chapter 4, the soleus is activated when the knees are bent. So, in a seated position, resting the balls of your feet on a step, place a weight (barbell, plate, free weight) on your knees and alternate between raising and dropping your heels.

STRENGTH TRAINING FOR INJURY PREVENTION

Injury is the biggest danger for any athlete, whether amateur or professional. A climbing injury might temporarily stop you from climbing, but it can also have very serious consequences, depending on where it is and how serious it is. It can even be life-threatening. A review conducted by Jones *et al.* (2018) found an injury rate of 2.71 ± 4.49 injuries per 1,000 hours of climbing. This may not seem that high, but in a study by Jones *et al.* (2008), 50 per cent of climbers had experienced at least one injury in the previous year. To begin, let's distinguish between three different types of injury:
- *Chronic or overuse injuries:* Grønhaug (2018) and Jones *et al.* (2008) agree that this is the most common type of climbing injury and they found a significant correlation between probability of injury and climbing grade. That is to say, climbers operating at a higher grade, especially boulderers, have a higher rate of injury due to overuse/excessive load. This could be down to the amount of training they do and/or the intensity of the moves on harder problems. Schöffl *et al.* (2015) conducted an interesting study that assessed and compared which were the most common climbing injuries. They found that finger injuries were by far the most common (52 per cent), followed at quite a distance by

shoulder injuries (17.2 per cent), hand injuries (13.1 per cent) and elbow injuries (9.1 per cent). Pulley injuries were the most common type of finger injury (15.4 per cent), mainly involving the C4, A4, A2 and A3 pulleys, and there was also a high percentage of capsulitis (9.5 per cent) and tenosynovitis (8.8 per cent).

- *Trauma:* a fall, bump or blow to the body. The percentage of these injuries is significantly lower (10 per cent), although 28 per cent of trauma injuries are caused by moves that are too difficult or demanding (Jones *et al.,* 2008).
- *Postural changes caused by training:* as with asymmetrical or unilateral sports, like tennis or javelin, where imbalances can occur between one side of the body and the other, certain postural 'deformities' can also arise in climbing. They mainly affect the spine and are referred to collectively as 'climber's back' (Förster *et al.,* 2009). As you'd expect, this adaptation/deformity is more pronounced in more advanced climbers. The upper back typically becomes rounded or hunched (kyphosis), causing the lower back to curve inwards (lordosis). As seen in chapter 5, if our joints are misaligned in any way, they become less efficient and are more prone to wear, which in turn can lead to chronic injury.

Having reviewed the most common climbing injuries, let's now look at how to prevent them, focusing on injuries caused by overuse and postural changes. As for physical trauma, this type of injury is perhaps the most difficult to predict and prevent. However, with the figures that we've looked at, we can take solace in the fact that this doesn't happen very often.

The most common climbing injuries – finger injuries – are caused by overuse of the hands, yet you can hardly not use your hands when climbing! As such, the best advice is to gradually introduce and build up external load in your training and to respect recovery times and the impact of internal load, which is something we don't always do. Even then, the physical demands of training and climbing can be too much on our body and lead to injury. As such, we need to know how and when to recognise this overload, before it results in a functional injury. Think for moment about a car – a typical, ordinary car. You'd only take it to the garage if it was broken, or at the very most for its MOT. However, a Formula 1 car is on the ramps all the time, even when it's not broken, with a team of mechanics working to prevent any problems out on the track. If you want to perform like a Formula 1 car, you need to treat your body like a Formula 1 car: go to a physiotherapist and let them get to work. If you're injured, they'll map out your recovery, steer you away from disaster and guide you back into training. As every injury is a world unto itself and needs to be assessed and treated by a healthcare professional, rehabilitation is not an area covered by this book. As such, we're going to focus solely on prevention, which in any case is always better than cure. However, having covered what causes climbing injuries, we'll also look at how and why they occur. This will make it easier to identify any process or exercise that may end up causing an injury.

- *Tendons:* as seen in chapter 4, the main job of our tendons is to transmit mechanical force. When they are repeatedly loaded, tendons experience what is known as fatigue damage. With sufficient recovery time, the body can compensate for and repair this damage, returning the tendon to a state of homeostasis. However, with insufficient recovery time and continued loading, or if there's a sudden increase in compressive or tensile load that the tendon isn't able to absorb, the cells in the tendon respond by drastically increasing in number and in water content. This reduces the load by increasing the diameter of the tendon. It's important to stress that this increase in diameter is an attempt to reduce load on the tendon, as per Young's modulus strategy, and not an inflammatory response (which is why ice and anti-inflammatories are of little use against tendonitis). If the load doesn't stop and this strategy fails, the cells will start producing extra collagen and proteoglycans. This destructures and disorganises the cell fibres, causing a pathological thickening of the tendon. If this process continues, it can cause almost irreversible damage with the onset of cell death and the appearance of new blood vessels, discontinuous fibres, and so on, leading, in 97 per cent of cases, to an inevitable rupture of the tendon (Cook *et al.*, 2017; Wiesinger *et al.*, 2015). This could be either a creep rupture if caused by progressive degeneration, or a crack rupture if caused by the accumulation of micro-cracks, leading to a full rupture or tear (Ker, 2007). Interestingly, a study by Earp *et al.* (2016) found that strength exercises at a slower tempo, as opposed to at maximum concentric speed, resulted in increased tendon compression at the start and end of the movement, causing increased time under tension and greater damage and degradation. This is another good reason for doing strength exercises at maximum speed and for questioning those super-slow pull-ups favoured by some coaches.
- *Pulleys:* pulleys are fibrous sheaths that closely tether tendon to bone. Imagine a fishing rod: the rod is the finger bone, the line is the tendon and the rings that guide the line along the rod are the pulleys (see image of the pulley system in chapter 4, page 39). Crimping puts a lot of stress on the pulleys (mainly the A2, which plays a key role in finger flexion) and can cause either a full or partial tear, or gradual stretching in the case of repetitive stress (Font *et al.*, 2005). After studying the biomechanics of climbers' pulleys, Schweizer (2008) confirmed that crimping can result in tenosynovitis and a full or partial rupture of the A2 and A4 pulleys, especially in the absence of a proper warm-up of at least 100 moves. In turn, Schreiber *et al.* (2015) studied pulley adaptations in a group of F7b+ to F9a climbers compared to a group of non-climbers. In climbers, the A2 and A4 pulleys were 62 to 76 per cent thicker and the tendons were up to 21 per cent thicker. These adaptations occurred after 15 years of climbing and training for climbing, so don't expect changes overnight!

8 WHAT CAN I OPTIMISE IN MY TRAINING SESSIONS? | 151

Exercises to curb the excesses caused by climbing, including the classic 'climber's back' and any form of joint instability, should be a common feature of any training programme. This is known as antagonist or compensatory training.

A 'climber's back' is synonymous with sway-back posture (upper and lower crossed syndrome) and with excessive tension in the AM and AP muscle chains (see pages 49 and 50). Regardless of what it's called, this condition involves an excess of muscle tone (hypertonia) in certain muscles (that need relaxing), which pulls segments of bone out of place and deforms our posture. This is linked to a lack of muscle tone (hypotonia) or inhibition in the antagonist muscles, which can't counter the excessive force of the agonist muscles and therefore can't stabilise the joint.

The table on the next page shows hypertonic muscles (to relax) and hypotonic or inhibited muscles (to strengthen) (adapted from PowerExplosive, 2017). Remember that the agonist/antagonist pairing isn't always as simple as front/back, biceps (flexor)/triceps (extensor). If you're unsure about this, take another look at chapter 4. It explains the key muscles and joints in the human body and will help you steer clear of bro science and popular myths. For example, the common misconception that the antagonist of the latissimus dorsi (a key muscle in climbing) is the pectoralis major: both are in fact internal rotator muscles. So, if to balance out the latissimus dorsi you go to town on the pectoralis major, you'll only be making your sway-back posture worse and destabilising the shoulder joint.

SWAY-BACK POSTURE

Hypertonic muscles	Inhibited muscles[†]
Latissimus dorsi	Middle and lower trapezius
Pectoralis major	Rhomboids
Anterior deltoid	Serratus anterior
Anterior trapezius	Longus colli
Sternocleidomastoid	Transversus abdominis
Quadratus lumborum	Multifidus
Erector spinae muscles	Gluteus maximus
Rectus abdominis	Infraspinatus
Iliopsoas	Teres minor
Rectus femoris	Semitendinosus
	Semimembranosus

For the best results from antagonist training (and to not cause a fight between one muscle and another), you need to relax or inhibit the hypertonic muscles (see chapter 3 on mobility) before working on the hypotonic muscles. The exercises in the previous section (plank, glute bridge, kneeling superman, face pull, Romanian deadlift and modified razor curl) are essential for helping to correct 'climber's back'.

Finally, and although it's not overly common, I feel it's important to dedicate a few lines to the prevention of medial and lateral epicondylitis.

- *Medial epicondylitis or golfer's elbow:* this is a proximal tendinopathy caused by overloading the flexor muscles of the wrist (flexor carpi ulnaris, flexor carpi radialis and palmaris longus), although it can also affect the biceps brachii. It can be treated by releasing tension through self-massage and physiotherapy (Nogueiras, 2016). Golfer's elbow can lead to excessive strain on the extensor muscles, which have to fight against the strong pull of the flexor muscles to keep the wrist stable, resulting in reactive lateral epicondylitis.
- *Lateral epicondylitis or tennis elbow:* unlike golfer's elbow, tennis elbow is a proximal tendinopathy caused by excessive tension in the extensor muscles of the wrist, mainly the extensor carpi radialis brevis. In terms of treatment, strengthening exercises have proved more effective than corticosteroid injections (Araya Quintanilla and Moyano Galvez, 2015). Kenas *et al.* (2015) propose doing at least two wrist extension exercises (such as wrist curls with added weight and eccentric pronation) three times a week, spending four to six seconds on the eccentric phase of the exercise (at a constant speed) and progressing, pain dependent, to loads of 70 to 80 per cent 1RM.

[†] NB: This table shows hypertonic and inhibited muscles, implying no agonist/antagonist relationship between these pairings.

CARDIOVASCULAR ENDURANCE TRAINING FOR CLIMBING. BASE ENDURANCE, HIIT, BODY COMPOSITION AND SIT

Do you need to run/swim/cycle (or do any other form of cardio) to get better at climbing? Does cardio have any real transfer to climbing? In truth, unless you're trekking for hours to get to the crag, aerobic endurance isn't really a limiting factor in any type of climbing. So, you shouldn't need a good level of cardiovascular endurance to get better at climbing. However, in reality, it isn't quite that simple. Endurance training can have a positive impact on two aspects of climbing performance:
- *Base endurance:* this can be defined as the ability to perform any type of activity, in any given sport, involving multiple muscle groups and systems (central nervous system, cardiovascular, respiratory, and so on) over a prolonged period of time, with an optimal effect on specific performance. It's a generic type of endurance needed in any sport that isn't specifically an endurance sport (such as trail running, or cross-country skiing). Cardiovascular endurance is measured using VO2 max, or maximal oxygen consumption. By definition, this is the maximum amount of oxygen we can get into our lungs, transport round the body and use to produce energy. Although they only had a small number of participants, a study by Billat *et al.* (1995) found that F7b climbers had a VO2 max of 54.8 ± 5 ml/kg/min, which we could use as a benchmark for optimal base endurance. That is, if you do a cardiopulmonary exercise test (effort test) and your VO2 max is lower than this, you might want to work on your base endurance. However, exceeding this benchmark isn't going to have a big effect on climbing performance, as even on the hardest routes, you're only using a fairly small fraction of your maximal aerobic capacity (Sheel, 2004).

How can you improve your VO2 max? On the one hand, VO2 max is largely determined by genetics (Wilmore and Costill, 2007); that said, the VO2 max recorded by Billat *et al.* (1995) is not completely unattainable for the average person. On the other hand, the oh-so-popular HIIT (high-intensity interval training) is the most efficient way to increase VO2 max for both elite athletes and normal people, including people with injuries or illness, young people or adults (Mallol *et al.*, 2019; Batacan *et al.*, 2017; García-Hermoso *et al.*, 2016). Although running is probably the simplest way to get the best results, if this isn't an option because of your knees, level of ability or any other reason, pick your activity (rowing, cycling) and be prepared to sweat. According to a meta-analysis performed by Wen *et al.* (2019), the best results are achieved with intervals of over two minutes, total work time (sum of the intervals) of over 15 minutes and training blocks of four to 12 weeks. With HIIT, you need to be working at maximum intensity, aiming for above 90 per cent of maximum heart rate, power, and so on, for the entire workout. Maintaining this level of intensity for a full 15 minutes isn't easy and will require some training. To build up to it, try playing with the rests between intervals: progressing from a 1:3 work:rest ratio to a 2:1 ratio.

The following example is for running training for beginners (in HIIT, not climbing):
7 sets × 2 minutes of running at 90–95 per cent of max heart rate × 6 minutes of active rest (easy jogging) at 60–70 per cent of max heart rate

And for advanced training:
10 sets × 2 minutes of running at 90–95 per cent of max heart rate × 1 minute of active rest at 60–70 per cent of max heart rate

- *Body composition:* another reason that people take up running is to maintain a low body fat percentage, to burn calories or to lose weight. Before explaining why cardio is a hugely inefficient way to lose weight, let's look at what constitutes ideal body composition for climbers. This will help us to set achievable, sensible targets for improving body composition. Fortunately, Couceiro (2010) covered this exact topic as part of his PhD thesis. He established the following parameters for three different groups:[‡]
  a) *Elite:* male, onsight F7b+/8a, redpoint F8a/8c and boulder Font 7b/8a+, weight 65.8 ± 7.5kg, body fat 8.8 ± 2.6 per cent.
  b) *Advanced:* male, onsight F6c+/7a+, redpoint F7a+/7c+ and boulder Font 6b/7a+, weight 67.2 ± 5.5kg, body fat 9.9 ± 4 per cent.
  c) *Female:* onsight F6a/7a+, redpoint F6b/7b+ and boulder Font 6b/7a, weight 51.6 ± 4.5kg, body fat 19.26 ± 3.5 per cent.

Without wishing to oversimplify what is a complex and sensitive topic in climbing, these parameters could allow you to measure your body fat percentage and sensibly establish how much fat you might want to lose to climb at a desired grade.

Let's return to how inefficient cardio is for weight loss and take an objective look at the numbers: meet Paco, a climber who took part in the study by Billat *et al.* (1995). Paco's VO2 max is 54.8 ml/kg/min, he weighs 71 kilograms and his max heart rate is 205bpm (which were the average measurements in this study). You could say that his absolute VO2 max is 54.8 × 71 = 3.9L/min. VO2 max is directly proportional to maximum heart rate, meaning that if Paco runs at maximum heart rate, he'll also be running at VO2 maximum and if he runs at 80 per cent of his maximum heart rate, he'll be running at 80 per cent of his VO2 max. In turn, we know that one litre of oxygen yields 5kcal of energy, one gram of carbohydrate yields 4kcal and one gram of fat yields 9kcal. Imagine that Paco runs for an hour and, as he

---

[‡] Editor's note: it should be noted this study appears to have a questionable approach to gender equality, by only assigning 'elite' or 'advanced' designations to men, and combining all women into one category with a lower grade range.

wants to burn lots of calories, he runs at a fast pace for the full hour: 175bpm and 85 per cent of his max heart rate. Let's see what the numbers say: if Paco runs at 85 per cent of 3.9 L/min, he's consuming 3.31 L/min and expending 3.31 x 5 = 16.6 kcal/min, making for a total of 16.6 x 60 minutes = 996 kcal. Even if Paco was burning 100 per cent fat (which is completely unviable as such high intensities produce large amounts of H^+, which inhibits lipolysis), he would have burnt 996/9 = 111 grams. One hour of running at 175bpm, with the fatigue this would entail, for just 111 grams. And what's more, this is based on very high levels of VO2 max, intensity and activity time. As you can see, cardio is not a very efficient way to burn fat.

So, what is the most efficient way to lose weight and lower body fat percentage? The key is to control your insulin levels and this means being very aware of what you eat. As nutrition is a vast and complex topic, which is beyond the limits of this book, I recommend reading *The Obesity Code* by Dr Jason Fung. This book explains why all diets work and why none of them provide a long-term solution. It also explains how to keep insulin levels in check by managing your intake of macronutrients and through intermittent fasting. That said, physical activity such as interval training does undoubtedly play a part in burning calories and reducing body fat percentage. SIT (sprint interval training) involves shorter intervals than HIIT (5, 15 and 30 seconds), and it uses a work-to-rest ratio of 1:8 (40, 120 and 240 seconds of rest, respectively), adding up to a total work time of two to three minutes going all-out, at maximum intensity (McKie *et al.*, 2018). There's no evidence to suggest one length of interval is more efficient than the others for burning fat. However, 30-second intervals create a higher increase in VO2 max (nearly double) than 5-second or 15-second intervals (McKie *et al.*, 2018), which is good to know if you want to use SIT to improve body composition and base endurance at the same time.

MOBILITY TRAINING FOR CLIMBING

In truth, there's not much to say about mobility training that's not already been said in previous chapters. However, I would like to distinguish between two different purposes of mobility training. One is to correct postural imbalances that can lead to joint misalignment, with the aim of preventing excessive wear and compensation elsewhere in the body, as per the biotensegrity principle. The other is to increase range of motion to optimise movement and technical ability (for example, the ability to get your foot above your hip to use a high foothold).

First, let's recall what mobility training is really about: reassuring the brain and ensuring that any new range of motion is functional (force can be applied within it). This highlights the need to include mobility in our wall-based training sessions, at least if the aim is to increase useful range of motion for climbing. However, if the aim is to correct postural imbalances or to reduce excessive tension in certain muscle chains, it might be best to save mobility training for days when you're not at the wall.

- *Mobility training to increase useful range of motion for climbing:* as seen in previous chapters, the best and most logical approach is to include mobility training as part of your warm-up. If you can get the brain to expand your ROM as you warm up, and you then use this range of motion during your session, it will become part of how you naturally move on the wall. This will reassure the brain that you can move safely within this new ROM and, by repeating this experience of expanding and then using your newly acquired ROM, you can gradually convince the brain to keep this ROM open to you all the time. Remember: active stretching, foam rolling, massage balls, local vibration and flossing will improve ROM without triggering the autogenic inhibition reflex and inhibiting contractile capacity.

- *Mobility training to correct postural imbalances:* physiotherapy here is key. On the one hand, your physiotherapist will use the most suitable techniques to relax muscle tissue and help reorganise bundles of muscle fibres, fascia cells, and so on, to promote healthy movement and function. Think back to the analogy of the Formula 1 car and the expert mechanics. On the other hand, your physiotherapist may also do a GDS muscle chain assessment, indicating which of your chains are causal or reactive and which muscles are being overworked. After finding out which areas you need to focus on, it's time to get to work.

    First, you need to create a neurophysiological environment that facilitates mobility training and reduces the chance of triggering pain signals in the brain. Begin with some deep breaths to boost muscle oxygenation and to reduce high alertness and activation of the sympathetic nervous system. Be aware of room temperature (colder temperatures cause muscle tension/spasm and reduced blood flow due to vasoconstriction; hotter temperatures increase blood flow and reduce muscle tension), lighting (lighting has a significant effect on serotonin, which regulates our sleep/wake cycle), noise, and so on. Once you've got the right environment, begin with some exercises to reduce descending inhibition so that less pain information reaches the brain and you can increase your stretch tolerance. Use a foam roller or massage ball in areas with the most tension, aiming for 8 to 10 passes per area. After this, the central nervous system will be more receptive and better prepared for stretching. Now you're ready for some stretches to safely inhibit the target muscles. Let's look at a technique that gives a greater increase in ROM than passive stretching (Hindle *et al.*, 2012): proprioceptive neuromuscular facilitation (PNF). PNF covers two different methods: the CR method (contract/relax) and the CRAC method (contract/relax/antagonist/contract).

In the CR method, the target muscle is stretched for a few seconds until you feel a light stretch. Once you start feeling the stretch, you isometrically contract the muscle and hold for 10 to 15 seconds. You then relax the muscle and stretch for a further 15 to 20 seconds. The CRAC method is an extension of the CR method: after isometrically contracting the stretched muscle (the agonist), instead of relaxing the muscle and stretching again, you contract the antagonist muscle for 6 to 10 seconds, then relax and go back to stretching the agonist muscle. For example, if you're stretching the hamstrings, first contract these muscles, then the quads. Depending on individual ability and tolerance, the study authors recommend two to four cycles per agonist muscle.

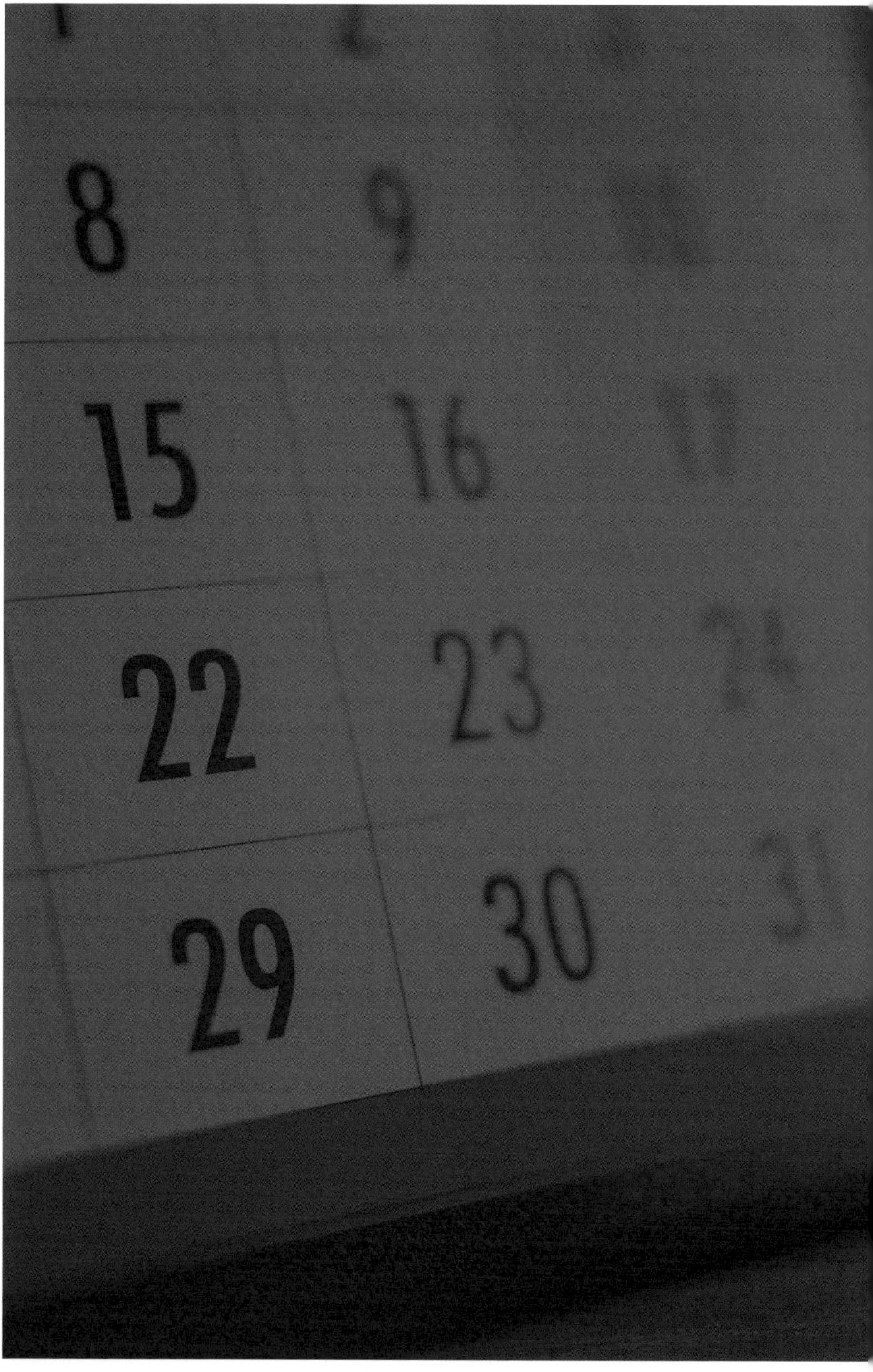
8
9
15
16
22
23
29
30

PART III

PLANNING YOUR TRAINING

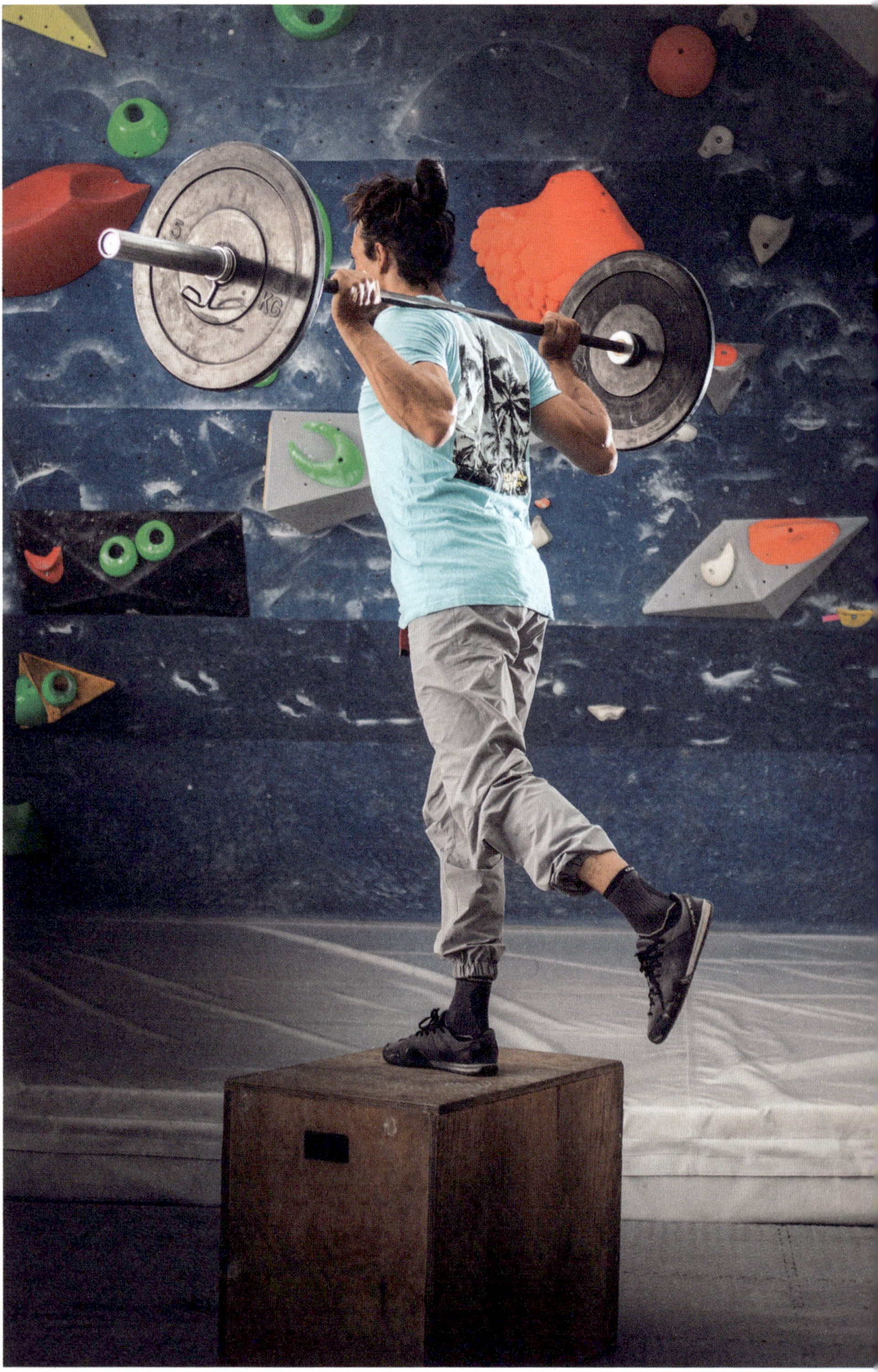

9

TRAINING SESSION DESIGN

Now you know what to train and how to train it, you need to bring together individual exercises, each type of training, into the basic unit of any training plan: a training session. You could work on one area or skill per session, or focus on multiple skills in the same session. However, if you train more than one skill per session, bear in mind that the order of these skills will change the end product. What's more, while there's a positive transfer between certain skills, some have a negative transfer and others can lead to training interference.

SINGLE-FOCUS SESSIONS. EXAMPLE SESSION

The first thing to decide is what to work on, then you need to decide how to work on it. You could do isolated exercises (for example, deadhangs to build maximum finger strength), climbing exercises (crimpy problems), or a combination of both. This choice will depend on your level of ability, training goals, strengths and weaknesses, and where you are in your training cycle.

Let's use the following model for the example session in this chapter:
1. **Warm-up:**
    - *General:* joint mobility, increasing ROM, muscle activation, etc.
    - *Specific/wall-based:* traversing, introducing the target technique, core, etc.
    - *For more advanced levels:* PAP exercises.
2. **Main part of the session:**
    - *Technique:* it's essential to train technique **without fatigue and at the actual intensity** at which you'd use the technique on a boulder problem, traverse, pitch, etc.
        a) Climbing exercises:
            › Boulder problems or routes featuring the skill that you want to work on (crimps, dynos, campusing, slopers, endurance, continuity), using the most suitable method for what it is that you want to train.
            › *Complementary isolated exercises:* depending on climbing ability, training needs and how much time you have left, you could also do some isolated exercises (such as deadhangs or pull-ups), **as long as you're able to maintain the right level of intensity** for your chosen exercise. For example, if you're tired and can't move at maximum speed, campusing would be a bad idea as you'd not produce the necessary power/RFD and you'd also be increasing your risk of injury.
            › *Antagonist training:* end your session with some antagonist training for injury prevention, activating and strengthening the antagonist muscles to balance out their agonist counterparts.
        b) Isolated exercises:
            › *Select the relevant exercises and methods:* deadhangs, pull-ups, lock-offs, campusing, etc. Remember that this type of session is for more advanced climbers looking to isolate specific aspects of physical conditioning for climbing.
            › *Antagonist training:* end your session with some antagonist training for injury prevention, activating and strengthening the antagonist muscles to balance out their agonist counterparts.

c) Isolated exercises + climbing exercises (intra-session transfer):
   › *Isolated exercises:* do your isolated exercises first to make sure you can maintain the right level of intensity.
   › *Complementary physical conditioning:* as you'll need a good amount of rest to ensure good technique and the right level of intensity in your climbing exercises, you could use this rest time for some physical conditioning. Focus on muscles which are often neglected or which might need a little extra attention (for example, hamstring strength for more powerful heel hooks).
   › *Climbing exercises:* this is when to focus on the inter-session transfer of skills. For example, in a finger strength training session, you could do a range of crimpy boulder problems after your max-weight deadhangs.

The following example is a maximum strength training session with both isolated exercises and climbing exercises for an intermediate/advanced climber:

Warm-up:
1. *Joint mobility:* 10 seconds per joint, from ankles to wrists/fingers.
2. *Cardio:* two minutes of skipping at an intensity of 3–4/10.
3. *Increasing ROM:* foam roll calves, hamstrings, glutes, back and between the shoulder blades. Hip abduction with local vibration on gluteus medius, pushing against a wall for resistance: five reps with five seconds of isometric contractions. Knee raises with local vibration on hip flexors (psoas and rectus femoris).
4. *Muscle activation:* two sets of: pull-ups (6 reps) + Bulgarian lunge (10 reps) + forearm plank (3 x 8 seconds × 2 seconds rest) + military press with resistance band (10 reps) + glute bridge (15 reps) + ab roll-out (8 reps) + biceps and triceps with resistance band (12 reps each). Rest for one minute between sets.
5. *Traversing:* four traverses with 40–30–20–15 moves. Incremental intensity: do the first three traverses on a vertical wall with the 20-move traverse on one-pad holds, then do the fourth traverse on a slightly overhanging wall also on one-pad holds. Rest for 30 to 45 seconds between each traverse.
6. *Wall-based core work:* feet forwards. Three sets of four to five moves, resting for one minute between sets.

Main part of the session:
1. *Deadhangs:*
   Preparation: 3 hangs × 20mm – 16mm –14mm × 8 seconds: 1 minute of rest
   Five max-weight hangs × 18mm × 8 seconds: 3–5 minutes of rest
2. *Complementary physical conditioning:*
   Two sets × modified razor curl with hands on chest × 8 reps × 90 seconds of rest
   Four sets × Nordic curl × 5 reps × 2 minutes of rest
3. *Bouldering:*
   Pick a five-move crimpy overhanging problem, EL 5(6). Rest for three minutes between each attempt. Have as many attempts as possible. End the exercise when you start falling, due to tiredness, on move three or lower. Focus on problems with lock-offs and heel hooks.

Cool down:
1. *Traversing:* two to three traverses on a vertical wall, 15 to 20 moves, intensity 3–4/10, using minimum two-pad holds. Rest for 30 to 60 seconds.

CRITERIA FOR PLANNING A MULTI-FOCUS SESSION. TRANSFER AND INTERFERENCE

If you want to work on multiple areas in one session, it's important to consider the following points:
- Effective maximum strength training requires rest. If you don't rest for long enough between sets and exercises, neither the nervous system (neurotransmitter replenishment) nor the metabolism (phosphagen replenishment) will be in the best condition for the next set or exercise. As such, you won't be able to perform at your best and will end up with fatigue instead of the intended training stimulus.
- Effective power and RFD training requires high levels of strength. You should never train power or RFD to exhaustion. Remember that if you're tired and can't produce enough force, the end product (power) will be lower and you won't achieve the intended training stimulus.
- Endurance training interferes with strength gains. Strength training activates the mTOR pathway (a series of metabolic chemical reactions involving the secretion of certain hormones and anabolic processes responsible for building up organic structures, among other physiological functions), while endurance training activates the AMPK pathway (a series of metabolic chemical reactions involving the secretion

of certain hormones and catabolic processes responsible for breaking down organic structures in order to produce energy, among other physiological functions). They are opposing and incompatible pathways (adapted from González-Badillo and Gorostiaga-Ayestarán, 2002). However, emerging evidence suggests that this interference can be reduced to a minimum if certain recovery times (specific to the training method and intensity) are observed.

With this in mind, some potential combinations include:
- *Maximum strength sessions:*
  a) Maximum finger strength + maximum pulling strength
  b) Maximum finger strength/pulling strength + power/RFD – only if strength and speed aren't limited by fatigue and only in this order (not power/RFD + max strength)
- *Power/RFD sessions:*
  a) Single focus
- *Endurance sessions:*
  a) Single focus
  b) Endurance + antagonist strength/non-targeted muscle groups: These sessions can be used to work on areas of weakness and to build antagonist strength for injury prevention.

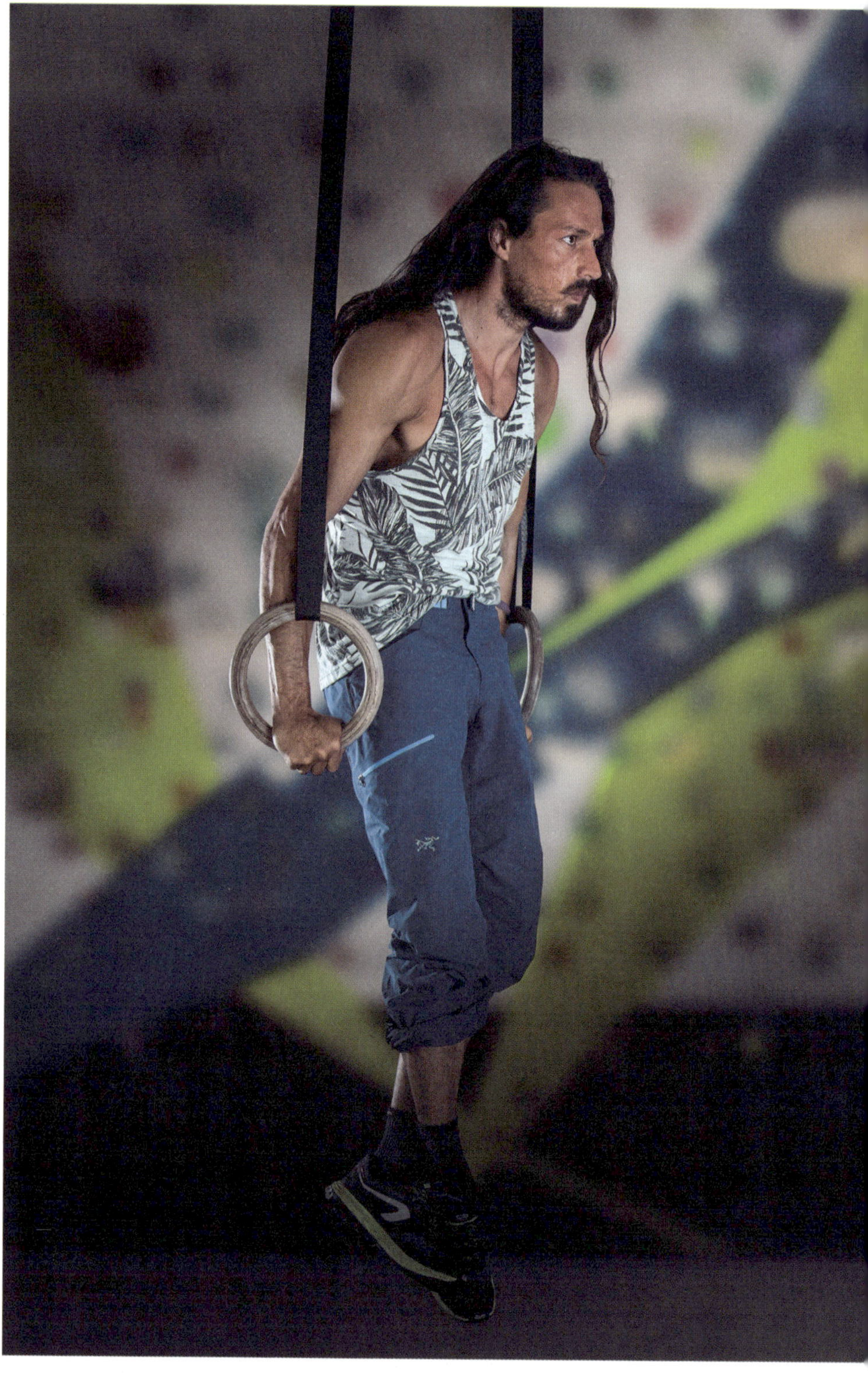

10

PERIODISATION MODELS: IN SEARCH OF OPTIMAL PEAK FORM

How was Usain Bolt able to hit peak physical, technical and mental form at 9.35 p.m. on 16 August 2009 at the World Athletics Championships in Berlin, when he ran the 100 metres in 9.58 seconds? Art? Science? Luck? Experience?

The planning of sports training is 10 per cent science and 90 per cent art – but don't turn your nose up at this 10 per cent! Compared to training with no plan at all, a well-designed training plan can improve performance by 1.5 to 2.3 per cent (Muñoz, 2017). Although it might seem trivial, you'll soon see the difference that this can make. A proper training plan also shows greater awareness of the biodynamic changes in your body, as governed by the principles of training, which translates into a lower chance of injury and, above all, a much greater respect for you and your body.

BASIC CONCEPTS: MACROCYCLE, MESOCYCLE AND MICROCYCLE

Before starting to cook (planning), you need to know what ingredients to use (skills to develop) and what utensils (units of planning) you're going to need.

- *Macrocycle:* the basic unit of planning. A macrocycle is defined as an extended period of training resulting in a higher level of performance (adapted from Solé, 2006). A macrocycle is divided into various mesocycles. It's important to stress that in order to improve performance, it's essential that the body can establish a state of homeostasis.
- *Mesocycle:* a medium-length block of training designed to achieve intermediate goals as part of the wider training process (Solé, 2006). A mesocycle is divided into various microcycles.
- *Microcycle:* a short block of training designed to work on individual skills or qualities.

Defining these three units as long, medium and short blocks of time avoids labelling the macrocycle as a year, the mesocycle as a month or a quarter, and the microcycle as a week. They may, or may not, coincide. You could have several macrocycles in a season, or just one. It all depends on which periodisation model you're using.

There are many periodisation models (linear, non-linear, block, integrated, and so on), each with their own advantages and disadvantages. The suitability of any given model depends on the sport, the athlete and their level of experience. This book will focus on two linear models (the most simple to understand and put into practice) and one block (ATR) model that allows for multiple points of peak form in a season, which, in my experience, is highly applicable and effective for climbing.

As these models are designed for use in (practically) any sport, they refer to periods of training for competitions. However, this doesn't mean they're only designed for competition climbers: simply take competition to mean any challenge, test, checkpoint or project.

LINEAR PERIODISATION: TRADITIONAL AND REVERSE. GENERAL AND SPECIFIC PREPARATION PERIOD. COMPETITION AND TAPERING PERIOD. ADVANTAGES AND DISADVANTAGES. EXAMPLE PERIODISATION

The classic periodisation model, referred to as traditional or linear periodisation, was developed by Matveyev (1977).

It uses the season as the basic unit of planning (the macrocycle). The end of the macrocycle and the point of peak form coincide with the final or most important competition of the season, although it is possible to have two points of peak form in the same macrocycle.

Matveyev divides the macrocycle into three periods:
- **Base or preparation period:** the aim of this period is to build up basic fitness and movement. It is further divided into:
  1. *General preparation period:* multilateral training (non-specific, varied, multicomponent) takes precedence over specific training (training specifically for climbing). The focus is on volume rather than intensity, creating a solid foundation for the training load in the specific preparation period. It's commonly referred to as the 'preseason'. The mesocycles in this period develop adaptation to strength, endurance and hypertrophy training, through general and non-specific exercises. In training for climbing, this phase should be equally non-specific. We should aim to introduce different types of movement, correct basic technique and amass a broad range of climbing experience (different disciplines, rock types, styles – slabs, cracks, overhangs, dihedrals, and so on), in addition to building continuity and endurance. The general preparation period could account for as little as 20 to 30 per cent of the base period for advanced climbers or as much as 60 to 70 per cent for less advanced climbers.
  2. *Specific preparation period:* specific training takes precedence over multilateral training. There's a notable increase in intensity and a slight reduction in volume. The mesocycles in this phase cover maximum strength, power and RFD. The climbing becomes more specific, applying and developing the skills introduced in the general period in order to maximise performance. The focus shifts to climbing on routes/boulder problems and rock types that are more specific to our end goal for the season.

- **Competition period:** in this period, which is also known as tapering, there's a significant drop in volume and the aim is to reach peak form for the final competition or end goal of the season. There's also a significant drop in specific physical conditioning (we should have already reached maximum potential in the specific preparation period and the goal now is to maintain it). Finally, the focus shifts to specific wall-based training, on either rock or plastic. We should be working at maximum intensity (no higher than in the specific preparation period) on routes where we can perfect the style, grade and skills (strength, continuity, endurance) of our end goal. According to Mujika and Bosquet (2016), tapering is beneficial at any level of ability whenever the training load needs to be reduced.

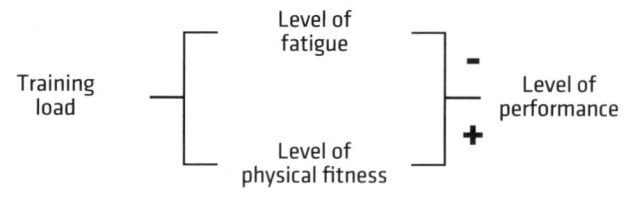

Training load [Level of fatigue — / Level of physical fitness +] Level of performance

TAKEN FROM MUJIKA AND BOSQUET (2016)

Any training load will cause some level of fatigue which, logically, will limit our level of performance (the more tired we are, the worse we perform). However, any training load will also raise our physical fitness and, as a result, will improve our level of performance. The success of tapering lies in finding the right balance between our level of fatigue (on a macrocycle level) and our level of physical fitness.

The average improvement in performance observed in quality research is 1.96 per cent. This might seem negligible or even laughable, but according to Mujika and Bosquet (2016):
- In a swimming event at the Sydney 2000 Olympic Games, the difference between first and fourth place was 1.62 per cent, while the difference between third and eigth place was 2.02 per cent.
- In the 1,500 metres at the Athens 2004 Olympic Games, the difference between first and second place was 0.012 seconds (0.05 per cent) and the difference between first and third place was 0.05 seconds (0.23 per cent).

As you can see, at an elite level, margins that might seem trivial are the difference between one medal or another. In climbing, although there are no similar studies, these small margins could make all the difference when it comes to sticking a hard move or using a crucial handhold.

10 PERIODISATION MODELS: IN SEARCH OF OPTIMAL PEAK FORM | 171

Mujika and Bosquet (2016) give the following guidelines for tapering:
- The volume of training should be reduced by 60 to 41 per cent over the four weeks prior to the competition.
- First reduce the number of training sessions, then reduce the duration of the sessions.
- The intensity should remain constant, not increase.
- The last few sessions shouldn't be used as a test.
- Calorie intake should be adapted to the new energy needs in order to avoid weight gain.
- Priority should be given to movement efficiency and the development of maximum power.
- For best results, favour heavy weights over light weights.
- It's essential to ensure full recovery.
- When done correctly, tapering increases the diameter of fast-twitch muscle fibres, boosts neural electrical activity and makes glycolysis more efficient at maximum intensity, in addition to modifying anabolic hormonal response.

Mujika and Bosquet refer to a quote from the world of competitive swimming, which we could all bear in mind when tapering or approaching our end goal(s): 'You don't need to feel good to swim fast.' Feelings are fundamental, especially when we're facing a win-or-lose situation after months and months of training. However, if we've trained properly and our body has adapted to the training load and is in a state of homeostasis, we're much more likely to top our target route, even if we start doubting our chances of success.

- **Transition period:** this is when we start losing form and begin the process of recovery and regeneration.

Micro 1 2 3	Micro 1 2 3	Micro 1 2 3	Micro 1 2 3	Micro 1 2 3	Micro 1 2 3	Period of peak form
Meso 1	Meso 2	Meso 3	Meso 4	Meso 5	Meso 6	
General period			Specific period		Tapering	
Preparation period				Competition period		
Macrocycle						

This model of planning is known as linear periodisation as there is a linear or proportional increase in intensity and a linear or proportional decrease in volume over the course of the macrocycle.

Months	Sept	Oct	Nov	Dec	Jan	Feb	Mar	Apr	May	Jun	Jul	Aug
Periods	\multicolumn{6}{c|}{Preparation}	\multicolumn{6}{c|}{Competition}

Load
Volume
intensity

What are the advantages and disadvantages of Matveyev's linear periodisation model?

Main advantages of linear periodisation:
- It lays strong foundations in each skill or quality as they are trained over a long period of time.
- The risk of injury is fairly low as it's a progressive system.
- It's a safe model for beginners.

Main disadvantages of linear periodisation:
- It takes a long time to reach peak form.
- There's no scope for readjustment until the first period of peak form.
- It's not recommended for advanced athletes as the skills aren't revisited during the year.
- It's fallen into disuse in many sports as it's less applicable to performance.

The following is an example of linear periodisation for a novice sport climber looking to up their grade from the F5s to F6s for a sport climbing trip in the Easter holidays, beginning their macrocycle at the start of September. It should give an idea of the nature of training in each period and mesocycle.
- **Macrocycle: September–April**
- **Preparation period: 1 September to 24 March**
    » **General preparation period: 1 September to 23 December**
        › **Mesocycle 1: 1 to 30 September (4 weeks)**
          Physical conditioning: strength training circuit including exercises for all muscle groups. Level of intensity: EL 8(20). Low-intensity steady-state aerobic endurance – working in Z1 (130 to 155bpm) for a total of 2 hours per week.

Climbing: long and easy traverses (below maximum grade), with short rests. Focus on building up the number of moves, not the difficulty. Easy boulder problems.

> **Mesocycle 2: 1 October to 11 November (6 weeks)**
> *Physical conditioning:* hypertrophy training. Level of intensity: EL 8(16). Special focus on core and shoulders. Low-intensity steady-state aerobic endurance – working in Z1 for a total of 1 hour 45 minutes per week. *Sprint interval training:* 2 minutes of effective work per session. *Climbing:* work on movement and technique, focusing on bicycles, foot swaps and movement efficiency. Endurance training – intermittent method, aiming for up to 12 minutes of effective work. Maximum pulling strength: EL 8(16).

> **Mesocycle 3: 12 November to 23 December (6 weeks)**
> *Physical conditioning:* hypertrophy training. Level of intensity: EL 6(12). Low-intensity steady-state aerobic endurance – working in Z1 for a total of 45 minutes per week and in Z3 (160 to 170bpm) for 30 minutes per week. *Sprint interval training:* 2 minutes 30 seconds of effective work per session. *Climbing:* work on movement and technique, introducing overhangs, dragging and heel hooks. Endurance training – long interval method, aiming for up to 20 minutes of effective work. Maximum pulling strength, intensity: EL 6(12).

» **Specific preparation period: 7 January to 17 March**

> **Mesocycle 4: 7 January to 17 February (6 weeks)**
> *Physical conditioning:* maximum strength training, multi-joint exercises only, special focus on pulling in different grip positions. Maximum intensity method II. SIT, with a total of 3 minutes of effective work.
> *Climbing:* endurance training. Continuous method, introducing active wall-based recovery. Maximum grip strength training, aiming to hang for 1 minute 30 seconds on a pull-up bar.

> **Mesocycle 5: 18 February to 24 March (5 weeks)**
> *Physical conditioning:* maximum strength training, multi-joint exercises only, special focus on pulling in different grip positions and upper body pushing strength. Maximum intensity method II. SIT, with a total of 3 minutes of effective work.

Climbing: endurance training. High-intensity interval method with very short intervals (three to six moves) and easy climbing between intervals on a vertical wall for as long as it takes to fully recover (active wall-based recovery). Maximum grip strength training, aiming to hang for 1 minute 30 seconds on a fingerboard, using a three-pad hold.

» **Competition period: 25 March to 21 April**
  › **Tapering: 25 March to 14 April (3 weeks)**
    Physical conditioning: none.
    Climbing: endurance training, interval method with short intervals (six to eight moves) on a slightly overhanging wall and easy climbing between intervals on a vertical wall for as long as it takes to fully recover (active wall-based recovery). Maximum pulling strength and maximum grip strength.
  › **Peak form: 15 to 21 April (1 week)**
    Sport climbing trip.

There's another linear model, known as reverse periodisation, which was developed by Ian King (2000). The main difference between the reverse model and Matveyev's model is that the levels of volume and intensity are reversed.

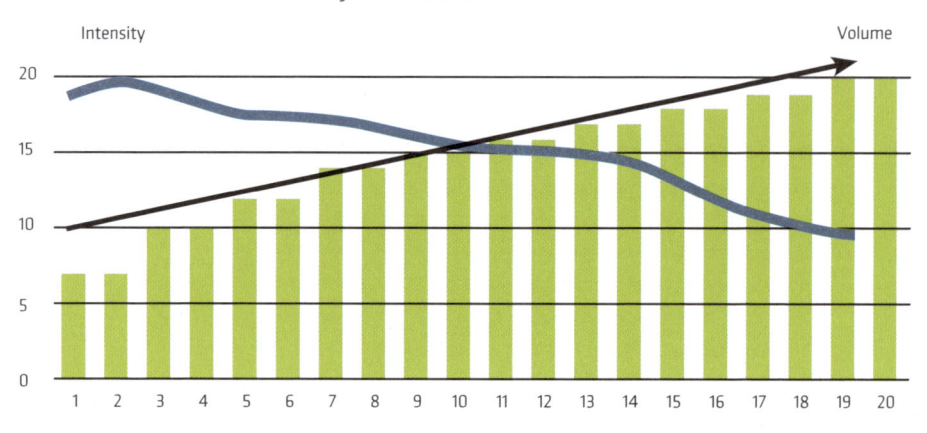

As seen in the image, and in contrast to linear periodisation, King suggests starting at maximum intensity and minimum volume, then gradually reducing the intensity and increasing the volume over the course of the season. That is, in the preparation period, you'd begin by training maximum strength and power, then move on to endurance. According to House and Johnston (2014), reverse periodisation is the best training method for climbers and mountaineers. This is because it begins by recruiting the greatest number of fast-twitch muscle fibres, through maximum strength (high-intensity) training, and then converts them into slow-twitch muscle fibres for a greater number of fibres that provide energy for longer periods of time. Reverse periodisation is also recommended by another great mountaineer, Mark Twight, in his book *Extreme Alpinism*.

Main advantages of reverse periodisation:
- Like linear periodisation, it lays strong foundations in each skill or quality as they are trained over a long period of time.
- It's the best option for trainee athletes or athletes with little training experience.
- It ensures a higher degree of fibril recruitment, the prevalence of type II muscle fibres and enhanced mitochondrial density, guaranteeing greater functional capacity.

Main disadvantages of reverse periodisation:
- Like Matveyev's model, it takes a long time to reach peak form.
- There's also no scope for readjustment until the first point of peak form.
- It's also not recommended for advanced athletes as the skills aren't revisited during the year.

The following is an example of reverse periodisation for an intermediate sport climber looking to consolidate at F6a to F6c and start pushing into the F7s. It should give an idea of the nature of training in each period and mesocycle.
- **Macrocycle: September–March**
- **Preparation period: 1 September to 24 February**
    » **General preparation period: 1 September to 2 December**
        › **Mesocycle 1: 1 to 16 September (2 weeks)**
        Physical conditioning: strength training circuit including exercises for all muscle groups. Level of intensity: EL 8(20). Low-intensity steady-state aerobic endurance – working in Z1 (130 to 155bpm) for a total of 1 hour per week.
        Climbing: long and easy traverses (at least one and a half to two grades below maximum grade), with short rests. Focus on building up the number of moves and the range of techniques, not the difficulty.
        › **Mesocycle 2: 17 September to 21 October (5 weeks)**
        Physical conditioning: maximum strength training. Level of intensity: EL 4(7). Low-intensity steady-state aerobic endurance – working in Z1 for a total of 45 minutes per week.
        Sprint interval training: 2 minutes of effective work per session.

Climbing: bouldering. Endurance training – continuous method, aiming for up to 30 minutes of effective work. Maximum grip strength – max weight deadhangs on a large edge.
> **Mesocycle 3: 22 October to 2 December (6 weeks)**
> *Physical conditioning:* maximum strength training. Level of intensity: EL 4(7).
> *Sprint interval training:* 2 minutes of effective work per session.
> *Climbing:* endurance training – long interval method, aiming for up to 40 minutes of effective work. Maximum grip strength – minimum edge deadhangs and lock-offs. Power training and RFD on the campus board.

» **Specific preparation period: 3 December to 24 February**
> **Mesocycle 4: 3 December to 13 January (6 weeks)**
> *Physical conditioning:* strength training with an emphasis on single-joint upper body exercises, intensity EL 8(18).
> *Climbing:* endurance training. Continuous method on an overhanging wall, with active wall-based recovery.
> **Mesocycle 5: 14 January to 24 February (6 weeks)**
> *Physical conditioning:* strength training with an emphasis on single-joint upper body exercises, intensity EL 8(18).
> *Climbing:* endurance training. Interval method with medium intervals (eight to ten moves) on an overhanging wall and easy climbing between intervals on an overhanging wall for as long as it takes to fully recover (active wall-based recovery). Intermittent deadhangs.

- **Competition period: 25 February to 24 March**
  > **Tapering: 25 February to 17 March (3 weeks)**
  > *Physical conditioning:* none.
  > *Climbing:* endurance training, continuous method on an overhanging wall, aiming for up to 30 minutes of effective work. Maximum pulling strength and maximum grip strength – max weight deadhangs on a large edge.
  > **Peak form: 18 to 24 March (1 week)**
  > Begin working routes graded F7a and above.

ATR PERIODISATION. ACCUMULATION, TRANSMUTATION AND REALISATION MESOCYCLES. TYPES AND ORDER OF MICROCYCLES. ADVANTAGES AND DISADVANTAGES. EXAMPLE PERIODISATION

The ATR model is one of the newer forms of periodisation and is based on the idea of training blocks. It was created by Issurin and Kaverin (1985) and developed by Fernando Navarro Valdivielso. It's the method used by top Spanish climber and coach Patxi Usobiaga, who has coached Adam Ondra, among others.

Each macrocycle is six to nine weeks long, meaning peak form can be achieved in a short period of time and multiple times across the season.

Each macrocycle comprises three mesocycles: accumulation, transmutation and realisation.
- *Accumulation:* this mesocycle lasts for two to three weeks. The aim is to build the athlete's technical and movement potential, which is similar to the general preparation period in linear periodisation; the technical and movement skills accumulated in this mesocycle would create a base for the specific preparation period. Accumulation covers basic endurance, basic strength and basic technique, focusing on the correction of errors. In climbing, this includes pulling strength, continuity, general increase in ROM and a range of non-specific boulder problems and routes that aren't too narrowly focused on the end goal. The volume of training is relatively high, with a moderate level of intensity.
- *Transmutation:* this mesocycle lasts for two to three weeks. The aim is to transform the athlete's technical and movement potential into specific skills, turning basic movement and technique into sport-specific abilities. Transmutation covers specific strength, specific endurance and specific technique in situations of fatigue. In climbing, this includes finger strength endurance, power and RFD, as well as endurance. This mesocycle places special emphasis on tolerance to fatigue and retaining good technique when fatigued. The training volume is lower than in the accumulation phase and the training intensity is high. It is important to be well rested for the training in this mesocycle.
- *Realisation:* this mesocycle lasts for two to three weeks. The aim is to achieve the best possible competition results by employing to the fullest possible extent all technical and movement skills developed in the previous cycles in the specific competition activity. The training involves competition-style exercises – boulder problems and routes that are specific to the end goal, maintaining maximum intensity, consolidating at the target grade and ensuring being properly rested

for training. To achieve supercompensation, it also includes recovery protocols and tapering. At the end of this block, you'd look to achieve the end goal of the macrocycle.

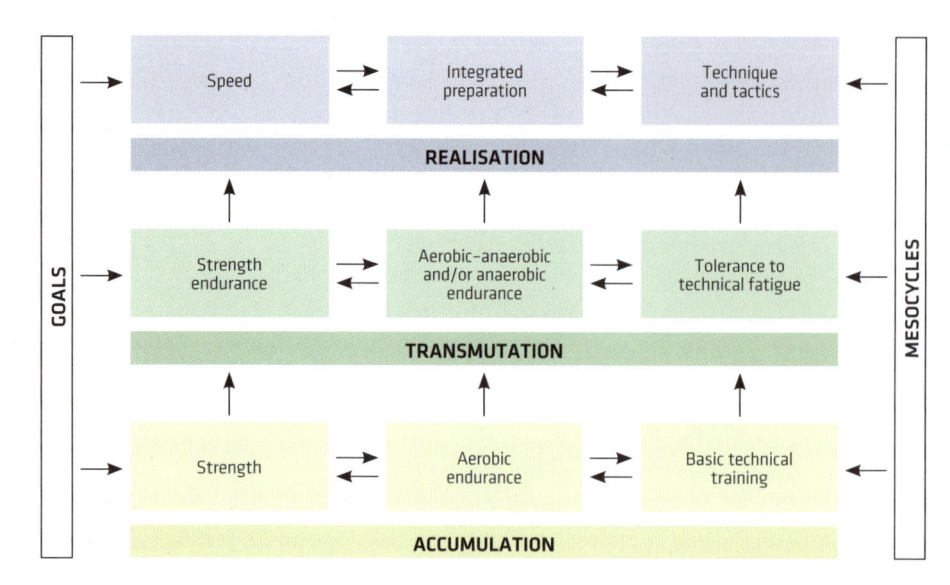

```
GOALS                                                                          MESOCYCLES

  → Speed   ⇄  Integrated preparation  ⇄  Technique and tactics  ←

                           REALISATION
                              ↑              ↑                  ↑

  → Strength endurance ⇄ Aerobic–anaerobic and/or anaerobic endurance ⇄ Tolerance to technical fatigue ←

                          TRANSMUTATION
                              ↑              ↑                  ↑

  → Strength  ⇄  Aerobic endurance  ⇄  Basic technical training  ←

                           ACCUMULATION
```

There are several types of microcycle for each mesocycle, and the microcycles that you might do would depend on where you are in the season, your specific goals, the level of physical/technical demand, your level of ability, and so on.

Accumulation	Transmutation	Realisation
Recovery and/or adjustment	Adjustment and load	Adjustment or load
Load and/or impact	Load and/or impact	Load or recovery
Load	Load and/or impact	Activation and competition

Here's a description of what each microcycle entails:
- **Adjustment:** medium training load. Medium intensity. Medium technical difficulty. Duration: 4 to 7 days.
- **Load:** *significant* load and total workload. Duration: 1 week.
- **Impact:** maximum total workload. Load increased to *extreme* limits. Duration: 1 week.

10 PERIODISATION MODELS: IN SEARCH OF OPTIMAL PEAK FORM | 179

- **Activation:** Low volume. Increased intensity. Modelling of upcoming competitions. Duration: 3 to 7 days.
- **Competition:** competition schedule and recovery protocols. Duration: 3 to 9 days.
- **Recovery:** low volume and intensity. Varied means of recovery. You'd use this microcycle when the previous macrocycle ends with a significant load and/or biological stress. Duration: 3 to 7 days.

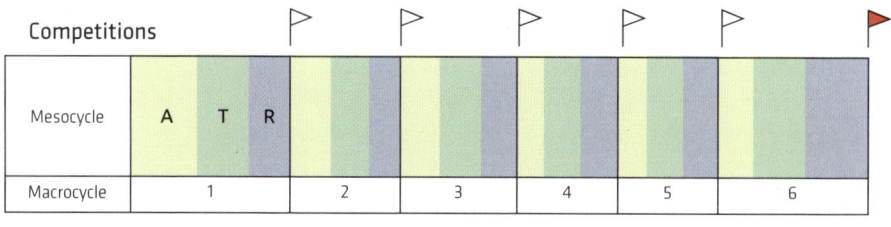

Competitions						
Mesocycle	A T R					
Macrocycle	1	2	3	4	5	6

A – Accumulation. T – Transmutation. R – Realisation

Competitions					
Mesocycle	Aerobic endurance / Maximum strength	Strength. Endurance		Anaerobic and mixed endurance	
Phases	1	2	3	4	
Months	Sept Oct Nov	Dec Jan Feb	Mar Apr May	Jun Jul Aug	
Periods	Preparation		Competition		

This graphic gives a comparison between reverse linear periodisation and ATR block periodisation.

Inevitably, there are also advantages and disadvantages to the ATR model.

Main advantages of ATR periodisation:
- It allows for multiple points of peak form and training adjustments throughout the season.
- Peak form can be reached in a very short period of time.
- It's the best option for high-level athletes with various competitions across the season.
- It helps keep the athlete motivated as the content of the training is very varied.

Main disadvantages of ATR periodisation:
- It's a complex model that's very time consuming for the coach.
- It doesn't allow any time to consolidate or stabilise the targeted skills.

The following is an example of ATR periodisation for an advanced sport climber looking to climb a F7c route that they've been working for some time. It should give an idea of the nature of training in each period and mesocycle.
- **Macrocycle: March to April**
- **Accumulation mesocycle: 4 March to 21 March**
  - » **Adjustment microcycle 1: 4 March to 7 March (4 days)**
    Physical conditioning: maximum strength, multi-joint exercises, intensity EL 1(4).
    Climbing: emphasis on technique. Bouldering.
  - » **Load microcycle 1: 8 March to 14 March (1 week)**
    Physical conditioning: maximum strength, multi-joint exercises, intensity EL 2(3).
    Climbing: bouldering. Maximum grip strength – max weight deadhangs on a large edge.
  - » **Load microcycle 2: 15 March to 21 March (1 week)**
    Physical conditioning: maximum strength, multi-joint exercises, intensity EL 2(3).
    Climbing: bouldering. Power training and RFD on the campus board.
- **Transmutation mesocycle: 22 March to 11 April**
  - » **Load microcycle 3: 22 March to 28 March (1 week)**
    Climbing: endurance training. Continuous method with blood flow restriction, aiming for 20 minutes of climbing. Continue climbing with no blood flow restriction, using the long interval method, for a total of 50 minutes of effective work.
  - » **Impact microcycle 1: 29 March to 4 April (1 week)**
    Climbing: intermittent deadhangs. Endurance training. Interval method with short intervals (six to eight moves), difficulty F7a/7a+, on an overhanging wall, and active wall-based recovery between intervals for 2 minutes, also on an overhanging wall, difficulty F6a/6b.
  - » **Impact microcycle 2: 5 April to 11 April (1 week)**
    Climbing: intermittent deadhangs. Endurance training. Interval method with medium intervals (ten to twelve moves), difficulty F7a/7a+, on an overhanging wall, and active wall-based recovery between intervals for 1 minute 30 seconds, also on an overhanging wall, difficulty F6a/6b.

- **Realisation mesocycle: 12 April to 21 April**
  - » **Adjustment microcycle 2: 12 April to 15 April (4 days)**
    Climbing: bouldering. Maximum grip strength – max weight deadhangs on a large edge.
  - » **Activation microcycle: 16 April to 18 April (3 days)**
    Climbing: bouldering. Maximum pulling strength, intensity EL 1(3) and maximum grip strength – minimum edge.
  - » **Competition microcycle: 19 April to 21 April (3 days)**
    Work on target route.

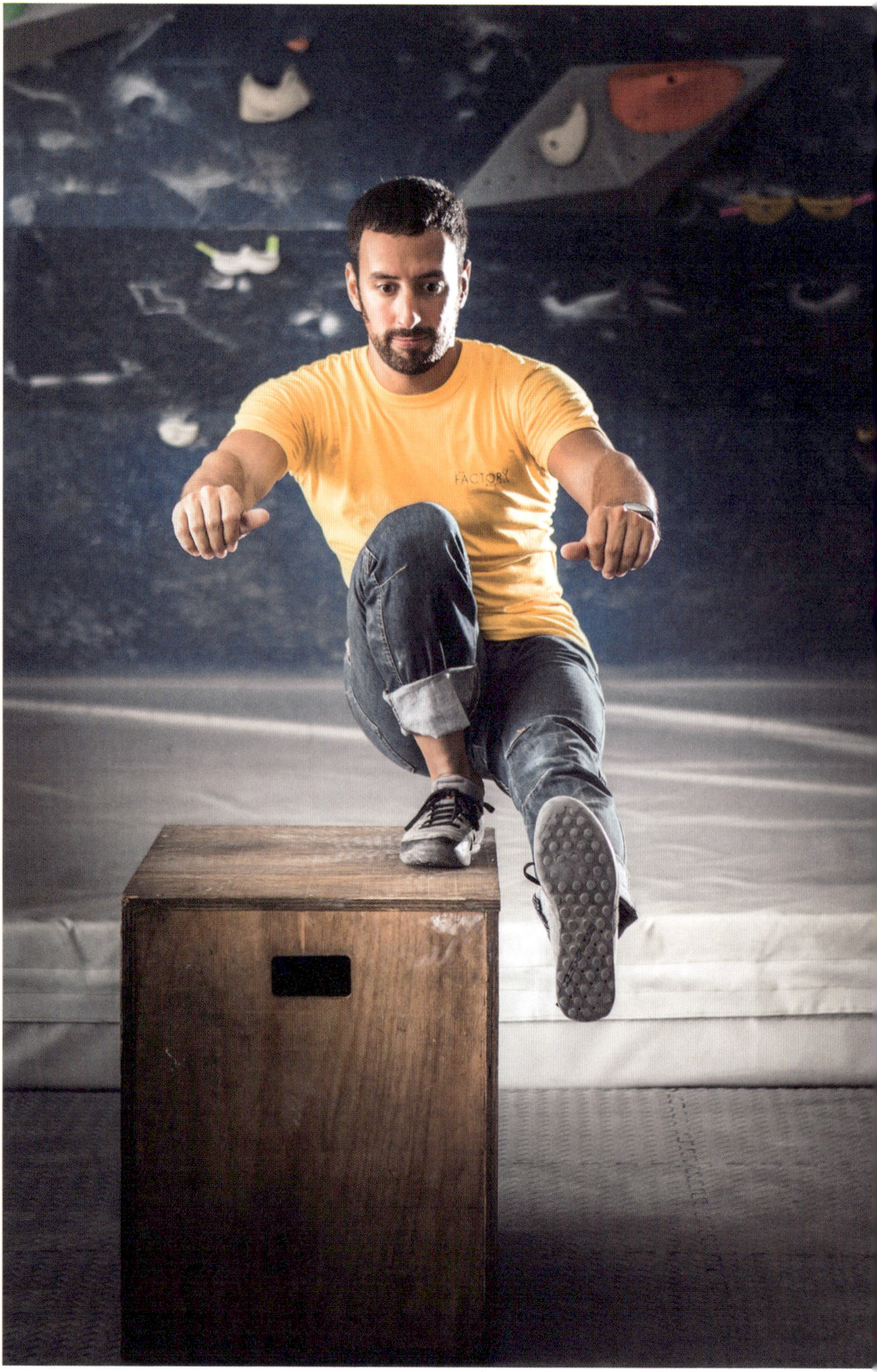
FACTORY

11

DETRAINING

The dreaded loss of the gains from so many hours of training (when a holiday, an injury or a busy period at work keeps you from training for a while), in other words detraining, comes down to the reversibility principle. Unfortunately, there's still no research into detraining in climbing but there are a number of studies on detraining strength and endurance in other sports which we can use for reference.

As a starting point, we know that the more extreme the adaptation, the faster it's lost. Usain Bolt has only once run the 100 metres in 9.58 seconds. If he had run the following day, he would probably have got a slower time. Adam Ondra made the first ascent of *Silence* (F9c) on 3 September 2017, after four years of training and trying the route. There's very little chance that he could have climbed it again the following day.

Let's look at some of the research into detraining:
- There's a 23 per cent reduction in the activity of mitochondria and oxidative enzymes after three weeks of inactivity, dropping by a further 23 per cent from weeks four to eight (Mujika, 2012).
- There's a 22 per cent increase in postprandial insulin (the hormone that makes us put on weight, which 'stores calories' after a meal) after 6.5 days of inactivity (Mujika and Padilla, 2003).

- There's an 86 per cent increase in lipoprotein lipase activity in adipose tissue (the storage of fatty acids in fatty tissue, storing fuel in subcutaneous fat) after just 14 days of inactivity. In contrast, there's a 75 per cent reduction in lipoprotein lipase activity in muscle (allowing us to burn these fatty acids) during the same 14-day period (Mujika and Padilla, 2003). In other words, a shift in enzyme activity meaning more fat is stored and less fat is burnt.
- A study by Alomari *et al.* (2010) examined the effects of handgrip training and detraining on vascular resistance. Participants did 20 minutes of rhythmic handgrip exercises, at 60 per cent of their MVC (maximum voluntary contraction), five days a week for a total of four weeks. After these four weeks of training, forearm blood flow had increased significantly but just one week after they stopped training, blood flow had returned to pre-training levels.
- There's a 39 per cent reduction in muscle glycogen stores after seven days of inactivity (Mujika and Padilla, 2003).
- A study on a group of swimmers who swam the 200 metres freestyle at 90 per cent of their best time for that distance examined levels of blood lactate and HCO_3 (bicarbonate, which is the main buffering system for lactate: it's the 'broom' that can 'sweep away' this metabolic waste) over four weeks of inactivity:

	Weeks without training			
	0	1	2	4
Lactate (mmol/L)	4.2	6.3	6.8	9.7
HCO_3 (mmol/L)	21.2	19.5	16.1	16.3

Costill *et al.* (1985)

The table shows a dramatic rise in blood lactate levels (the swimmers lost oxidative capacity in favour of anaerobic lactic metabolism) and significantly lower levels of HCO_3 (an impaired ability to flush out metabolic waste) after just four weeks of inactivity.

- Luckily, similar studies on detraining strength are a little more encouraging. Kraemer *et al.* (2002) studied the loss of maximum strength and power in a group of men involved in recreational strength training (not at elite level). After six weeks of inactivity, the group experienced an almost negligible loss of maximum strength and around 10 per cent loss of power.
- García-Pallarés *et al.* (2010) studied the effects of five weeks of inactivity on world-class kayakers. Five weeks after they stopped training, the participants had lost around 9.8 per cent on their 1RM bench press.

This gives a good indication of what happens when we stop training. A house can take years to build but be demolished in a matter of minutes. The same can be said of physical fitness and performance, especially in relation to endurance. Use this chapter as motivation to never give up on training. Use this book to understand that to perform at your best, in most cases it's counter productive to train at your absolute limit.

No pain, more gain. Don't train more: train better.

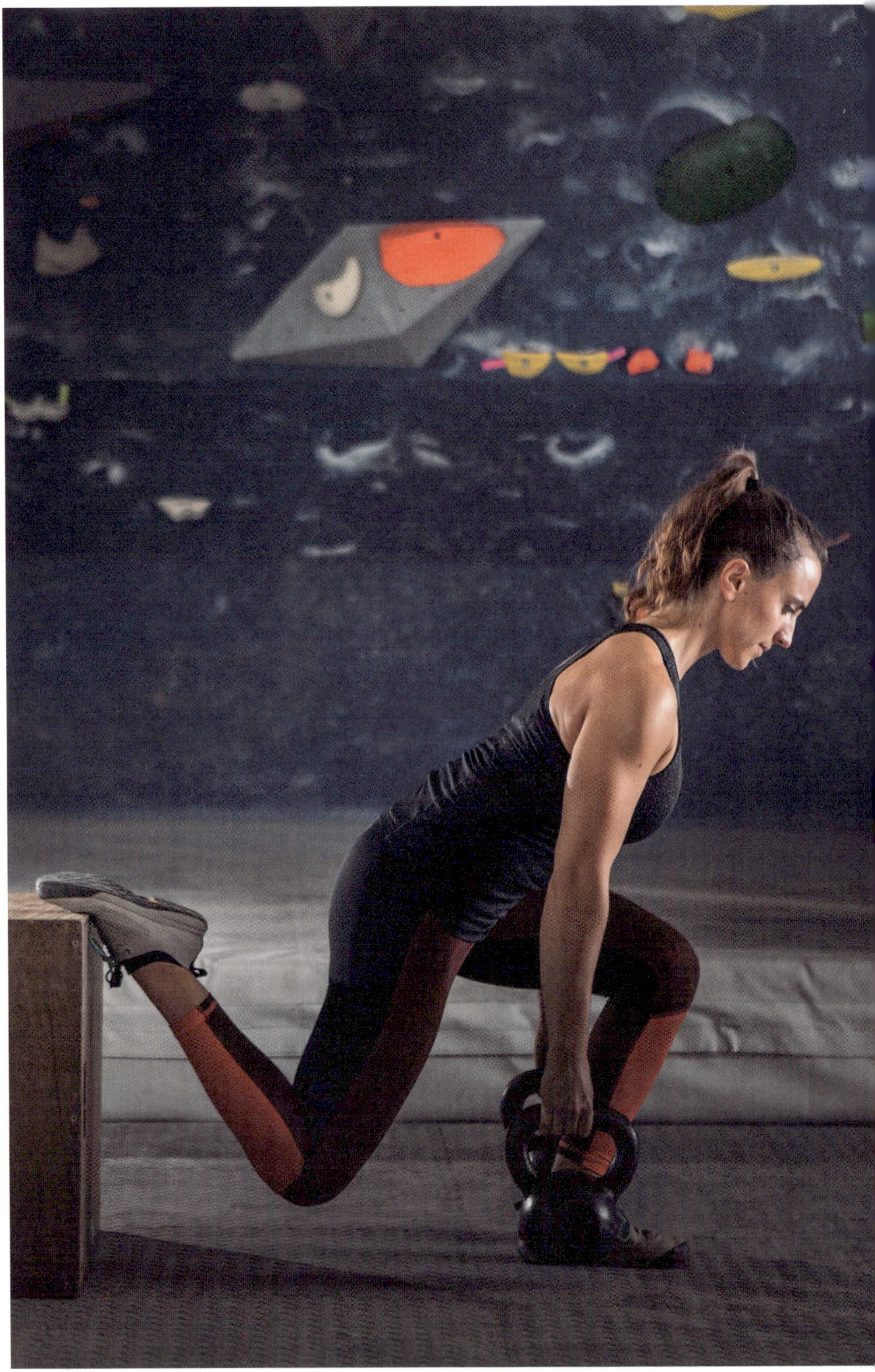

BIBLIOGRAPHY

Alomari, M.A., Mekary, R.A. and Welsch, M.A. (2010), 'Rapid vascular modifications to localized rhythmic handgrip training and detraining: vascular conditioning and deconditioning', *European Journal of Applied Physiology,* Volume 109:5, pp. 803–809, doi: 10.1007/s00421-010-1367-0.

Amani-Shalamzari, S., Rajabi, S., Rajabi, H., *et al.* (2019), 'Effects of blood flow restriction and exercise intensity on aerobic, anaerobic, and muscle strength adaptations in physically active collegiate women', *Frontiers in Physiology,* Volume 10, Article ID: 810, doi: 10.3389/fphys.2019.00810.

Andersen, J.L. and Aagaard, P. (2010), 'Effects of strength training on muscle fiber types and size; consequences for athletes training for high-intensity sport', *Scandinavian Journal of Medicine & Science in Sports,* Volume 20:s2, pp. 32–38, doi: 10.1111/j.1600-0838.2010.01196.x.

Anderson, M.L. and Anderson, M.L. (2014), *The Rock Climber's Training Manual: A Guide to Continuous Improvement,* Fixed Pin Publishing.

Araya Quintanilla, F. and Moyano Galvez, V. (2015), 'Ejercicio terapéutico para epicondilalgia lateral: revisión sistemática', *Revista de la Sociedad Española del Dolor,* Volume 22:6, pp. 253–270.

Arshad, R., Zander, T., Dreischarf, M., *et al.* (2016), 'Influence of lumbar spine rhythms and intra-abdominal pressure on spinal loads and trunk muscle forces during upper body inclination', *Medical Engineering & Physics,* Volume 38:4, pp. 333–338, doi: 10.1016/j.medengphy.2016.01.013.

Baechle, T. and Earle, R. (2000), *Principios del Entrenamiento de la Fuerza y del Acondicionamiento Físico*, Editorial Médica-Panamericana [*Essentials of Strength Training and Conditioning*, Human Kinetics Publishers (2000)].

Baláš, J., Panáčková, M., Jandová, S., *et al.* (2014a), 'The effect of climbing ability and slope inclination on vertical foot loading using a novel force sensor instrumentation system', *Journal of Human Kinetics*, Volume 44, pp. 75–81, doi: 10.2478/hukin-2014-0112.

Baláš, J., Panáčková, M., Strejcová, B., *et al.* (2014b), 'The relationship between climbing ability and physiological responses to rock climbing', *The Scientific World Journal*, Volume 2014, Article ID: 678387.

Balsalobre-Fernández, C. and Jiménez-Reyes, P. (2014), *Entrenamiento de Fuerza: Nuevas Perspectivas Metodológicas,* available at: www.carlos-balsalobre.com/Entrenamiento_de_Fuerza_Balsalobre&Jimenez.pdf

Batacan, R.B., Jr, Duncan, M.J., Dalbo, V.J., *et al.* (2017), 'Effects of high-intensity interval training on cardiometabolic health: a systematic review and meta-analysis of intervention studies', *British Journal of Sports Medicine*, Volume 51, pp. 494–503, doi: 10.1136/bjsports-2015-095841.

Baxter, C., McNaughton, L.R., Sparks, A., *et al.* (2017), 'Impact of stretching on the performance and injury risk of long-distance runners', *Research in Sports Medicine*, Volume 25:1, pp. 78–90, doi: 10.1080/15438627.2016.1258640.

Benito, P.J. (2008), *Conceptos Básicos del Entrenamiento con Cargas: De la Musculación al Wellness,* Kinesis.

Bernal Ruiz, J.A. (2006), *La Fuerza y el Sistema Muscular en la Educación Física y el Deporte,* Wanceulen.

Bertuzzi, R.C., Franchini, E., Kokubun, E., *et al.* (2007), 'Energy system contributions in indoor rock climbing', *European Journal of Applied Physiology*, Volume 101:3, pp. 293–300, doi: 10.1007/s00421-007-0501-0.

Biazon, T.M.P.C., Ugrinowitsch, C., Soligon, S.D., *et al.* (2019), 'The association between muscle deoxygenation and muscle hypertrophy to blood flow restricted training performed at high and low loads', *Frontiers in Physiology*, Volume 10, Article ID: 446, doi: 10.3389/fphys.2019.00446.

Billat, V. (2002), *Fisiología y Metodología del Entrenamiento de la Teoría a la Práctica,* Editorial Paidotribo.

Billat, V., Palleja, P., Charlaix, T., *et al.* (1995), 'Energy specificity of rock climbing and aerobic capacity in competitive sport rock climbers', *The Journal of Sports Medicine and Physical Fitness*, Volume 35:1, pp. 20–24.

Bompa, T.O. and Cornacchia, L.J. (2002), *Musculación: Entrenamiento Avanzado,* Hispano.

Boyle, M. (2010), *Advances in Functional Training,* On Target Publications.

Boyle, M. (2017), *El Entrenamiento Funcional Aplicado a los Deportes*, Ediciones Tutor [*New Functional Training for Sports*, Human Kinetics Australia P/L (2016)].

Cairns, S.P. (2013), 'Holistic approaches to understanding mechanisms of fatigue in high-intensity sport', *Fatigue: Biomedicine, Health & Behaviour*, Volume 1:3, pp. 148–167.

Calatayud, J., Casaña, J., Martín, F., *et al.* (2017), 'Progression of core stability exercises based on the extent of muscle activity', *American Journal of Physical Medicine & Rehabilitation*, Volume 96:10, pp. 694–699, doi: 10.1097/PHM.0000000000000713.

Chopp, J.N., O'Neill, J.M., Hurley, K., *et al.* (2010), 'Superior humeral head migration occurs after a protocol designed to fatigue the rotator cuff: a radiographic analysis', *Journal of Shoulder and Elbow Surgery*, Volume 19:8, pp. 1137–1144, doi: 10.1016/j.jse.2010.03.017.

Clements, J. (2015), *Confirmed: Voodoo Flossing Helps Climbing Injuries*, available at: www.hcrbeta.com/confirmed-voodoo-flossing-helps-climbing-injuries

Cook, J.L, Rio, E., Purdam, C.R., *et al.* (2017), 'El continuum de la patología de tendón: concepto actual e implicaciones clínicas', *Apunts. Medicina de l'Esport*, Volume 52:194, pp. 61–69. [Cook, J.L., Rio, E., Purdam, C.R., *et al.* (2017), 'The continuum of tendon pathology: Current view and clinical implications', *Apunts. Medicina de l'Esport*, Volume 52:194, pp. 61–69, doi: 10.1016/j.apunts.2017.05.002].

Costill, D.L., Fink, W.J., Hargreaves, M., *et al.* (1985), 'Metabolic characteristics of skeletal muscle during detraining from competitive swimming', *Medicine & Science in Sports & Exercise*, Volume 17:3, pp. 339–343.

Couceiro, J. (2010), *Perfil Antropométrico y Respuesta Psico-Fisiológica en Escalada Deportiva en Roca: Diferencias entre Modalidades*, PhD Thesis, Universidad Politécnica de Madrid.

Counts, B.R., Dankel, S.J., Barnett, B.E., *et al.* (2016), 'Influence of relative blood flow restriction pressure on muscle activation and muscle adaptation', *Muscle & Nerve*, Volume 53:3, pp. 438–445, doi: 10.1002/mus.24756.

Davies, R. (2008), 'Low back pain', *InnovAiT*, Volume 1:6, pp. 440–445, doi: 10.1093/innovait/inn056.

Del Castillo, J.M. (2019), *Progresiones de Dominadas Unilaterales (a una mano) – Fuerza Extrema*, available at: www.josemief.com/progresiones-de-dominadas-unilaterales-fuerza-extrema

Delavier, F. (2004), *Guía de los Movimientos de Musculación: Descripción Anatómica*, Paidotribo.

Denys-Struyf, G. (2008), *El Manual del Mezierista*. Paidotribo.

Dickie, J.A., Faulkner, J.A., Barnes, M.J., *et al.* (2017), 'Electromyographic analysis of muscle activation during pull-up variations', *Journal of Electromyography and Kinesiology*, Volume 32, pp. 30–36.

Domínguez, R. (2015), 'Entrenamiento con restricción del flujo sanguíneo e hipertrofia muscular', *RICYDE. Revista Internacional de Ciencias del Deporte*, Volume 10:38, pp. 367–382, doi: 10.5232/ricyde2014.03806.

Dones, V.C., III, Milanese, S., Worth, D., *et al.* (2013), 'The anatomy of the forearm extensor muscles and the fascia in the lateral aspect of the elbow joint complex', *Anatomy & Physiology: Current Research*, Volume 3:1, Article ID: 1000117, doi: 10.4172/2161-0940.1000117.

Earp, J.E., Newton, R.U., Cormie, P., *et al.* (2016), 'Faster movement speed results in greater tendon strain during the loaded squat exercise', *Frontiers in Physiology*, Volume 7, Article ID: 366, doi: 10.3389/fphys.2016.00366.

Fanchini, M., Violette, F., Impellizzeri, F.M., *et al.* (2013), 'Differences in climbing-specific strength between boulder and lead rock climbers', *The Journal of Strength and Conditioning Research*, Volume 27:2, pp. 310–314.

Font, J., Doreste, J.L., Garea, A., *et al.* (2005), 'Rotura de la polea A2 en escalada libre', *Archivos de Medicina del Deporte*, Volume 22:109, pp. 419–421.

Förster, R., Penka, G., Bösl, T., *et al.* (2009), 'Climber's back – form and mobility of the thoracolumbar spine leading to postural adaptations in male high ability rock climbers', *International Journal of Sports Medicine*, Volume 30:1, pp. 53–59, doi: 10.1055/s-2008-1038762.

Fradkin, A.J., Zazryn, T.R. and Smoliga, J.M. (2010), 'Effects of warming-up on physical performance: a systematic review with meta-analysis', *The Journal of Strength and Conditioning Research*, Volume 24:1, pp. 140–148, doi: 10.1519/JSC.0b013e3181c643a0.

Fry, A.C., Smith, J.C. and Schilling, B.K. (2003), 'Effect of knee position on hip and knee torques during the barbell squat', *The Journal of Strength and Conditioning Research*, Volume 17:4, pp. 629–633.

Fryer, S.M., Stoner, L., Dickson, T.G., *et al.* (2015a), 'Oxygen recovery kinetics in the forearm flexors of multiple ability groups of rock climbers', *The Journal of Strength and Conditioning Research*, Volume 29:6, pp. 1633–1639, doi: 10.1519/JSC.0000000000000804.

Fryer, S., Stoner, L., Lucero, A., *et al.* (2015b), 'Haemodynamic kinetics and intermittent finger flexor performance in rock climbers', *International Journal of Sports Medicine*, Volume 36:2, pp. 137–142, doi: 10.1055/s-0034-1385887.

Fryer, S., Stoner, L., Scarrott, C., *et al.* (2015c), 'Forearm oxygenation and blood flow kinetics during a sustained contraction in multiple ability groups of rock climbers', *Journal of Sports Sciences*, Volume 33:5, pp. 518–526, doi: 10.1080/02640414.2014.949828.

Fryer, S., Stoner, L., Stone, K., *et al.* (2016), 'Forearm muscle oxidative capacity index predicts sport rock-climbing performance', *European Journal of Applied Physiology*, Volume 116:8, pp. 1479–1484.

Fryer, S., Stone, K.J., Sveen, J., *et al.* (2017), 'Differences in forearm strength, endurance, and hemodynamic kinetics between male boulderers and lead rock climbers', *European Journal of Sport Science*, Volume 17:9, pp. 1177–1183.

Fung, J. (2017), *El Código de la Obesidad*. Sirio [*The Obesity Code*, Scribe (2016)].

García-Hermoso, A., Cerrillo-Urbina, A.J., Herrera-Valenzuela, T., *et al.* (2016), 'Is high-intensity interval training more effective on improving cardiometabolic risk and aerobic capacity than other forms of exercise in overweight and obese youth? A meta-analysis', *Obesity Reviews*, Volume 17:6, pp. 531–540, doi: 10.1111/obr.12395.

García-Pallarés, J., Sánchez-Medina, L., Pérez, C.E., *et al.* (2010), 'Physiological effects of tapering and detraining in world-class kayakers', *Medicine & Science in Sports & Exercise*, Volume 42:6, pp. 1209–1214, doi: 10.1249/MSS.0b013e3181c9228c.

Gáspari, A.F., Berton, R., Lixandrão, M.E., *et al.* (2015), 'The blood lactate concentration responses in a real indoor sport climbing competition', *Science & Sports*, Volume 30:4, pp. 228–231, doi: 10.1016/j.scispo.2015.05.002.

González-Badillo, J.J. and Gorostiaga-Ayestarán, E. (2002), *Fundamentos del Entrenamiento de la Fuerza: Aplicación al Alto Rendimiento Deportivo*, Inde.

González-Badillo, J.J., Rodríguez-Rosell, D., Sánchez-Medina, L., *et al.* (2016), 'Short-term recovery following resistance exercise leading or not to failure', *International Journal of Sports Medicine*, Volume 37:4, pp. 295–304, doi: 10.1055/s-0035-1564254.

González-Badillo, J.J., Sánchez-Medina, L., Pareja Blanco, F., *et al.* (2017), *La Velocidad de Ejecución como Referencia para la Programación, Control y Evaluación del Entrenamiento de Fuerza*, Ergotech.

Green, J.G. and Stannard, S.R. (2010), 'Active recovery strategies and handgrip performance in trained vs. untrained climbers', *The Journal of Strength and Conditioning Research*, Volume 24:2, pp. 494–501.

Grenier, S.G. and McGill, S.M. (2007), 'Quantification of lumbar stability by using 2 different abdominal activation strategies', *Archives of Physical Medicine and Rehabilitation*, Volume 88:1, pp. 54–62.

Grønhaug, G. (2018), 'Self-reported chronic injuries in climbing: who gets injured when?', *BMJ Open Sport & Exercise Medicine*, Volume 4:1, Article ID: e000406, doi: 10.1136/bmjsem-2018-000406.

Hindle, K.B., Whitcomb, T.J., Briggs, O.W., *et al.* (2012), 'Proprioceptive neuromuscular facilitation (PNF): its mechanisms and effects on range of motion and muscular function', *Journal of Human Kinetics*, Volume 31, pp. 105–113.

Hirvonen, J., Nummela, A., Rusko, H., et al. (1992), 'Fatigue and changes of ATP, creatine phosphate, and lactate during the 400-m sprint', *Canadian Journal of Sport Sciences*, Volume 17:2, pp. 141–144.

Horiuchi, M. and Okita, K. (2012), 'Blood flow restricted exercise and vascular function', *International Journal of Vascular Medicine*, Article ID: 543218, doi: 10.1155/2012/543218.

Hörst, E. (2006), *Entrenamiento para Escalada*, Desnivel [*Training for Climbing*, Falcon (2004)].

Hörst, E. (2016), *4 Fingerboard Strength Protocols That Work*, available at: www.trainingforclimbing.com/4-fingerboard-strength-protocols-that-work

Hörst, E. (2018), *Entrenamiento para Escalada: El Manual Definitivo para Mejorar tu Rendimiento*, Desnivel [*Training for Climbing* (3rd edition), Falcon (2016)].

House, S. and Johnston, S. (2014), *Training for the New Alpinism,* Patagonia.

Issurin, V. and Kaverin, V. (1985), 'Planning and design of annual preparation cycle in canoeing', in *Grebnoj Sport (Rowing, Canoeing, Kayaking),* Fizkultura i Sport, pp. 25–29 (in Russian).

Jeffries, O., Waldron, M., Pattison, J.R., et al. (2018), 'Enhanced local skeletal muscle oxidative capacity and microvascular blood flow following 7-day ischemic preconditioning in healthy humans', *Frontiers in Physiology*, Volume 9, Article ID: 463, doi: 10.3389/fphys.2018.00463.

Jelmini, J.D., Cornwell, A., Khodiguian, N., et al. (2018), 'Acute effects of unilateral static stretching on handgrip strength of the stretched and non-stretched limb', *European Journal of Applied Physiology*, Volume 118:5, pp. 927–936, doi: 10.1007/s00421-018-3810-6.

Jenkins, N.D.M., Housh, T.J., Buckner, S.L., et al. (2016), 'Neuromuscular adaptations after 2 and 4 weeks of 80% versus 30% 1 repetition maximum resistance training to failure', *The Journal of Strength and Conditioning Research*, Volume 30:8, pp. 2174–2185, doi: 10.1519/JSC.0000000000001308.

Jones, G., Asghar, A. and Llewellyn, D.J. (2008), 'The epidemiology of rock-climbing injuries', *British Journal of Sports Medicine*, Volume 42:9, pp. 773–778.

Jones, G., Schöffl, V. and Johnson, M.I. (2018), 'Incidence, diagnosis, and management of injury in sport climbing and bouldering: a critical review', *Current Sports Medicine Reports*, Volume 17:11, pp. 396–401, doi: 10.1249/JSR.0000000000000534.

Kapandji, A.I. (2019), *The Physiology of the Joints* (three volumes), Handspring Publishing [first published in 1971].

Kay, A.D. and Blazevich, A.J. (2012), 'Effect of acute static stretch on maximal muscle performance: a systematic review', *Medicine & Science in Sports & Exercise*, Volume 44:1, pp. 154–164, doi: 10.1249/MSS.0b013e318225cb27.

Kenas, A., Masi, M. and Kuntz, C. (2015), 'Eccentric interventions for lateral epicondylalgia', *Strength and Conditioning Journal*, Volume 37:5, pp. 47–52, doi: 10.1519/SSC.0000000000000175.

Ker, R.F. (2007), 'Mechanics of tendon, from an engineering perspective', *International Journal of Fatigue*, Volume 29:6, pp. 1001–1009, doi: 10.1016/j.ijfatigue.2006.09.020.

King, I.J. (2000), *Foundations of Physical Preparation*, King Sports International.

Kraemer, W.J., Koziris, L.P., Ratamess, N.A., et al. (2002), 'Detraining produces minimal changes in physical performance and hormonal variables in recreationally strength-trained men', *The Journal of Strength and Conditioning Research*, Volume 16:3, pp. 373–382.

La Torre, A., Crespi, D., Serpiello, F.R., et al. (2009), 'Heart rate and blood lactate evaluation in bouldering elite athletes', *The Journal of Sports Medicine and Physical Fitness*, Volume 49:1, pp. 19–24.

Laffaye, G., Levernier, G., and Collin, J.-M. (2016), 'Determinant factors in climbing ability: influence of strength, anthropometry, and neuromuscular fatigue', *Scandinavian Journal of Medicine & Science in Sports*, Volume 26:10, pp. 1151–1159, doi: 10.1111/sms.12558.

Latash, M. L. and Zatsiorsky, V.M. (1993), Joint stiffness: myth or reality?, *Human Movement Science*, Volume 12:6, pp. 653–692, doi: 10.1016/0167-9457(93)90010-M.

Laursen, J.B., Bertelsen, D.M. and Andersen, L.B. (2014), 'The effectiveness of exercise interventions to prevent sports injuries: a systematic review and meta-analysis of randomised controlled trials', *British Journal of Sports Medicine*, Volume 48:11, pp. 871–877, doi: 10.1136/bjsports-2013-092538.

Levernier, G. and Laffaye, G. (2019), 'Four weeks of finger grip training increases the rate of force development and the maximal force in elite and top world-ranking climbers', *The Journal of Strength and Conditioning Research,* Volume 33:9, pp. 2471–2480, doi: 10.1519/JSC.0000000000002230.

Levernier, G. and Laffaye, G. (2021), 'Rate of force development and maximal force: reliability and difference between non-climbers, skilled and international climbers', *Sports Biomechanics*, Volume 20:4, pp. 495–506, doi: 10.1080/14763141.2019.1584236.

Li, T., Hua, X.-Y., Zheng, M.-X., et al. (2015), 'Different cerebral plasticity of intrinsic and extrinsic hand muscles after peripheral neurotization in a patient with brachial plexus injury: a TMS and fMRI study', *Neuroscience Letters*, Volume 604, pp. 140–144, doi: 10.1016/j.neulet.2015.07.015.

López-Rivera, E. (2009), *Entrenamiento de Fuerza de Dedos: ¿Suspensiones con Lastre, o sin Lastre en un Canto Pequeño?*, available at: www.eva-lopez.blogspot.com/2009/05/entrenamiento-de-fuerza-de-dedos.html

López-Rivera, E. (2011), *Una nueva Herramienta para Entrenar tus Dedos: Multipresa PROGRESSION*, available at: www.eva-lopez.blogspot.com.es/2011/08/una-nueva-herramienta-para-entrenar-tus.html

López-Rivera, E. (2014a), *[Actualización 1] Objetivos y Bases de Planificación del Entrenamiento de la Continuidad*, available at: www.eva-lopez.blogspot.com/2014/09/actualizacion-objetivos-y-bases-de.html [*Objectives and Bases for Designing an Endurance Training Program in Sport Climbing*, available at: https://en-eva-lopez.blogspot.com/2014/09/objectives-and-bases-for-designing.html]

López-Rivera, E. (2014b), *[Actualización 3] Entrenamiento de Continuidad. La Capacidad (II). Componentes de la Carga: Objetivos, Intensidad y Volumen*, available at: www.eva-lopez.blogspot.com/2014/11/actualizacion-entrenamiento-de_27.html [*Aerobic Endurance Training in Sport Climbing: Capacity (II). Training Load Elements: Objectives, Intensity and Volume*, available at: http://en-eva-lopez.blogspot.com/2014/12/aerobic-endurance-training-in-sport.html]

López-Rivera, E. (2014c), *[Actualización 4] Entrenamiento de Continuidad. La Capacidad (III): Métodos de Entrenamiento*, available at: www.eva-lopez.blogspot.com/2014/12/actualizacion-entrenamiento-de.html [*Aerobic Endurance Training in Sport Climbing. Capacity (III): Training Methods*, available at: http://en-eva-lopez.blogspot.com/2014/12/aerobic-endurance-training-in-sport_29.html]

López-Rivera, E. (2014d), *Efectos de Diferentes Métodos de Entrenamiento de Fuerza y Resistencia de Agarre en Escaladores Deportivos de Distintos Niveles*, PhD Thesis, Universidad de Castilla La Mancha.

López-Rivera, E. (2017), *¿Por qué Suspensiones Intermitentes?*, available at: www.eva-lopez.blogspot.com/2017/08/english-version-coming-soon-tal-como.html [*Why do intermittent dead hangs?*, available at: http://en-eva-lopez.blogspot.com/2017/08/why-do-intermittent-dead-hangs.html]

López-Rivera, E. (2018a), *Guía de Entrenamiento de Suspensiones (I). Estudio de la situación actual y evaluación inicial*, available at: www.eva-lopez.blogspot.com/2018/05/programas-de-entrenamiento-de-Suspensiones-i-evaluacion-inicial.html [*Fingerboard training guide (I). Preliminary evaluation*, available at: http://en-eva-lopez.blogspot.com/2018/05/fingerboard-training-guide-i-preliminary-evaluation.html]

López-Rivera, E. (2018b), *Guía de Entrenamiento de Suspensiones (II). Métodos para Mejora de la Fuerza Máxima y Resistencia de Agarre y Control de la Carga*, available at: www.eva-lopez.blogspot.com/2018/05/guia-de-entrenamiento-de-suspensiones-II-metodos.html [*Fingerboard Training Guide (II). Maximal grip Strength and Endurance Methods and Load Training management*, available at: http://en-eva-lopez.blogspot.com/2018/05/fingerboard-training-guide-II-Maxhangs-SubHangs-and-Inthangs-methodology.html]

López-Rivera, E. (2018c), *Guía de Entrenamiento de Suspensiones (III). Pautas de Planificación para SuspMax, Suspint y SuspSub y Ejemplos de Planning para SuspMax*, available at: www.eva-lopez.blogspot.com/2018/06/guia-de-entrenamiento-de-suspensiones-III-planificacion-y-planes-SubMax.html [*Fingerboard Training Guide (III). Program design and Periodization of MaxHangs, IntHangs and SubHangs. Samples of MaxHangs training programs*, available at: http://en-eva-lopez.blogspot.com/2018/07/fingerboard-training-guide-iii-periodization-samples-of-maxhangs-training-programs-.html]

López-Rivera, E. and González-Badillo, J.J. (2019), 'Comparison of the effects of three hangboard strength and endurance training programs on grip endurance in sport climbers', *Journal of Human Kinetics*, Volume 66, pp. 183–195, doi: 10.2478/hukin-2018-0057.

Macleod, D., Sutherland, D.L., Buntin, L., et al. (2007), 'Physiological determinants of climbing-specific finger endurance and sport rock climbing performance', *Journal of Sports Sciences*, Volume 25:12, pp. 1433–1443, doi: 10.1080/02640410600944550.

Magiera, A., Roczniok, R., Maszczyk, A., et al. (2013), 'The structure of performance of a sport rock climber', *Journal of Human Kinetics*, Volume 36, pp. 107–117, doi: 10.2478/hukin-2013-0011.

Mallol, M., Bentley, D.J., Norton, L., et al. (2019), 'Comparison of reduced-volume high-intensity interval training and high-volume training on endurance performance in triathletes', *International Journal of Sports Physiology and Performance*, Volume 14:2, pp. 239–245, doi: 10.1123/ijspp.2018-0359.

Malone, S., Hughes, B., Doran, D.A., et al. (2019), 'Can the workload–injury relationship be moderated by improved strength, speed and repeated-sprint qualities?', *Journal of Science and Medicine in Sport*, Volume 22:1, pp. 29–34.

Manini, T.M. and Clark, B.C. (2009), 'Blood flow restricted exercise and skeletal muscle health', *Exercise and Sport Sciences Reviews*, Volume 37:2, pp. 78–85.

Marchante, D. (2015), *Powerexplosive. Entrenamiento Eficiente. Explota tus Límites*, Luhu.

Marshall, P.W.M., McEwen, M. and Robbins, D.W. (2011), 'Strength and neuromuscular adaptation following one, four, and eight sets of high intensity resistance exercise in trained males', *European Journal of Applied Physiology*, Volume 111:12, pp. 3007–3016, doi: 10.1007/s00421-011-1944-x.

Martuscello, J.M., Nuzzo, J.L., Ashley, C.D., et al. (2013), 'Systematic review of core muscle activity during physical fitness exercises', *The Journal of Strength and Conditioning Research*, Volume 27:6, pp. 1684–1698, doi: 10.1519/JSC.0b013e318291b8da.

Matros, P., Korb, L. and Huch, H. (2013), *Gimme Kraft! Effektives Klettertraining*, Café Kraft [*Gimme Kraft! Effective Climbing Training*, Café Kraft (2013)].

Matveyev, L.P. (1977), *Periodización del Entrenamiento Deportivo*, Instituto Nacional de Educación Fisica.

McKean, M.R., Dunn, P.K. and Burkett, B.J. (2010), 'Quantifying the movement and the influence of load in the back squat exercise', *The Journal of Strength and Conditioning Research*, Volume 24:6, pp. 1671–1679.

McKie, G.L., Islam, H., Townsend, L.K., *et al.* (2018), 'Modified sprint interval training protocols: physiological and psychological responses to 4 weeks of training', *Applied Physiology, Nutrition, and Metabolism*, Volume 43:6, pp. 595–601, doi: 10.1139/apnm-2017-0595.

Medernach, J.P.J., Kleinöder, H. and Lötzerich, H.H.H. (2015), 'Fingerboard in competitive bouldering: training effects on grip strength and endurance', *The Journal of Strength and Conditioning Research*, Volume 29:8, pp. 2286–2295, doi: 10.1519/JSC.0000000000000873.

Mermier, C.M., Janot, J.M., Parker, D.L., *et al.* (2000), 'Physiological and anthropometric determinants of sport climbing performance', *British Journal of Sports Medicine*, Volume 34:5, pp. 359–365; discussion 366, doi: 10.1136/bjsm.34.5.359.

Meunier, D., Lambiotte, R. and Bullmore, E.T. (2010), 'Modular and hierarchically modular organization of brain networks', *Frontiers in Neuroscience*, Volume 4, Article ID: 200.

Michailov, M. (2014), 'Workload characteristics, performance limiting factors and methods for strength and endurance training in rock climbing', *Medicina Sportiva*, Volume 18, pp. 97–106, doi: 10.5604/17342260.1120661.

Michener, L.A., McClure, P.W. and Karduna, A.R. (2003), 'Anatomical and biomechanical mechanisms of subacromial impingement syndrome', *Clinical Biomechanics*, Volume 18:5, pp. 369–379.

Moseley, G.L. and Butler, D.S. (2015), *The Explain Pain Handbook: Protectometer*, NOI Group.

Mostoufi-Moab, S., Widmaier, E.J., Cornett, J.A., *et al.* (1998), 'Forearm training reduces the exercise pressor reflex during ischemic rhythmic handgrip', *Journal of Applied Physiology*, Volume 84:1, pp. 277–283.

Mujika, I. and Padilla, S. (2003), 'Physiological and performance consequences of training cessation in athletes: detraining', in *Rehabilitation of Sports Injuries: Scientific Basis* (Editor: Frontera, W.R.), International Olympic Committee, pp. 117–143.

Mujika, I. (Editor) (2012), *Endurance Training: Science and Practice,* Iñigo Mujika.

Mujika, I. and Bosquet, L. (2016), *El Afinamiento Precompetitivo*. Iñigo Mujika.

Muñoz, M., (2017), *¿Verdaderamente Sirve de Algo Planificar?*, available at: www.powerexplosive.com/verdaderamente-sirve-de-algo-planificar

Muñoz-López, M., Marchante, D., Cano-Ruiz, M.A., *et al.* (2017), 'Load-, force-, and power-velocity relationships in the prone pull-up exercise', *International Journal of Sports Physiology and Performance*, Volume 12:9, pp. 1249–1255, doi: 10.1123/ijspp.2016-0657.

Muscolino, J.E. (2014), *Kinesiology: The Skeletal System and Muscle Function*, Mosby.

Nascimento, M.A., Cyrino, E.S., Nakamura, F.Y., *et al.* (2007), 'Validation of the Brzycki equation for the estimation of 1-RM in the bench press', *Revista Brasileira de Medicina do Esporte*, Volume 13:1, pp. 40e–42e.

Navarro Valdivielso, F. (1998), *La Resistencia,* Gymnos.

Nogueiras, D. (2016), *Tratamiento Recomendado para la Lesión de Epitrocleitis o Codo de Golfista*, available at: www.fisioterapia-online.com/videos/epitrocleitis-o-codo-de-golfista-que-es-y-cual-es-su-tratamiento

Nuckols, G. (2016), *How to Deadlift: The Definitive Guide,* available at: www.strongerbyscience.com/how-to-deadlift

Ozimek, M., Staszkiewicz, R., Rokowski, R., *et al.* (2016), 'Analysis of tests evaluating sport climbers' strength and isometric endurance', *Journal of Human Kinetics*, Volume 53, pp. 249–260, doi: 10.1515/hukin-2016-0027.

Ozimek, M., Rokowski, R., Draga, P., *et al.* (2017), 'The role of physique, strength and endurance in the achievements of elite climbers', *PLOS ONE*, Volume 12:8, Article ID: e0182026.

Pareja-Blanco, F., Rodríguez-Rosell, D., Sánchez-Medina, L., *et al.* (2017), 'Effects of velocity loss during resistance training on athletic performance, strength gains and muscle adaptations', *Scandinavian Journal of Medicine & Science in Sport*, Volume 27:7, pp. 724–735, doi: 10.1111/sms.12678.

Peláez Maza, P. (2015a), *Estiramientos I: Flexibilidad, Amplitud de Movimiento y Tensión Muscular*, available at: www.renentrenamiento.com/2015/07/15/estiramientos-i-flexibilidad-amplitud-de-movimiento-y-tension-muscular

Peláez Maza, P. (2015b), *Mejorar la Movilidad Usando el Cerebro: Mental Imagery,* available at: www.renentrenamiento.com/2015/09/25/mental-imagery-mejorar-la-movilidad-usando-el-cerebro

Peláez Maza, P. (2016), *Tendinopatías Patelares II: Reduciendo el Dolor con Ejercicios Isométricos en una Sola Sesión*, available at: www.renentrenamiento.com/2016/07/05/tendinopatias-patelares-ii-reduciendo-el-dolor-con-ejercicios-isometricos-en-una-sola-sesion

Peña, G., Heredia, J.R. and Segarra, V. (2013), *El Entrenamiento Oclusivo (Kaatsu) a la Palestra*, available at: https://g-se.com/el-entrenamiento-oclusivo-kaatsu-a-la-palestra-bp-t57cfb26d48403

Philippe, M., Wegst, D., Müller, T., *et al.* (2012), 'Climbing-specific finger flexor performance and forearm muscle oxygenation in elite male and female sport climbers', *European Journal of Applied Physiology*, Volume 112:8, pp. 2839–2847.

Piepoli, A. (2019), *¿Está la Movilidad Articular Limitada por Músculos Acordados?*, available at: www.antoniopiepoli.com/descargables

Pilgramm, S., de Haas, B., Helm, F., *et al.* (2016), 'Motor imagery of hand actions: decoding the content of motor imagery from brain activity in frontal and parietal motor areas', *Human Brain Mapping*, Volume 37:1, pp. 81–93.

PowerExplosive (2013), *Tutorial Dominadas a un Brazo // How to do your First One Arm Pull Up (Subs)*, available at: www.youtube.com/watch?v=pc_L0PolKzQ

PowerExplosive (2015), *La Famosa Retracción Escapular: ¿Por qué es Obligatoria?*, available at: www.youtube.com/watch?v=e_f8GD8oVP0

PowerExplosive (2016), *Cómo hacer Abdominales: Plancha Abdominal Perfecta*, available at: www.youtube.com/watch?v=5JMakqxdT5c&t=19s

PowerExplosive (2017), *Cómo Corregir la Postura: ¡No Hagas Esto!*, available at: www.youtube.com/watch?v=fywuuBtAGD0

Prinold, J.A.I. and Bull, A.M.J. (2016), 'Scapula kinematics of pull-up techniques: avoiding impingement risk with training changes', *Journal of Science and Medicine in Sport*, Volume 19:8, pp. 629–635, doi: 10.1016/j.jsams.2015.08.002.

Rippetoe, M. (2011), *Starting Strength*, 3rd edition, Aasgaard.

Rogan, S., Riesen, J. and Taeymans, J. (2014), 'Core muscle chains activation during core exercises determined by EMG: a systematic review', *Praxis*, Volume 103:21, pp. 1263–1270, doi: 10.1024/1661-8157/a001803.

Saul, D., Steinmetz, G., Lehmann, W., *et al.* (2019), 'Determinants for success in climbing: a systematic review', *Journal of Exercise Science and Fitness*, Volume 17:3, pp. 91–100, doi: 10.1016/j.jesf.2019.04.002.

Schaefer, L.V. and Bittmann, F.N. (2017), 'Are there two forms of isometric muscle action? Results of the experimental study support a distinction between a holding and a pushing isometric muscle function', *BMC Sports Science, Medicine & Rehabilitation*, Volume 9, Article ID: 11, doi: 10.1186/s13102-017-0075-z.

Schöffl, V.R., Möckel, F., Köstermeyer, G., *et al.* (2006), 'Development of a performance diagnosis of the anaerobic strength endurance of the forearm flexor muscles in sport climbing', *International Journal of Sports Medicine*, Volume 27:3, pp. 205–211.

Schöffl, V.R., Popp, D., Küpper, T., *et al.* (2015), 'Injury trends in rock climbers: evaluation of a case series of 911 injuries between 2009 and 2012', *Wilderness & Environmental Medicine*, Volume 26:1, pp. 62–67.

Schreiber, T., Allenspach, P., Seifert, B., *et al.* (2015), 'Connective tissue adaptations in the fingers of performance sport climbers', *European Journal of Sport Science*, Volume 15:8, pp. 696–702, doi: 10.1080/17461391.2015.1048747.

Schuenke, M.D., Herman, J.R., Gliders, R.M., *et al.* (2012), 'Early-phase muscular adaptations in response to slow-speed versus traditional resistance-training regimens', *European Journal of Applied Physiology*, Volume 112, pp. 3585–3595, doi: 10.1007/s00421-012-2339-3.

Schünke, M., Schulte, E., Schumacher, U., *et al.* (2005), *Prometheus: Texto y Atlas de Anatomía, Tomo I, Anatomía General y Aparato Locomotor*, Editorial Médica-Panamericana.

Schweizer, A. (2008), 'Biomechanics of the interaction of finger flexor tendons and pulleys in rock climbing', *Sports Technology*, Volume 1:6, pp. 249–256, doi: 10.1080/19346182.2008.9648482.

Sheel, A.W. (2004), 'Physiology of sport rock climbing', *British Journal of Sports Medicine*, Volume 38, pp. 355–359, doi: 10.1136/bjsm.2003.008169.

Smith, E. and Blumenthal, K. (2016), *Hang Right: Shoulder Maintenance for Climbers*, available at: www.blackdiamondequipment.com/en_US/stories/experience-story-esther-smith-shoulder-maintenance-for-climbers

Solé, J. (2006), *Planificación del Entrenamiento Deportivo*, SicropartSport.

Souron, R., Farabet, A., Féasson, L., *et al.* (2017), 'Eight weeks of local vibration training increases dorsiflexor muscle cortical voluntary activation', *Journal of Applied Physiology*, Volume 122:6, pp. 1504–1515, doi: 10.1152/japplphysiol.00793.2016.

Staszkiewicz, R., Rokowski, R., Michailov, M., *et al.* (2018), 'Biomechanical profile of the muscles of the upper limbs in sport climbers', *Polish Journal of Sport and Tourism*, Volume 25, pp. 10–15, doi: 10.2478/pjst-2018-0002.

Støve, M.P., Hirata, R.P. and Palsson, T.S. (2019), 'Muscle stretching – the potential role of endogenous pain inhibitory modulation on stretch tolerance', *Scandinavian Journal of Pain*, Volume 19:2, pp. 415–422, doi: 10.1515/sjpain-2018-0334.

Taylor, C.W., Ingham, S.A. and Ferguson, R.A. (2016), 'Acute and chronic effect of sprint interval training combined with postexercise blood-flow restriction in trained individuals', *Experimental Physiology*, Volume 101, pp. 143–154.

Thacker, S.B., Gilchrist, J., Stroup, D.F., *et al.* (2004), 'The impact of stretching on sports injury risk: a systematic review of the literature', *Medicine & Science in Sports & Exercise*, Volume 36:3, pp. 371–378.

Thompson, E.B., Farrow, L., Hunt, J.E.A., *et al.* (2015), 'Brachial artery characteristics and micro-vascular filtration capacity in rock climbers', *European Journal of Sport Science*, Volume 15:4, pp. 296–304.

Valenzuela, P.L., de la Villa, P. and Ferragut, C. (2015), 'Effect of two types of active recovery on fatigue and climbing performance', *Journal of Sports Science & Medicine*, Volume 14:4, pp. 769–775.

Van Dyk, N., Behan, F.P. and Whiteley, R. (2019), 'Including the Nordic hamstring exercise in injury prevention programmes halves the rate of hamstring injuries: a systematic review and meta-analysis of 8459 athletes', *British Journal of Sports Medicine*, Volume 53:21, pp. 1362–1370, doi: 10.1136/bjsports-2018-100045.

Viana, R.B., Naves, J.P.A., Coswig, V.S., et al. (2019), 'Is interval training the magic bullet for fat loss? A systematic review and meta-analysis comparing moderate-intensity continuous training with high-intensity interval training (HIIT)', *British Journal of Sports Medicine*, Volume 53, pp. 655–664, doi: 10.1136/bjsports-2018-099928. Article retracted December 2020.

Vigouroux, L. and Quaine, F. (2006), 'Fingertip force and electromyography of finger flexor muscles during a prolonged intermittent exercise in elite climbers and sedentary individuals', *Journal of Sports Sciences*, Volume 24:2, pp. 181–186, doi:10.1080/02640410500127785.

Wen, D., Utesch, T., Wu, J., et al. (2019), 'Effects of different protocols of high intensity interval training for VO_2max improvements in adults: a meta-analysis of randomised controlled trials', *Journal of Science and Medicine in Sport,* Volume 22:8, pp. 941–947, doi: 10.1016/j.jsams.2019.01.013.

Wiesinger, H.-P., Kösters, A., Müller, E., et al. (2015), 'Effects of increased loading on in vivo tendon properties: a systematic review', *Medicine & Science in Sports & Exercise*, Volume 47, pp. 1885–1895, doi: 10.1249/MSS.0000000000000603.

Wilmore, J.H. and Costill, D.L. (2007), *Fisiología del Esfuerzo y del Deporte*, Paidotribo [*Physiology of Sport and Exercise*, Human Kinetics Publishers (2004)].

Zabala, M., Peinado, A.B., Calderón, F.J., et al. (2011), 'Bicarbonate ingestion has no ergogenic effect on consecutive all out sprint tests in BMX elite cyclists', *European Journal of Applied Physiology*, Volume 111:12, pp. 3127–3134, doi: 10.1007/s00421-011-1938-8.

Zatsiorsky, V.M. (1995), *Science and Practice of Strength Training*, Human Kinetics.

ACKNOWLEDGEMENTS

This chapter would be far too long if I listed everyone who has in some way contributed to this book, so my apologies to anyone who isn't mentioned by name. Keeping it as brief as possible, I'd like to thank:

Alba for her support and patience during the (long) process of writing this book.

Pedro J. Benito (@pedrojbenito), who's probably had the biggest influence on me in my professional life. Thank you for teaching me the importance of backing up action with evidence.

Jesús, for introducing me to the world of climbing, which has had such a huge impact on my life.

Gerar, Isa, Raúl and everyone at RockOMadrid (@madridrocko) and Boulder Madrid (@bouldermadrid), for the opportunity to teach the courses and classes that have led to this book.

Edu (@educalzada), Elías (@eliasdelapedra) and all the other coaches who have helped me to learn, improve and understand climbing performance.

María (@mery_itur) and Alba and Elías again, for appearing in the photos in this book.

Javi (@javierfdc_art), for his incredible graphics.

Rubén (@rubencrespo_filmmaker), for the energy he's brought to this project and for all his hard work on the outstanding photography.

Pedro Bergua (@p_bergua), for helping me structure my thoughts and for showing me the many things I need to unlearn and relearn.

The Factory Boulder (@thefactoryboulder) and Crossfit Koroibos, for use of their centres and Sparta Sport Center Jaca (@spartasportcenterjaca) for use of the equipment in the photographs in this book.

The team at Cadenas Musculares GDS (cadenasmuscularesgds.com) and Ibai López (efmh.es) for providing images for this book.

Everyone at Desnivel for their support and collaboration on this project that means so much to me.

To everyone who in one way or another has helped bring this project to life, my sincerest thanks.

The world's best climbing training books

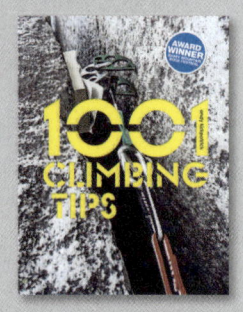

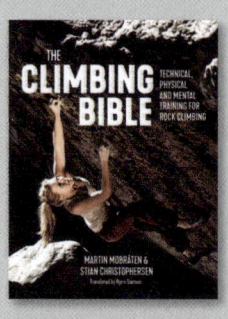

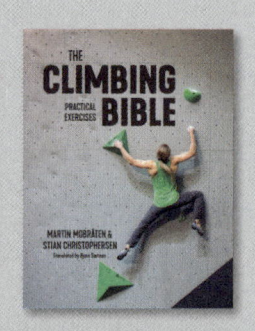

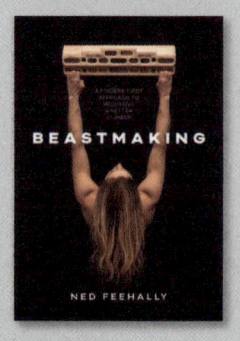

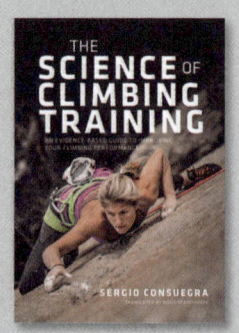

Find out more and order direct
www.adventurebooks.com/tsct

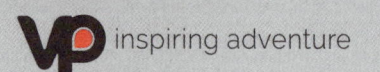

vp inspiring adventure   www.adventurebooks.com/tsct